SHARPER STROKES

Living Smarter — Not Harder

SHARPER STROKES

Third Printing

Golden Oak Publishers
P. O. Box 330385
Fort Worth, Texas 76163

ISBN 1-929248-14-8

To order online go to **haroldbullock.com**

Cover design by Jon Holiday, www.ImageOneMedia.com

DEDICATION

To Lula Mae (Mrs. Carl) Mathis

Amazingly wise and loads of fun,
Bold as a lion and welcoming as home,
Smiling with wisdom's brightness,
Mentor to generations of "young people,"
Delightful friend,
Now with the Lord.

SHARPER STROKES

Living Smarter—Not Harder

TABLE OF CONTENTS

FOREWARD

From The Author

Ours is the Prozac Era.

Earlier, philosophers wanted to live the *examined* life. Later, Christians wanted to live the *holy* life. Today, we live the *medicated* life.

Our times are awash in emotion, swamped in passion. Perhaps no period in history has been so thoroughly "romantic" as ours. Fearing "repression," the greatest secular sin, we have freed our emotions to fill the sails of our lives and drive us wherever they will.

Indeed, at this "post-modern" moment in time, emotion is about all we have left to give our lives meaning. Coached by the media, we have relegated religion to the realm of the irrational. Ethics and values then become mythical; life itself is meaningless.

Following the cues of our media instructors, we try to feel strongly and act with style (cheering others' strong feelings and style also, of course). We are told that this is about as close as we can come to a meaningful and enjoyable life.

Refusing to worry about values, morals or meaning, we simply "try to be happy." That usually means we aim for whatever gratification we can achieve. So, we go about seeking our next gratification in food, drugs, sex, relationship, security, status, conquest, vengeance, venting—or just entertainment—taking great care to "feel strongly" and "act stylishly" along the way.

Without the restraint of morals or values or the direction set by meaning and purpose, our quest for gratification leads us into slavery to our passions amid a relational wasteland. And—we aren't happy! Occasionally we stumble across a sense of excitement and joy, *but we can't seem to make happiness last!*

There is a reason our happiness doesn't last: no matter how zealously or with what style a person sets out on a *foolish* course of action, disappointment will be the natural result. Repeated attempts to pursue folly with verve and style lead to repeated disappointment. Repeated disappointment leads to discouragement and loss of heart.

Over time our repeated disappointment and discouragement spiral into depression—which is very definitely an *emotion*, but a *terrible* emotion to fill one's sails and carry one's life forward. We may occasionally manage a fresh burst of passion to give our ship a sudden jolt of life—perhaps as we listen to a motivational speaker. But, as we act again in folly, it is only a matter of time until the "prevailing winds" of disappointment fill our sails and drive our lives toward depression. The day comes that we convert to the medicated life. We enter the Prozac age.

Even in the Christian realm, fervor, passion and feelings of faith have come to displace actual reflection about which of our choices are pleasing to the Lord. Though the Scripture says that "zeal without knowledge is not good" (Pro 19:2), in our day zeal is the popular *replacement* for knowledge. "I feel the Lord wants me to" has become the adequate reason to act. Yet, even for Christians, foolish actions still lead to disappointment, no matter how full of righteous conviction one felt when he set out on the foolish course. And disappointment leads to discouragement and discouragement to depression. So, in the Christian realm, we, too, are in the age of Prozac.

We have turned our faces away from the lessons of the past. For more than four thousand years, sages in different cultures have taught their observations that,

- No matter how one feels in the moment, all paths in life are *not* equally true or false.
- *Some* paths in life are *better* than others. Some paths are wiser—and some paths are downright *foolish*.
- And the one who chooses the *wiser* path comes out *better* than the others.

I write these words on the day that we celebrate the occasion when the "Word became flesh," when Jesus Christ, in whom are hidden all the treasures of wisdom and knowledge (Col 2:3), was born into human history.

How badly we need genuine knowledge of how life works—knowledge from the Designer and Director of life, God, Himself! How badly we need His wisdom and His understanding of the best ways to approach the matters and decisions of our lives.

This book has been written to help you discover God's perspective on how success is actually achieved and how a rich life is lived both in time and eternity.

Amid this depressed and medicated age, there is *still* the possibility of genuine and enduring joy in life, a joy available to those who genuinely seek wisdom!

Harold Bullock
Christmas Day, 2002

INTRODUCTION

Read Me!

If the ax is dull, and one does not sharpen the edge, then he must use more strength; but wisdom brings success. (Ecc 10:10 NKJ)

My grandfather owned a coal business. Until the late 1960's, coal was a major home and commercial heating fuel in East Tennessee where I grew up. When I was twelve years old, during Christmas season, I chopped "kindling wood" for my grandfather to sell. Bundled up because of the cold, I hunched over in the half-basement of our home and used a heavy hand-ax to split leftover lumber into short, narrow sticks that would catch fire easily. People used the sticks to kindle a fire that would ignite the coal in their stoves or furnaces.

I learned the truth of the above verse. Sharpening the ax took time, time that I could be chopping wood and making money. But the duller the ax became, the more strength it took for each stroke. When I would take the time to sharpen the ax, the wood split quickly and easily. A sharp ax meant speedy work. A dull ax meant a very tired chopper.

The writer of Ecclesiastes, a book in the Old Testament of the Bible, compares chopping wood to achieving success in life. The sharper the ax, the more effective the stroke, and the more easily the wood pile is chopped. The duller the ax, the more exhausting the work, and the more effort it takes to chop.

The sharper the person, the more effective are his strokes in life, and the more easily he creates success—in work, in relationships, and in creating a good future for himself. The duller the person, the harder he works to get the same things done—and the less he has to show for the effort he invested.

What is the difference between a sharp ax and a dull one? Time spent with the right tools putting an edge on the metal of the sharp ax.

What is the difference between a sharp person and a dull one? Wisdom—wisdom gives the edge that brings one success. The person who has wisdom cuts through the situations of life to achieve his goals. The person without wisdom labors on, getting tired and frustrated as he hacks away at life, and so few of his dreams are realized.

We live in a driven society; we are in a rush. We are in a rush to get on with life, to get through school, to get a job, to get married, to have kids, to raise kids, etc. And, the rush eats up the days of the week and the minutes of the day. We are in a rush to get to class, to get to work, to get our work done, to get home, to get our chores done. And, when we get a break in our schedule, we get in a rush to have a good time.

We chop, chop, chop away at life. And, we get wearier and wearier. At some point, we need to sharpen the ax. We need to sharpen *us*. We need to put time, effort and money into gaining *wisdom.*

So...what is wisdom? Ecclesiastes provides a clue when it says,

...the wise heart will know the proper time and procedure. (Ecc 8:5 NIV)

The wise person is able to read a situation and pick out both the best responses to make and the right timing for each one. He slices through the situation.

The dull person may encounter the same situation and respond to it, but he does not have the capacity to read it perceptively like the wise. Nor does he have resources to construct excellent, well-timed responses. Since he must deal with the situation, he hacks away at it, doing the best he can with his dull procedures and timing, growing tired as it takes so much energy just to make any progress.

Wisdom is the fund of understandings and skills that allow one to accurately assess the flow of life and construct excellent, well-timed responses to it. So, how do you become "wise?" How do you *get the edge you need* in life?

One way to start is by reading this book. Through it, I hope to help you start on the journey into growing wisdom. As you read it, you are going to be challenged to a larger perspective on life. Yet, it will be a perspective that allows you to deal with the details of everyday situations—and deal with them quite differently from the normal viewpoint encountered in pop culture and the media, the shaper of pop culture.

Wisdom involves more than an alteration of perspective, however. At some point, you must personally engage the truths you are going to encounter. The secular proverb says, "A journey of a thousand miles begins with a single step." If you want to take the journey, at some point, you must start stepping. The wisdom journey will require you, at some point, to take action.

The chapters of this book are intended to help you understand what wisdom is, how it touches down into the situations of daily life, and how you can acquire it.

Chapter one overviews the practical advantages of wisdom.

Chapter two lays out the manner in which all of us make our decisions. Whether we make decisions more emotionally on the spur of the moment or we make them more rationally, a step at a time, there is a pattern to the way human beings make decisions.

Chapter three investigates what wisdom really is.

Chapter four looks at what appears to be wisdom, but actually is not.

Chapter five details wisdom's two prerequisites. Without these in place, the ax must remain dull.

Chapter six identifies the characteristics of wise people and wise strategies.

Since one's god-concept impacts one's strategies for responding to life, chapter seven looks at wisdom's god-concept.

Wisdom has several facets to it. It also has differing levels. And, it demonstrates a domino effect on different areas of life. These are surveyed in chapter eight.

The opposite of wisdom, in English, is "folly." Chapter nine summarizes wisdom's opposite in the Bible and the different life patterns that are generated by the opposite.

Chapter ten details some key principles of wisdom that are upside down to our society's normal approach to living. Understanding the principles sets the stage for creating sharper responses to the situations we encounter.

Chapter eleven identifies the track to gaining wisdom and gives practical steps one can take.

One of the major channels for developing wisdom turns out to be rather surprising. Chapter twelve looks at this pipeline of wisdom.

According to the Bible, God has His people in a training program, wanting to teach them wisdom. Chapter thirteen looks at that training program in detail, and indicates how to cooperate with it.

Chapter fourteen looks at life in the church of today in light of learning wisdom.

Chapter fifteen surveys the causes of a decline in one's wisdom.

An epilogue gives a broad summary of the book.

The appendices are quite important. The first summarizes the current society's concept of what is wise and the problems generated by a modernist or post-modernist view. The second details one of the prerequisites for wisdom in a manner to show how it comes up in daily life. The third surveys the ups and downs of wisdom in the flow of Biblical history. The fourth actually summarizes the key books and passages of the Bible that relate to wisdom. The fifth outlines some of the key issues in interpreting wisdom literature.

The insights contained in this book are based on eighteen years of extensive research into the Biblical concepts of wisdom and folly and more than thirty years of work helping people turn their lives in a God-ward direction.

My desire is that this book will help you make sharper strokes as you create your life. May you avoid just hacking away and instead be able to cut through to genuine success!

NOTES:

1. Use of Italics

Hoping to increase the ease of reading, I have used italics frequently in this book, mainly for emphasis. Direct quotes of the Bible also appear in italics.

2. Abbreviations Used

OT	Old Testament	NT	New Testament
KJV	King James Version	NKJ	New King James Version
NAS	New American Standard Version	NAU	NAS Update
TLB	The Living Bible	NLT	New Living Translation
TEV	Today's English Version	RSV	Revised Standard Version

3. Personal Pronouns.

To deal with the awkward English-language lack of a singular generic possessive pronoun that refers to either men or women, I shall use the more traditional "his."

4. Resources

Of great help in the studies that lie behind this book have been

- ***PC Study Bible*** copyright 19880-2002 by Jim Gilbertson and distributed by Biblesoft. The transliteration and pronunciations for Greek and Hebrew terms used herein are according to Biblesoft's New Exhaustive Strong's Numbers and Concordance with Expanded Greek-Hebrew Dictionary, copyright © 1994, Biblesoft and International Bible Translators, Inc.

- *Merriam-Webster's Tenth Collegiate Dictionary*, Electronic Edition V. 1.5 copyright © 1994-96 by Merriam Webster Inc.

Chapter 1

WISDOM? WHY BOTHER?

The answer is quite simply *pain or prosperity.*

Life demands we develop ways of dealing with it. We cannot simply sit, like a bump on a log, and let life pass while we grow old. We have to figure out how to deal with parents, with friends, with school, with working on a job, with dating, with marriage, with handling money, with raising kids, with problems, and etc.

To the extent we come up with good ways of handling life, we *prosper.* To the extent we don't, we create *pain* for ourselves.

In our youth, it is easy for us to have grand, untested, but strong opinions about how we think life works. After operating for a few years based on strong opinions and having to grapple with the consequences of choices made, many people re-evaluate their ideas about how life works.

"I don't ever want to do *that* again!" is the motto of life's School of Hard Knocks. After time spent in that relentless school, many realize that some of their big ideas about how to enjoy life have brought them only pain, not enjoyment—and that some of the real enjoyment they have found has come to them on paths earlier thought to lead only to pain. Over time, it becomes obvious to many that, regardless what they originally thought, *some* choices and lifestyles lead to a truly *better* life, and *other* choices and lifestyles appear to promise a better life, but lead to a *worse* one instead.

I knew a man who had entered the military as a teenager and was trained thoroughly in martial arts. He learned that he could overpower people who annoyed him. Since he was serving in the military in *wartime*, his combative release of anger was excused. And, his way of handling annoyance or insult was highly effective. After the war, however, he frequently landed in jail for fighting or for knocking out people who annoyed him. He told me that he was nearly thirty-four years old before it finally dawned on him that hitting people didn't really *help* him. It only caused more trouble for him. He decided he had to learn *another way* to handle annoyance.

A similar thing occurs with parenting. Regardless what they thought before they had children, most people *eventually* come to believe that children must be intentionally taught and trained in how to manage their own desires—rather than being left to figure out how to handle their desires on their own. Undisciplined children, left to themselves, tend to have life-long problems and fail to become responsible citizens. Some people realize this as they see the children of others develop problems because of a lack of self-discipline. Others sorrowfully realize it later as they see their grown-up children failing in life because in earlier years they, as parents, failed to teach and develop discipline in the child. Now, grappling with the problems of an irresponsible adult child, their on-going sorrow confirms their failure.

After just a few experiences in the School of Hard Knocks, anyone who possesses a basic amount of common sense wants to discover *which* choices and *which* ways of living lead to a *better* life—prosperity—and which lead into trouble—pain. And, of course, we all want to be able to recognize the paths to a better life and the paths to a worsening life *in advance, before* we have to choose one path or the other.

SOURCES OF WISDOM

Over the centuries, people have sought out *different sources* to come up with the insight and understandings, the "wisdom" they have needed in order to pick the better path in life.

Religions. The vast majority have turned to different kinds of *religions.* As time has rolled on, different religions have risen to promulgate their ideas about which god or gods are behind the flow of everyday life and how people can appease them or earn their favor. The basic idea behind religion is that the person who is properly tuned into the god or gods that affect the world will be able to live a better life. That is, the one who properly tunes into the god/gods may be able to spend his days on this planet with a greater measure of prosperity—whether it be spiritual, material, emotional or other form—and with less difficulty and pain. And, the various religions indicate that whatever future lies beyond one's death will also be made more amenable if one properly tunes into the god/gods behind the universe.

Tradition And Wise People. Most people through the ages have not had great depth in their religion or in the philosophy that has shaped their society. Their approach to finding the wisdom has been much less theoretical and much more practical. They have simply sought out people with a reputation for wisdom, such as a wise man or wise woman. In nearly every society, a few people have stood out above their fellows in their understanding of life and in their ability to make better choices. Their contemporaries, wanting to choose the paths to a better life rather than a worse one, have sought them out for guidance in making decisions. The "wise ones" usually have an awareness of both the religion of their society and the traditional views and morals of their people. In tribal societies, the wise men have often been the story-tellers, retelling the legends that carry the values of the tribe and give the listeners clues about how to deal with life.

In contemporary America, the role of the *wise one* is usually played by several groups of people. The authors of "self-help" books/CDs/DVDs are offering advice on "how to" for those seeking a better way, whether the subject is Wall Street investing, emotional health or childrearing. Some TV/music/movie celebrities (Oprah, Dr. Phil, Madonna, Susan Sarandon, etc.) expound their views on what really matters in life and which choices need to be made. Writers and directors of movies now function as our society's "story-tellers;" their productions tend to shape the values (concept of what's more important) of those who are exposed to them and provide a kind of "life script" for living out the "better" life.

Reason/Philosophy. A very few people, usually in more urbanized societies, have turned to *philosophy* to find wisdom. The realm of study we call "philosophy" has developed over the centuries as "thinkers" have attempted to come up with a *non-religious* explanation of the world and how it operates—explanations that involve little or no reference to God. So, various thinkers through the ages have tried to use their mental powers to observe life, to evaluate experiences, and by the use of *reason* (consecutive, logical thinking), to come up with an explanation of what the universe *really is* and how life in it *really works.*

In earlier days, at least, the driving force behind the philosophical approach to life was the hope of a better life. The idea was that, if one could really grasp the ultimate nature of life and the principles by which it operates, he or she could have a better life by acting in line with the way things *really are* and how they work.

The religions of man, the philosophers through the centuries, and the wise men and women of various societies all reflect our human awareness that *some paths* in life are *better* than others, and the one who can find the better path finds, in time, *a better life*. Though their prescriptions for how to live life may vary, in essence they have affirmed the Biblical sentiment about the key role wisdom plays in life:

If you are wise, your wisdom will reward you; if you are a mocker, you alone will suffer. (Pro 9:12, NIV)

Regardless of what we originally thought when we started our adventure into life, the quest for wisdom later turns out to be *very important.*

No human beings, except those severely mentally impaired, are exempt from having to make decisions about how they will spend time and money, how they will deal with problems, with opportunities, with people and with the ups and downs of life. Every one decides how he or she will handle the "stuff on their plate" in life.

We *choose.* And, our decisions keep on producing consequences, *whether or not* we anticipated the particular consequences or wanted them. So, the question arises: "Is there a way to make decisions that will bring *good* consequences in such arenas as career, marriage, childrearing, emotional health—and *long-term* good consequences, not just short-term good followed by disaster?"

Every person reading self-help books on how to handle relationships with one's family is essentially asking this question. Every person reading the latest biography of a world class business executive is likely searching for clues to answer the same question. Every couple sitting before a marriage counselor is basically asking the same question. Every parent begins to ask the same question. Every fifteen-year-old seeking a friend's advice on how to solve a boyfriend or girlfriend problem is dealing with the same basic question.

What can I do with the situation before me in order to create a better life rather than a worse one?

This is the question addressed by Wisdom.

THE FABULOUS ADVANTAGES OF WISDOM

According to the Bible, genuine wisdom generates fabulous advantages in life:

- Favor from the LORD, the true God of the universe (Pro 8:35), the One who has adequate power to change situations for us. As we act in wisdom, He will look favorably on (enable and sustain) what we are doing.
- Protection from
  - o Bad decisions that lead to entrapment and long term pain (Pro 2:10-12, 16-19; 4:10-12; 28:26)
  - o Enemies who would damage and destroy us (Pro 3:21-26, 4:6)
- A life of *enduring* well-being (prosperity) (Pro 8:18; 19:8)
  - o A *long* life (Pro 3:16; 4:10-11)
  - o Emotional/psychological *health;* life itself (Pro 2:10; 3:17-18; 24:14; 8:35)
  - o *Power* to deal with circumstances and people (Pro 21:22; 24:5)
  - o *Honor* and esteem in the eyes of others (Pro 3:16; 4:8-9; 8:18; 12:8)
  - o Ability to build an estate (Pro 24:4), enduring *wealth* (Pro 3:16; 8:18, 21)
  - o Being a source of continuing *joy to one's family* (Pro 23:24; 29:23)
- Ability to *lead others effectively* and create just and highly effective organizational systems (Pro 8:15-16; 28:2)

THE PRIORITY OF WISDOM—AND DANGER OF MISSING IT

Given the blessings that come from wisdom, it is no surprise that the Scriptures place an *ultimate priority* on acquiring it—a priority above acquiring silver or even fine gold (Pro 3:14; 8:10; 16:16), above rubies (the most costly jewel, the "diamonds" of ancient Palestine) (Pro 3:15; 8:11) and *above anything else* one could desire (Pro 3:15; 8:11). Wisdom is the supreme thing, worth *spending all that one has* in order to acquire it (Pro 4:7). Indeed, it would appear that the primary use of money is to enable one to acquire wisdom (Pro 17:16).

On the "flip side," if acquiring wisdom brings blessing, the failure to acquire it brings problems and pain. Those who fail to find it *harm themselves* (Pro 8:36). The Hebrew word translated "harm" is "hamas" (khaw-mas') meaning violence. If someone *fails to find wisdom*, he does not merely fail to succeed, he ends up *actively damaging himself.* Indeed, the passage continues, the one who *hates wisdom* loves death. That is, knowingly or unknowingly, he is zealously *withering* his life and pursuing his *own termination.*

In the Bible, one faces a three-fold choice:

- *Find* wisdom and be blessed through it,

- *Fail to find* wisdom and repeatedly damage yourself in life, or
- *Hate* (have hostility toward and turn away from) wisdom and set yourself on a swift course to early termination.

Many people simply fail to find wisdom. They have never thought of pursuing wisdom, or have not exerted themselves to acquire it, or they have looked diligently in all the wrong places. As a result they have chosen unhelpful ways to handle their attitudes, the authorities over them, the relationships around them, the decisions that confront them, the work they must attempt, the way they talk to others, their approach to possessions and finances and their manner of dealing with trouble. At first, their choices seemed to promise the results they hoped for, such as an easier life, a greater sense of security, a sense of importance, gaining the esteem of others, etc. As time goes on, however, they discover they have set out on a course of piling up damage to themselves and to others. The day comes when they enter into intense, continuing emotional (and perhaps, physical) pain and difficulty because of the ways they have chosen to handle life.

Some finally go to professional counselors in hopes of discovering how to stop the damage and perhaps reverse it. However, while professional counselors may have some skill in giving advice, many lack the genuine wisdom with which they might help people to cease the self-damage. *Without genuine wisdom, self-damage will continue to accumulate.*

Other people have not merely failed to find wisdom; they have *despised* it. They have picked a more cavalier path in life, and have mocked the very idea of trying to use good sense to make decisions—especially the idea of trying to live in a way that pleases God. They intend to gratify their desires in the moment. Knowingly or not, they are in the process of withering the very satisfaction they hope to achieve. Even more, they swiftly pursue their own death, either by accidents brought on by their recklessness, or by their own hand in suicide as their disappointment with life piles up, or at the hands of others as they get involved with criminals, or at the hands of the state as they increasingly flout the law to satisfy their own impulses.

Pain or prosperity—in the long run, there's really not much middle ground. Which will it be for you?

Think About It

Have any of your opinions about how to handle life changed over time—that is, handling such things as parents, siblings, friends, school, homework, relating to the opposite sex, handling money, behavior at work, or ways of relating to people? Which ones? How?

Are there some areas of your life in which you have been chopping away but getting more and more tired and frustrated? If so, which ones? What needs to change in you or your approach in order to slice on through?

WE ALL WANT SOME THINGS IN LIFE.
AND, WE HAVE SOME STRATEGY FOR GETTING THEM.
WHAT IS THE PROCESS BY WHICH WE CHOOSE STRATEGIES?
YOU MIGHT BE SURPRISED!

Chapter 2

WHY DID YOU DO THAT?

How We Choose Our Strategies

Human beings tend to be motivated by what they *want.* We want something, and if we want it bad enough, we set out to get it. We want a meal. We want to go to the bathroom. We want friends. We want popularity. We want to date. We want a car. We want to get through school. We want to get married. We want a house. We want children. We want...

When we set out to get what we want, most of us *intend* to *succeed* in getting what we want. For example,

- If we have a date on Friday night, most of us want it to go well. Especially if we *want* a long-term relationship with our date, we want our date to enjoy our time together and desire to go out with us again.
- If we study for a test, most intend to make better grades rather than worse.
- Few parents intentionally want to mess up their kids. Most parents would like to raise their children to do well.
- Workers usually want to do well in their jobs.

We *want* to succeed in our endeavors. Some of us have a passionate drive to succeed; others have less drive. But, most of us don't *intentionally* set out to *fail.*

A COURSE OF ACTION PLUS EFFORT

So, what does it take to succeed? Most of us realize that if we are going to succeed, we will have to put out some effort. We will have to "work at it" if we are going to achieve what we want. Success is going to take some effort.

Many of us *also* realize that we will do much better if we can come up with a *good plan of action* to direct our efforts. So, we adopt a certain course of action and then exert effort to implement our plan. Success also takes a game-plan. For example,

- If we have a date Friday night, we decide to shower and dress appropriately beforehand, and then meet the other person and do some activities together.
- If we have a project due at work or for a class, we lay out *a series of steps* that will enable us to succeed.

Some of us plan thoroughly; others only sketch out plans. In some arenas of life, we have developed habitual ways of handling some types of situations so that we are only vaguely conscious of our goals or game plans; we proceed almost on "auto-pilot." Some of us simply act without planning. But, whether we plan a lot or little, very few of us *intend to fail.*

HANDLING UNCERTAINTY

Success entails some risk. We usually understand that the best plans and hardest efforts can be frustrated by things beyond our control. Life just has a certain unpredictability to it. Even the best plans can be ruined by an accident. A few years ago I watched a women's foot race in the Summer Olympics. One woman was highly favored to win the race. But going into a turn, she slipped and fell. Another won.

As the ancient book of Ecclesiastes says,

The race is not to the swift or the battle to the strong, nor does food come to the wise or wealth to the brilliant or favor to the learned; but time and chance happen to them all. (Ecc 9:11 NIV)

Accidents and intervening circumstances potentially could rob us of success that we have worked hard to achieve. For that reason, some people refuse to act until the circumstances are exactly right to ensure success. They don't want to waste effort and then fail. But, by refusing to start, they guarantee failure.

The writer of Ecclesiastes lived in a society heavily dependent on farming. He writes about the tendency of farmers to wait for the perfect moment to do time-sensitive things like planting a crop or harvesting it. Instead of delay, he urges his readers to take aggressive action while there is time:

If clouds are full of water, they pour rain upon the earth...
Whoever watches the wind will not plant; whoever looks at the clouds will not reap.
Sow your seed in the morning, and at evening let not your hands be idle, for you do not know which will succeed, whether this or that, or whether both will do equally well. (Ecc 11:3-4, 6 NIV)

Circumstances such as a strong wind could intervene, blow away some seed and make the farmer's efforts *less* fruitful. However, if the farmer does not plant at the *right time*, there will be *no* harvest at all. And, though rain could make harvesting difficult and ruin some of the crop at harvest time, if the farmer does not complete the harvest within a very short time frame, the crops will rot in the field soon after ripening. *All the crop* will be *lost*.

PATTERNS OF SUCCESS

Life is not totally predictable. However, neither is it totally unpredictable.

There *are patterns* of life and action that *tend to produce* success. The fastest person usually does win, so runners work to increase their speed. The strongest in battle is *likely* to conquer, so countries build their armies and armament.

Success usually grows out of our *efforts*. Our actions—or inactions—produce results. The farmer who plants on a windy day may have less than a maximum harvest—but he *will* have a harvest. The farmer who keeps waiting for the perfect day to plant is likely to plant nothing and have no harvest.

Success also grows out of our *strategy*.

If we are going to succeed, whether in dating, academics, parenting, career or finances, we have to make *decisions that lead to success* rather than failure—and not just occasional success, but repeated success. We must choose courses of action and act—and of course, reap the results. If you choose courses of action that repeatedly lead to success, you will gain a reputation as "wise," at least in the arena of your success, whether it be parenting or investing in the stock market. And vice-versa, repeated failures add to your reputation for folly.

All of us have to make decisions. Life simply will not let us refuse to make any decisions, and, thereby avoid all failure. Indeed, much of the time, to refuse to make a decision when needed is actually to have *made* a decision by default. *All* of us will reap the consequences of the actions we take, or fail to take, for better or worse.

Since consequences are hooked to our actions, and we do have to live with the consequences we generate, a question quite naturally arises: Can I learn to pick mostly *better* courses of action and come up with *better* consequences all across life?

The answer is yes! What one has to learn is called "wisdom."

HOW WE PICK OUR STRATEGIES

Before we get to the topic of wisdom however, we must understand how we human beings usually come up with our strategies (chosen courses of action) for handling life's situations (a date, parenting a three-year-old, relating to my boss, etc.).

To better understand the way we make decisions, consider the following situation:

Suppose you were lost in the woods for three days without food and were beginning to get extremely hungry. You come to a clearing and see a hundred feet ahead an empty campsite with food on the table. Would it be a wise course of action to run to the table and eat some food? If there are no dangers around, do it!

But, what if you hear what sounds like a bear grunting behind the tent. You know that grizzly bears are in the area and are drawn to food. So the bear will probably discover the table soon. You also know that grizzlies can run as fast as a racehorse in the short distance. There is no way you would be able to outrun it! Your hunger pains are intense. Do you head for the food on the table or not?

Notice that your choice of the best (most likely to give you what you want) course of action depends on:

- **What you want most of all.** You are hungry, so you want food. However, you also want to stay alive. In a way, the food will help you stay alive. However, trying to satisfy your hunger with a bear close at hand now might end up costing your life. If you have to choose, which do you want *more*—easing the hunger pains or staying alive? Your ranking of your desires (your value structure or the ranking of which things are really more important to you than others) determines your strategy.

- **The factors you discern.** If you discern no danger in the situation, you might proceed to the table and eat. However, discerning the presence of a grizzly bear might cause you to take a different course of action. *What* we discern impacts the course of action (strategy) we choose in handling the situations we face daily.

- **Your understanding of the factors.** In this case, your grasp of the nature of grizzlies affects what you decide to do. If you knew almost nothing about grizzlies, you might think you could probably outrun the bear. So, you may conclude that you can get to the table quickly, grab the food, and out-distance the bear if it accosts you. What we consider to be *true about the factors* we observe in the situation impacts the choices we make. For example,

- o *Consider going on a date Saturday night.* If you have a good understanding of how the opposite sex tends to respond to various situations, there is a fair chance you will pick a good way to handle your date. If you have a poor understanding of how the opposite sex responds, your poor understanding will likely beget poor choices, and the date may turn out to be a miserable experience.
- o *Suppose you are preparing for a test.* You know that you have a limited amount of time to prepare. If you have developed good study techniques (you know and understand how to study), and you know how the professor tends to create tests, your strategy for preparing for the test is likely to result in a good grade. If you have little understanding of good study techniques, and no grasp of the professor's testing inclinations, your efforts to prepare are not likely to produce a high grade.

- **Your ability in making "judgment calls."** Your choice of a way to handle the situations in your life is also affected by your skill in deciding which, among opposing factors, is likely to dominate and shape the situation. How much do your hunger pains weigh in the decision of whether or not to approach the table? How quietly can you swiftly approach the table? How likely is the bear to hear you or smell you? How fast can you run? How fast can the bear run? How much does your fear of the bear/death weigh in the decision? Which should be given priority?

Experience, especially experience under the guidance of a wise coach, really helps in sharpening your skill in making "judgment calls." People with a history of making good judgment calls are usually said to have "good sense." People who tend to make poor judgment calls are said to be "foolish."

Based on your *value structure* (what is *most* important), your *discernment* of the situation, your *accumulated knowledge* and *understanding* of the things you discern and your *skill in judgment* (weighing the factors), you make your decisions—and live with the consequences.

THE ULTIMATE INDICATOR OF GOOD STRATEGY

Suppose you assess a situation and pick a course of action. How do you know if your assessment of the situation is a good one? How do you tell if you exercised good judgment, both in choosing the goals and the strategy?

There is one way to tell how good your decision-making process is: *consequences*. The *results or consequences* of your chosen course of action will tell you how adequate your goals, discernment, understanding and judgment *really are.*

Goal Choice. Did you get what you wanted? Did it turn out to be what you *really* wanted, or did you mistake the relative importance of things? Perhaps, you chose and got what you wanted. But now you are disappointed because, when all was said and done, something else actually turned out to be more important, and you didn't get that. Consequences should now cause you to re-examine your "value structure."

Accuracy of Discernment. The accuracy of your discernment dramatically affects your success. Did you "see" all the factors influencing the situation you were trying to deal with? Or, were you surprised by things you didn't detect?

For example, *suppose you hungrily survey the scene at the campsite (above) and see only food on the table. There is no sign of a bear anywhere. You rush to the picnic table and begin to gulp down some food. You sit down at the table because you are tired. Unknown to you, a six-foot rattlesnake lies in the grass under the table. As you sit down to eat more, you accidentally kick the snake and it bites you—twice. It is likely you would die before getting to the outside world. In this case, the consequences of your actions are impacted dramatically, not only by the things you did discern, but also by something you did not discern.*

The keenness and thoroughness of your discernment are important to choosing a successful course of action. It is important to do everything you can to increase your discernment of the situation *before* you decide on a course of action. For example, in the campsite illustration, if you were nearsighted, putting on your glasses for better distance vision might help discern the presence of the snake. Even better, surveying the campsite with a pair of binoculars, if you had them, would give greater detail of the situation. Another way to improve your discernment might be to draw closer to the table and re-examine the site for signs of danger, that is, to investigate the situation more fully before committing to a definite plan. If you had a hungry friend with you, *and* you were willing to listen to his perspective on the campsite, you might also increase your chances of accurate discernment and greater success by getting his perspective.

In the words of an old proverb: "Look before you leap."

Our human tendency is to let our desires override the need for accurate discernment. We get excited when we see the chance to get what we want so badly. We want it now! We *don't want to* discover any data that would indicate our gratification has to be delayed!

Some examples?

- I see a beautiful car—the kind I have wanted for so long! It's *sooooo* beautiful! And, the seller is willing to make me an exceptional deal today, *right now!* I ask for more time in order to have the car mechanically checked out by an auto shop. He tells me to "take it or leave it," for he has another buyer coming in about an hour who has said he definitely wants the car. I look at the car again. It is *sooooo* beautiful!

- I have needed a job badly. I have just finished an interview and have satisfied the interviewer's questions. He pulls out a three year contract and asks me if I want the job. The salary is good, but I am not exactly sure of everything the job involves. The number of hours per week has not been discussed. Neither have vacation and benefits. I have not met my supervisor or seen the working conditions. But, the salary is good, and, I see the line of people waiting for an interview! And, I need a job really badly!

- I want so much to be married, and here is a person who appears to be pleasing to me—and wants to marry me! Investigate the person? How unromantic! Delay the marriage until I am certain I know and actually like the person? The person might get interested in someone else! I may not get another chance like this!

How easy it is to decide before really knowing the facts! We humans *want what we want when we want it!* So, we tend to do a quick survey of a situation and then rush toward the gratification we want—and miss important details (the rattlesnake). This is why the Bible says:

It is not good to have zeal without knowledge, nor to be hasty and miss the way. (Pro 19:2 NIV)

The way of a fool seems right to him, but a wise man listens to advice. (Pro 12:15 NIV)

A simple man believes anything, but a prudent man gives thought to his steps. (Pro 14:15 NIV)

The wise are cautious and avoid danger; fools plunge ahead with great confidence. (Pro 14:16 NLT)

What a shame—yes, how stupid!—to decide before knowing the facts! (Pro 18:13 TLB)

Adequacy Of Knowledge And Understanding. A person's fund of knowledge and understanding of the *parts of life* and *how life works* greatly impacts his ability to make good decisions and choose good strategies. As with the campsite illustration above, one's *understanding* of what he discerns affects how he evaluates its importance in the decision he has to make.

What do the consequences of your decision or course of action say about your knowledge and understanding? Was your understanding of the people and factors accurate? Was it extensive enough? Or, were you mistaken in your ideas about what was going on or about how people and events would respond to the course of action you chose?
Consequences may indicate that you are ignorant of key factors, that is, that you do not know well enough their nature and tendencies. If so, you need to strive for a greater understanding if you want *different* (better) consequences.

Because our understanding does dramatically impact the choices we make, Western society has been a champion of education for individuals in order for them to be able to make better decisions as citizens in a democratic republic. The more a person can know about how life operates, the better off he is in making choices about what he will do. Citizens of a republic could make better choices if they had a better informed understanding of life.

A part of the contemporary crisis in public educational programs across the USA is the decision about *which information* should be taught (which information is more crucial for a rising generation to grasp in order to make good decisions about life).

At an earlier period in America, the concepts and categories taught in the public educational system were, to an extent, harmonious with the

Bible. Biblical categories influenced how people interpreted life and understood it. As the Biblical understandings of life have been replaced by "secular" (atheistic philosophical) concepts, the society has been increasingly unable to evaluate its life situations effectively—people simply do not have the knowledge and understanding needed to deal well with life. The result has been increasing divorce, declining family life, increasing medication-as-a-way-of-life, etc.

Valid Judgment. Usually, a given life situation has several factors influencing it, each tugging the situation in its own unique direction. If one knows and understands the factors involved and the strength of influence they exert on the other factors, he can often predict which of the factors in the situation will prevail. Knowing which will prevail, he can decide upon a course of action that will deal adequately with the "winner" of the situational tug-of-war.

For example, if a power struggle develops at work and you have a good estimate of the power of each participant, you can guess who will win. Then you can conduct yourself so that you don't alienate the most powerful contender.

Or, suppose there is a conflict in your extended family. One particularly difficult aunt is demanding that certain things happen "her" way. You know that repeatedly in the past, this aunt has become so disagreeable that other people finally gave in to her out of disgust or exhaustion. Currently, two brothers and a sister of the aunt oppose her, but they have "folded" and given in to her in the past. Whom do you think will prevail in the current conflict?

Or, suppose you are a leader with unmotivated followers. You need to motivate them. You know that they can be motivated by a variety of things: greed, hatred, fear, opportunities to grow, altruistic sacrifice, the desire to leave a legacy for others, etc. Given the people whom you lead, you must decide to which "motivators" you will appeal.

Excellent judgment is often the result, not simply of having had *experiences*, but of being *coached* through a variety of decisions so that one learns good judgment. With the increasing breakdown of the family (the normal source to provide coaching), adults are emerging with minimal or no coaching on how to make good decisions.

If you tend to misjudge the strength of factors shaping situations, you need to find a coach or mentor to guide your decision-making and teach you how to weigh factors.

WHAT ABOUT LUCK?

It is true that sometimes a poor strategy is chosen, and it accidentally ends up with good results. Just *one* instance of good consequences doesn't prove your strategy was excellent. It could just be "good luck."

This, by the way, is the *"Hollywood version"* of reality. On the screen, people make foolish choices, and a "kind fate" intervenes to make the foolish choices produce happy endings. For example, in the older movie "Bill And Ted's Excellent Adventure," two likeable guys who have procrastinated on preparing a history project face failure and will not be able to graduate from high school. By a marvelous sequence of events, things still work out for them to score big and graduate. Story after story has a similar plot. The movie may be fun for entertainment, but it is terrible as a "life-script" with which to approach a *real* person's future.

Luck could intervene in real life. However, miraculous or fortuitous outcomes are *usually* limited to the TV or movie screen.

God is merciful, but He tends to let us experience the results of our choices in life so that we learn lessons and develop into the right kind of person.

God "will give to each person according to what he has done." (Rom 2:6 NIV)

...the Lord disciplines those He loves, and He punishes everyone He accepts as a son." Endure hardship as discipline; God is treating you as sons. For what son is not disciplined by his father? (Heb 12:6-7 NIV)

It is also possible that an excellent plan might produce bad results because of unforeseen accidents. "Bad luck" might undermine a good strategy.

It is true that luck might occasionally intervene, but usually we get the results of the course of action we have chosen. Thus, a *pattern of good consequences* indicates good discernment, understanding and judgment about how to handle situations. A pattern of *poor or bad consequences* indicates, not that you are "unlucky," but that something is wrong with your values, your discernment, your understanding or your judgment.

It is amazing how, when we improve our discernment, understanding, and judgment, our *luck* improves!

VIEW OF ULTIMATE REALITY: THE HIDDEN SHAPER OF STRATEGY

Besides our process of discerning, grasping and evaluating, another very significant but often *hidden* factor shapes the decisions we make and the strategies we create.

The way we answer the question "What is the best course of action to take in this situation?" does depend on our *goals*, the factors we *discern* in the situation, our *understanding* of them, and our ability (or lack of ability) to make a *good judgment* call. *But, it also depends on what we think is the nature of "ultimate reality."*

"Ultimate reality" is the reality that lies behind the universe we experience, behind the world we see, hear, touch, smell and taste.

We are aware of a physical universe made up of plants, animals, people and inorganic matter—a universe that functions by the laws of chemistry and physics. Is that universe all there is, or is there something behind it? Did something create it? If so, what is that creator like?

There are different possible answers to these questions.

Perhaps "ultimate reality" is *several divine persons* (gods), as some tribal religions, adherents of New Age thought, and Mormons assert. Or, maybe it is a *single* god, as Islam, Judaism, Christianity and Jehovah's Witnesses affirm. Or, as Hinduism suggests, perhaps there is a non-personal *"something"* that we can not really describe that lies behind everything.

Then again, perhaps there is *nothing at all* behind the universe. Perhaps the physical universe is, itself, the ultimate reality. Atheists affirm that the raw universe is the only reality. It simply exists. It always has been and always will be. And it operates according to the laws of physics and chemistry without a supernatural managing director.

Though few people specifically think about it beforehand, *most people select strategies in life that line up with their view of "ultimate reality."*

For example, if the ultimate reality is *"gods,"* one would do well to factor those gods into selecting his course of action. It would be good if he could know how the gods are related to one another and which one has the greatest power. He would then want to make sure he conducts his life in line with the wishes of the most powerful without offending others who could damage him. There may even be one or two gods he could get on his side to help him in his quest for success. If there were a way to get a divinity behind your plan—that would indeed be wise! Supernatural power could really help!

If the ultimate reality is a single *god*, one would want to know if it is *aware of all* that goes on, or does it miss some information? Is it possible to sneak past the deity, or does he catch everything that happens? Especially, to what extent is the deity *aware of individuals such as you*, their thoughts, and the details of their lives? If it is unaware of humans, you probably can choose any course of action you please. But, if the god is quite aware of all that goes on, you will have to take it into account as you strategize, for it will know about the progress of your operations, and you don't want to anger it.

It would also be helpful to know: Is the god absolutely in *control* of everything or does it occasionally have difficulty handling the universe? Is it *actively involved* in governing the world of people, or does it pay scarce attention to humans? If it is fully in control and actively involved, then you would be well-advised to take it's preferences into consideration as you choose your goals, strategies, and the courses of action you will take.

If it is both *quite powerful* and *quite engaged*, one would also want to know more about the god. It would be good to know the god's *characteristic attitudes*, *habits* and *mode of operations*—and the god's *goals and methods* of achieving them. It would also help to know what *really pleases* that god and what really *ticks him/her/it off*. You certainly wouldn't want to pursue your success in a way that would block a powerful god's goals and draw his anger, or unknowingly tick the god off and bring disaster on yourself.

If that which is behind the universe is a *non-personal something*, as in Hinduism, you would want to know as much about it as possible and take those facts into account as you shaped your decisions in life.

If there is *no god*, and the ultimate reality is *only* the raw physical universe, then one would not have to worry about divine displeasure as he plotted his life's course and made his decisions. It would still be helpful to *know about the universe* and how it operates (that is, learn some physical and biological science). And, it would be helpful to accurately *understand people* and how they "tick," both individually and in groups (learn some social sciences: psychology, sociology, economics, etc.). Then one would be free to manipulate the universe of things and people in order to achieve *whatever goals he wanted* to pursue in life—*without any worry about ethics or morals, or even values.*

One would not have to worry, because without a god, there is no *ultimate* right or wrong (ethics), and there are no *ultimate* values. Concepts of right and wrong would be based merely in personal opinion or cultural preference. Without a god, there are no *intrinsically* noble things—such as freedom, justice, or love. Nor are there *intrinsically* despicable things, such as greed or preying on others. Without a god, there is no way to assign an ultimate high value to hatred or an ultimate low value to it, for there is no ultimate person to tell us whether hatred is noble or depraved. Without a god behind the universe, values are merely personal or socially acceptable preferences. Without a god, values become merely the "fashion statements" of the times, reflecting ideas in vogue at this place and in this day.

If there is no god, then a perceptive person would simply pick out the things that made him feel good and pursue them, without concern whether those things were right or wrong, moral or immoral. And, if that person were really shrewd, he probably would not worry about whether or not things were illegal or legal.

Particularly in decisions dealing with values and morals/ethics, the existence or non-existence of a deity can make a major difference. *If the Christian God exists*, for example, violations of sexual morals or perpetrating fraud upon investors will have consequences—it is a matter of time until they arrive. A person who genuinely believes in the existence of the Christian God sets definite boundaries on his behavior and the choices he makes in life.

If there is no god at all, then a person could be free of consequences for even predatory sexual behavior or for bilking investors out of billions of dollars and stealing their life savings—if he is simply shrewd enough to evade the law and block prosecution. If there is no God, fortunes almost beyond imagination sit waiting to be made by those bold enough to deceive and shrewd enough to avoid prosecution!

At a practical level, most Americans factor very little about a god into their decisions. Though most claim to believe in a god (about 96% in one survey), the god they believe in is only semi-cognizant of what goes on in the world, and does not really impact the flow of human lives. It is a remote, disengaged, preoccupied god of rather limited power with little impact on daily life or the flow of major events in the world. Therefore, most Americans pursue their strategies for living with little reference to that god.

To say it a different way, whether we are religious or not, our "god-concept" (whether it is a person, a thing or no god) shapes our view of what is the wise course of action in life. It is foundational to our strategy for living.

We will examine wisdom's "god-concept" in chapter seven.

TRUE VERSUS REAL

Americans tend to have a peculiar view of "reality." At a practical level, they tend to sort "facts" and "ideas" (the components of information) into one of three categories:

- True
- Real
- False (Not True or Real)

Ideas that we "feel" to be true, but which do not have any real *practical* impact or consequences for our lives, we affirm to be "true." For most of us, the fact that the world is approximately 25,000 miles around is "true." We affirm the idea, knowing it has no relationship to our daily lives (unless we are intercontinental airline pilots). We will never use the idea to guide our decisions in daily life.

Ideas that we feel are not only true but also *have real practical consequences* in our daily lives, we affirm as "real." Thus, gravity is *real.* To step off a twenty-story building engages the law of gravity, and gravity has real consequences, especially for those who violate it. Because of the real consequences, we guide our lives by what we consider "real." What is *real* guides our choices in daily situations. *"I'm not climbing that ladder—I might fall!"*

For us, the difference between the true and the real is pain or prosperity.

Most Americans, including most "born-again Christians," tend to put God and God's law in the "true but not real" category. These may affirm the truth of the ideas, and perhaps even argue vehemently about them. But they don't *really* think those laws bring consequences into daily life. Thus, they guide "generally" by the Scriptures, but don't really bother with specific obedience to God in the small situations of daily life.

For this reason, the lives of many church-going Christians is much the same as that of people in the general culture.

As we have seen above, if there is a god at home in the universe, and it is only dimly aware of human proceedings or only minimally involved in the flow of consequences in daily life and history, then that god deserves to be placed in the "true-but-not-real" box.

However, if the god is infinitely aware and wise, good, holy and absolutely, completely and powerfully in charge, then it would be really smart of us to put it in the same category as gravity. That god will definitely be a factor in shaping the consequences that come to us as we make our decisions about how we handle daily life.

WHY DO WE DO WHAT WE DO?

Why do we do what we do? Why do we pick certain courses of action? Because we think that course of action will bring us the results we desire!

Four-year-olds throw temper tantrums because they have come to believe that this is the way to get parents to relent and give them what is being demanded. Fifteen-year-olds pierce lips, eyebrows, cheeks and tongues because they are convinced the multiple piercing will make them "cool"—either acceptable to a certain group of people or at least, impressive to those who reject them. Fifty-year-olds drive Lamborghini sports cars for much the same reason. Ruthless CEO's make millions of dollars draining the stock value of their companies because they believe the money they will reap is the key to all the things they want in life.

We want some things in life. Those things differ depending on our age: a rubber ducky at age two, a car at sixteen, a marriage at twenty-five, an excellent retirement plan at sixty-five. Whether it is a small thing we want in a given situation, such as enjoying the attention of my friends, or getting an annoying person to shut up, or it is a major life goal, like getting married, we more or less consciously *adopt a course of action* in order to *get what we want.*

Over time, we play out our course of action and discover whether we chose a good strategy or a poor one. *Consequences let us know.*

The one who can consistently pick strategies that produce the results that he really wants—that one is often called "wise" by those who know him.

In summary, a person chooses a course of action based on his:

- Desires—what he wants more than other things
- Discernment—perception of the factors in his situation
- Knowledge and understanding of the factors and how to deal with them
- Judgment—skill in weighing the various opposing factors to decide which will most strongly influence the outcome of the situation
- God-concept (whether it is a "something," a god, multiple gods, or no god at all)

We *all* do what we do because we think it will get us what we really want.

However, some strategies produce good results and others produce poor results.

People who want to create a successful business or career must do more than merely hang around at a job. They must come up with *courses of action.* They must develop strategies to handle the *problems they encounter* on the job. And, they should devise a course of action in order to *advance their careers.* They must learn what the *components of job-success* really are. They must learn *how to make good decisions.* They have to learn how to *deal with people* in the job environment.

If they remain ignorant of many of the factors affecting their jobs, or if they are undiscerning as difficult situations approach, or if they cannot weigh the relative importance of job factors, or if they choose to go for the wrong goals—or if they think God will not be a factor in the consequences that come to them—they will do poorly. They have to learn a better way to pursue their work and career.

People who want to have a happy family life must do more than simply hang out in the same apartment. They must come up with *courses of action* to handle the *problems they face* in their marriage and in their working together. They must develop wisdom about *relating intimately* to a person of the opposite sex, about *communicating* with a person whose perceptual framework is significantly different from theirs, about *controlling their own anger and depression,* about *organizing the household* to get the necessary work done, and about raising children.

If they remain ignorant and undiscerning—or, if they think God will not be a factor in marital happiness—they will do poorly. They must learn a better way to pursue marital harmony.

People who want to live an emotionally healthy life must do more than simply have emotions. They must come up with *courses of action* to handle the *difficulties and pressures* of life in a positive way. They must learn *how reality operates* and develop *realistic expectations* regarding it. If they remain ignorant and undiscerning—or if they think God is not a factor in having an emotionally healthy life—they will do poorly. They must learn a better way to pursue emotional health.

What people have to learn is called "wisdom."

Think About It

Pick a previous decision you've made to set out on a course of action—perhaps how you chose a person to date. Analyze it with regard to what you wanted most, what factors you discerned would affect the decision, your understanding about those factors, how you weighed the pros and cons, and how your god-concept fit into it.

Which ideas about God are TRUE but not REAL to you?

LIKE TO KNOW WHAT WISDOM REALLY IS?
IT IS JUST AHEAD.
READ ON!

Chapter 3

EXACTLY WHAT IS WISDOM?

In a *basic* sense, a wise person is one who is able to create strategies that accomplish the results he desires. Wisdom is the capacity possessed by the wise person that enables him to create the strategies. In this chapter we will look at wisdom in a broader sense, and then in the Biblical sense.

WISDOM IN ENGLISH

In the English language, "wise" is an adjective that can be used in a positive or negative way.

Used *negatively*, it describes someone who is

- **Crafty** and shrewd, that is, someone who is able to achieve his goals but does so by deceit and by deviating from what is right
- **Insolent** and smart-alecky (a wise guy, a wisecrack)
- **An insider** or one who possesses inside information (the mafia "wise guy")
- **Occultic**, skilled in magic lore, astrology or other divination techniques

Used *positively*, "wise" indicates someone who demonstrates three capacities in exceptional amounts:

- Deep *understanding*, an exceptional grasp of the nature of people and of situations or of life itself
- Keen *discernment*, the ability to see into problems, situations and people and determine the factors influencing what is occurring
- Sound *judgment*, a trained, matured, reliable ability to make decisions which lead to success

We earlier met the terms *discernment, understanding* and *judgment* when we considered the campsite/food/bear situation. There we found that people tend to respond to a situation based on their *discernment* of the factors in the situation, their *knowledge and understanding* of the nature of the factors, and their *judgment* in weighing which factors will influence the situation most.

A wise person possesses these abilities in an *exceptional measure*: *deep* understanding, *keen* discernment, *and sound* judgment. A wise strategy would be one rooted in these capabilities. A wise person has an exceptional ability to analyze situations, people or life and reach extremely good conclusions about the best way to proceed.

"Wisdom" is basically an ability to reach intelligent conclusions (see *Webster's*). Wisdom has three basic components:

- Accumulated *knowledge*, whether it be scientific or philosophic
- *Insight*, the ability to *discern* inner qualities and relationships, to analyze people and situations
- *Judgment*, the use of good sense in decision-making

The term "wisdom" can be used to describe technical knowledge and skill in a certain arena, as sheet metal work or plumbing—or medicine. However we normally use the term to imply an exceptional ability to deal with the broad complexities and issues of life.

MORE THAN KNOWLEDGE

Knowledge is a building block of wisdom. But wisdom involves more than knowledge.

There are those who possess knowledge without wisdom. They have collected information or experiences but have not yet really developed understanding, insight or good judgment. The term "sophomore" applies to a person in the second year of higher education. The adjective "sophomoric" refers to someone who is overconfident of his knowledge but who is actually immature and ill-informed *(Webster's Tenth Collegiate Dictionary).* One wit has said that to be a "sophomore" was to *possess knowledge without understanding.*

The fact that wisdom involves more than just knowledge means that a *wise* person is more than an "educated" person. An educated person has been provided with information—but may have only *collected* information. Wisdom, however, takes information (facts and ideas about) and turns it into understanding (a grasp of the nature of), and discernment (how to determine if) and judgment (how to choose which). One with knowledge can explain *what* has occurred. One with understanding can explain *why* it occurred as it did. One with good judgment can grasp *what to do about it.*

"Education" as practiced in most American schools and universities tends to provide only *information* for students to collect. The academic setting of teacher-student tends to hinder the development of judgment, except at minimal levels.

In some *trades* (such as sheet metal working) and professions (such as medicine), the educational scheme provides both formal instruction and supervised practice in the trade (an apprenticeship) or profession (medical internship/residency). Supervised practice allows the trainee to take their knowledge and turn it into insight and judgment. Under the oversight of a skilled practitioner, the trainee gets to assess problems and opportunities and make a "judgment call" as he applies his skill. If the trainee's judgment turns out to be faulty, the supervisor intervenes to prevent serious errors in practice. A degree of discernment and judgment can be developed in such "vocational" educational settings. A well-trained apprentice or intern may actually develop a measure of wisdom in his field.

For the most part, however, "education" tends to produce a collection of information, not the ability to utilize the information in decision-making. Indeed, in the Biblical sense of wisdom, a child who simply trusts and obeys God has more wisdom than the greatest intellectual who does not. The intellectual may possess far more information and sophistication than the child, but the child possesses the key to wisdom: the fear of the LORD. This is why Jesus said we must become like children (Matt 18:2-4; Luke 18:16-17) in order to enter His kingdom. And, it is why His relatively uneducated disciples had more wisdom than the contemporary "wise and learned" (Matt. 11:25-26; see Acts 4:13).

Wisdom is also more than sophistication. To "sophisticate" is to remove someone's naïveté and bring them into a practical but shrewd view of life *(Webster's)*. "To sophisticate" is practically a synonym for "to disillusion." A sophisticated person has come to a "refined" view of life and the knowledge of appropriate behavior by wide experience of both good and bad. Based on his experience, he arrives at some discretion in the choices he makes. The "sophisticated" person may have had a mentor or tutor to sharpen his acquired tastes. However, "sophisticated" tends to imply a less than happy career in learning from experience. It connotes a lot of time spent slogging through a sad history of disappointing experiences in order to develop discretion.

Like the sophisticated, a wise person does learn appropriate behavior. And, a wise person usually has some breadth of experience and has learned from it. However, his wisdom has arisen from more than just experience. A wise person *also* learns by instruction from wise instructors, and from the example of others without necessarily having to directly engage in ugly experiences in order to develop "taste."

BIBLICAL WISDOM

The Biblical understanding of wisdom corresponds fairly well with the English-language idea of wisdom. However, the Biblical understanding adds important elements to the English concept.

The primary Hebrew root word translated as wise is *"chakam"* (khaw-kam'), sometimes Anglicized as *"hakam."* The term means to be wise in mind or word or act. It is usually a positive concept but occasionally occurs in the negative sense of "crafty." The noun related to *"hakam"* is *"hokma"* (khok-maw') translated as "wisdom." The focus of *"hakam"* and *"hokma"* is *skill.*

The *"hakam"* person is a *person of skill.* The term could apply to a person of skill in a *certain field,* such as the skill of a sculptor, weaver (Ex 35:31-35), or a politician (Isa 19:11). Or, used in the general sense, the word can refer to skill in dealing with the *broad range of life.*

A *chakam* person is one who possesses a fund of information and skill that allows him to analyze people and situations accurately, and construct successful strategies for dealing with them. He or she has a remarkable sense of both the procedures needed and the timing for executing the procedures (Ecc 8:5-6). And, the strategies of the *chakam* lead to enduring blessing, not just momentary relief or brief success followed by a flood of problems (Pro 8:18).

In the Bible, wisdom about life involves more than just a fund of *scientific* or *philosophic knowledge.* Biblical wisdom has a dimension that is lacking in the English understanding—a *spiritual* dimension that turns out to be crucial.

In order to gain wisdom in the Biblical sense, a person must have a *certain kind of relationship* to the God of the Bible.

THE TWO REALMS OF LIFE

The wisdom writings in the Old Testament present life as having two domains or two realms in which people operate: wisdom and its opposite. In English, the opposite of wisdom is "folly," a realm characterized by the use of poor judgment and frustrated efforts.

While the English translation of the Old Testament uses the word "folly," the Hebrew of the Old Testament actually has *nine different* word groups that indicate various ways to use poor judgment and so, to act foolishly. Five of the word groups describe persons who have built a lifestyle around a particular way to be foolish. There is no one Hebrew term that captures all the ideas of the different ways to be foolish. There is, however, an activity common to all fools, and that activity serves as the adequate alternative in Hebrew to the wisdom of the wise. The name of the activity is *mockery.*

If you are wise, your wisdom will reward you; if you are a mocker, you alone will suffer." (Pro 9:12 NIV)

The Two Realms Of Life

WISDOM: Realm of the Righteous and Wise
SIMPLICITY
MOCKERY: Realm of the Foolish and Wicked

Mockery involves making light of or ridiculing the things important to God and the ways that God chooses to operate in the world. The five fools of the Old Testament all mock holy matters in one way or another. People who are committed to pursuing their goals in life independently of God tend to have a scornful attitude about the things of God. Ultimately, one either functions in the realm of wisdom, or in the realm of the mockers.

As adolescents mature, they may for a time, function in the realm of *"Simplicity."* The simple person has not yet decided to become a mocker and a fool. He is, however, naïve about how difficult and deceptive life can be. The "simple" tend to trust the wrong people, to easily believe things without checking them out, and they do not think ahead before they commit to tasks, projects or people (Pro 15:14, 18; 27:12). Their naiveté makes them easy prey for ruthless people, such as the adulteress or adulterer (Pro 5, 6, 7). *"Simplicity"* is not a stable realm, however. Unless the simple (naïve) person aggressively turns toward wisdom, he/she will gradually drift into folly (Pro 15:18), into the realm of the mockers.

Wisdom is the realm of enduring success in life and eternity. The wise begin to understand God's ways of working in the world and in the lives of people. More and more, they can penetrate to the heart of matters and bring clarity out of confusing situations. Their ability to assess people and situations keeps improving. Their decision-making becomes increasingly perceptive and successful. Over time, they blossom as a person.

Those who enter wisdom do not leave the world's problems behind. But, they *do* develop the resources that enable them to meet and deal with problems and to wonderfully capitalize on opportunities. And, they develop a capacity for enjoying life far beyond that of ordinary people (Ecc 2:26).

THE PRECURSORS OF WISDOM

The person who wants to acquire wisdom must realize that wisdom has two precursors—two things that precede wisdom. Until these arrive in the life of a person, that person cannot enter the Wisdom realm. Each precursor deals with our relationship to God. We will investigate the precursors more fully in the next chapter. Here, we will quickly survey them.

The *first* precursor to wisdom is *humility.* We are to walk in humility before God.

When pride comes, then comes disgrace, but with humility comes wisdom. (Pro 11:2 NIV)

As pride comes first, and then later, disgrace arrives, so humility comes first, and later, wisdom arrives. Humility involves a spirit of deference and submission. Humility shapes our relationship to God—we defer to His wishes and submit to His will. It also affects our relationship to people — we recognize them as equal to us before God and as worthy of just and kind treatment as we are. Humility also shapes our self-concept. Out of a proper humility, we do not think of ourselves more highly than we ought, rather we think about ourselves with sober judgment (Rom 12:1-2; Ps 131:1). Humility sets the stage for Wisdom's arrival. A proud, arrogant person simply misses the opportunity to experience wisdom that only humility can bring.

The *second* precursor to wisdom is the *fear of the LORD.* In the fear of the LORD, our concern in life becomes to please God in our thoughts, attitudes, words and actions.

The fear of the LORD is the beginning of wisdom, and knowledge of the Holy One is understanding. (Pro 9:10 NIV)

For a person to develop wisdom in the full Biblical sense of great skill in dealing with the broad range of life, he must enter into a relationship with God described as the fear of the LORD. The LORD is the God of the Bible. The fear of the Lord is a profound respect for God. We will look at it more fully in another chapter. When one arrives at the fear of the LORD, wisdom has begun. As one lives in the fear of the LORD, it becomes his instructor teaching him wisdom.

WALKING IN WISDOM: 3-D SUCCESS

In Proverbs, Wisdom is personified as a woman who speaks to the reader. Personified "Wisdom" describes her "walk" (manner of living and operating) in the world.

I walk in the way of righteousness, along the paths of justice, bestowing wealth on those who love me and making their treasuries full.
(Pro 8:20-21 NIV)

In the passage, Wisdom has already declared the tremendous capacities she can grant. She will bless those who love and seek her. Those who want to find her have chosen certain paths (among many).

Based on her statement in the verses, one could say that Wisdom walks a two lane road that is going in her direction of success. One lane is righteousness, what is right before God. The other is the lane of just treatment of others. She walks the road of righteousness and justice. It is along this road that people who love her meet their success and find her rewards. Off this road, one never finds Wisdom or her blessings. Though they seek all their lives, those who do not walk in righteousness and justice will never encounter her and will never receive her blessings.

Another way of picturing this is to understand Wisdom as a "three-dimensional concept."

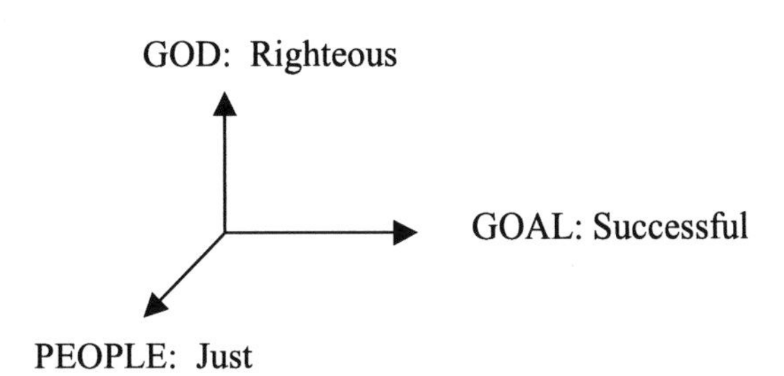

The 3 Dimensions Of Wisdom

A wise strategy is one in which the goal and all the individual steps are *righteous toward God, just toward people,* and *successful toward a goal.*

A godly person is righteous and just. Wisdom *adds* to godliness the ability to accomplish goals in a manner that pleases the LORD. God, Himself, is not only righteous and just. He, by His wisdom, achieves eminent success in what He attempts (Pro 8:22-31; Eph 1:11).

A strategy that is successful in accomplishing its goals, but *violates* righteousness or justice, is not of God. And it may be successful for the time, but it will draw punishment and problems from God in the long run. The gains achieved by ill-means will be lost (Job 5:12-13). Such a strategy is crafty but not "wise." God turns the crafty strategy around so that it finally ensnares the crafty person.

Many people attempt to solve marriage, parenting, business or personal problems with strategies that violate God's will and treat other people unjustly. As long as a person remains selfish in his approach to relational problems, the strategy he uses will bring limited success followed by more problems.

GROWING IN WISDOM

God does *no*t grow in wisdom. His wisdom has always been infinite and unlimited (Ps 147:5; Rom 11:33; 16:27).

Human beings, however, can always increase in wisdom (Pro 1:5). Indeed, at a given time, some of the wise will have greater wisdom than others (1 Kings 4:30-31).

There is a path to increasing wisdom. We will explore it in a later chapter.

Wisdom has several facets: knowledge, understanding, discretion, judgment, strategizing, complex management, etc. We will also look at these later.

There is a sense in which we can both accumulate greater amounts of wisdom and higher levels of wisdom. We will survey those levels later.

Wisdom also has several key arenas of operation. We will survey them and look at the key principle for dealing with each arena.

As a person's wisdom grows he begins to blossom as a person. Rather than a withered, narrow preoccupation with abstract religious ideas, wisdom brings a glad interest in the breadth and beauty of life. Solomon, wise beyond other people, was intrigued, not only with God, but also God's world. He became not only an exceptional ruler but also an accomplished poet and a naturalist, teaching about varieties of plant life, animals, birds, reptiles and fish (1 Kings 4:32-33 NIV). Wisdom even changes the appearance of our faces. A brighter, more joyful countenance is another benefit of wisdom's blossoming (Ecc 8:1).

With an increase in wisdom comes an increase in ability to deal with life and to experience the blessing of God. At the same time, however, an increase in wisdom brings with it a tinge of sorrow and pain (Ecc 1:18). The more one begins to see life from God's perspective, the more tragic the human condition is revealed to be. The more the possibilities of goodness and the beauty of what God intended are grasped by us, the more clearly we see how our rebellion against God has marred and scarred the world and our own lives. The sorrow that wisdom brings is, however, a sorrow wrapped up in happiness (Ecc 2:26).

Wisdom is not something that is fixed and unchanging. It can grow. It can also decline or be destroyed. The one who enters Wisdom's realm can also exit it.

When a person decides to stop walking in the fear of the LORD, his or her wisdom begins to deteriorate. Participation in extortion will do it quickly (Ecc 7:7), turning a wise man into a fool. The wretched career of the older Solomon is an example of declining wisdom. Once the wisest of men, he began to violate the law of God in accumulating wealth, armament, and multiple wives (Deu 17:16-17). Even worse, he violated the prohibition against marrying idolatrous wives (Deu 7:3-4). As God's word predicted, as he aged, his wives turned his heart from following God. He built temples to their idols, and worshipped with them before stone and metal. A man who in youth had brilliant wisdom trusting God, ended life as a crass idolater (1 Kings 11:1-10).

Proverbs speaks of the dimming of a person's perception as the individual continues rebellion against God.

The path of the righteous is like the first gleam of dawn, shining ever brighter till the full light of day. But the way of the wicked is like deep darkness; they do not know what makes them stumble. (Pro 4:18-19 NIV)

As day begins, the indistinct grays that announce the coming dawn give way to the appearance of the sun. As the sun climbs to its height at the noon hour, the light keeps increasing. So is the perspective of the person who keeps on walking in obedience to God: the light of spiritual insight keeps increasing. Looking around, he can see clearly both the nearby dangers and opportunities lying near him.

Those who have decided to walk in wickedness, doing wrong before the Lord, do not have the advantage of such perspective. Like a person in a dark room at midnight, they hit things that hurt them and cause them to trip, but they cannot perceive what it is that makes them hurt. Stumbling in the darkness, they only experience pain, unable to avoid what will cause the next problem.

I once hiked through a series of gigantic tunnels. Starting into a tunnel, I could see the ground in front of me and could avoid holes and obstacles. But the further back into the tunnel I went, the dimmer the light became. I finally came to a point where I had to turn on a flashlight. It was a different matter coming back out of the tunnel, now walking toward the light. Before long the light was illuminating the ground in front of me, and I could turn off the flashlight. It had been off for several minutes before I reached the place I had first turned it on. I struck me that, at the same place, I did not need additional light if I walked toward the light. But if I walked away from the light, I was in darkness. It is not just *where we are* in life that determines our ability to see spiritually, but *which direction we are walking*, toward the light or toward the darkness.

Like someone walking out of a cave or a tunnel, the righteous person—the one who is doing God's will—finds increasing light illuminating the ground in front of him. The longer he walks toward the light at the cave entry, the brighter and clearer things become. More and more easily, he can see his way around rocks that might otherwise trip him. But, like someone walking into a tunnel is the person resisting God's will. The longer he walks in disobedience, the darker his understanding becomes until he can no longer see why he is hurting so badly. Once the lights go out, all we have left is pain.

It is important that people who are trying to solve life problems understand this. They will only get the light they need if they are walking toward obedience, toward the light. To try to seek insight in solving major problems in life while walking further into the darkness is an exercise in frustration.

Not only does insight decrease during disobedience, if someone, believer or unbeliever, decides to oppose God, he may lose what practical wisdom he once possessed as God intervenes to make that person's "wisdom" become foolish (2 Sam 15:31; 17:14; Isa 19:11-15; 44:24-25).

WISDOM AND JESUS CHRIST

The high priority the Bible places on wisdom seems, at first glance, to compete with giving our highest priority to Jesus Christ. However, the two are related, not opposed.

The pursuit of Biblical wisdom is about trying to understand the world around us in line with God's perspective and living life God's way, that is, living in a way that is pleasing to the God of the Bible.

And He said to man, 'The fear of the Lord—that is wisdom, and to shun evil is understanding.'" (Job 28:28 NIV)

The fear of the LORD is the beginning of wisdom: and the knowledge of the holy is understanding. (Pro 9:10 KJV)

Wisdom is concerned with picking out the right "way" in life (Pro 4:10-12), the way of truth (Ps 119:30), the way of righteousness (Pro 8:20; 12:28), the way of understanding (Pro 9:6), the way of wisdom (Pro 4:11), the way of life (Pro 5:6; Jer 21:8), and the way of the LORD (Gen 18:19; Judg 2:22).

In contrast to the way of wisdom, the way of a sluggard is painful and frustrating (Pro 15:19). The way of the unfaithful is unendingly hard (Pro 13:15), and the way of the wicked leads to perceptual darkness and pain (Pro 4:19). The LORD detests the way of the wicked, but He loves those who pursue righteousness (Pro 15:9).

Ultimately, we need to find the way to God and the way to live in line with God's wishes while we remain in this world.

By the New Testament times, the Greeks had developed their own concept of the right way to approach deity involving their own reason. And, they were quite proud of their possession of such "wisdom." However, because of *the way God had chosen* to operate based on *His* wisdom, the way to God could never have been conceived by mere human reason (1 Cor 1:20-21). It had been revealed by God in the Gospel of Jesus Christ, through which the world could be saved (1 Cor 1:21-24).

Jews of the time wanted miracles to be done to prove Jesus was the way to God. Greeks wanted reasons, a logical layout of the wisdom that showed, based on reason, the way to God (1 Cor 1:22). But God sent, not a book, but a person, the word of God wrapped up in human flesh. God had sent not a miracle, but a powerful miracle-worker, Jesus. Jesus Christ was both the Wisdom of God and the power of God (1 Cor 1:24). In the person of Jesus is wrapped up all the treasures of wisdom and knowledge (Col 2:3).

Jesus is the truth (John 14:6). Whatever is true will conform to the reality of who He is, and how He made and runs the world. Jesus is the way

(John 14:6). He is the way to God (1 Tim 2:5-6; 1 Pet 3:18). He has set the example of the way to live aligned with God in the world (Luke 9:23; John 13:34-35; 1 John 2:6). And, through His Spirit, He guides and empowers us to live in the world in line with the will of God (Gal 5:22-23).

The way that wisdom seeks is the way provided in and by Jesus. They are not competing journeys but one and the same path. We will see this more clearly as we discuss the fear of the LORD in chapter five. Here, however, note that it is the one who calls Jesus "Lord" that really fears the LORD. The person who follows Jesus does not disregard the concerns of wisdom. Rather, that person is concerned to live wisely, not foolishly, in this difficult age and make the most of the opportunities that God sends us (Eph 5:15-18).

Jesus Christ opened a door for us to know God by His sacrifice on the cross in our place and His resurrection. By trusting Him, we begin to walk with God. As we walk with Him in the Holy Spirit, He empowers us and teaches us how to obey His Father in line with the word of God.

Walking in the way of wisdom is walking with Jesus Christ, learning from Him, trusting Him, and obeying Him. To walk with Jesus and put His teachings into practice is the very definition of "wise" (Matt 7:24). For those who seek the "way of wisdom," Jesus is the way.

SUMMARY

Wisdom is the possession of greater than ordinary learning, along with keen ability to see into people and situations (discernment), and good judgment in decision-making. While "wisdom" could describe such expertise in a limited arena (such as medicine or plumbing), it is normally used of these abilities applied to life in general. A wise person is able to create successful strategies for reaching his/her goals.

In the Bible, genuine wisdom begins when a person, in humility, decides to fear the LORD, that is, to live out of a profound respect for the LORD and in a manner that is pleasing to the God of the Bible. The strategies of the wise reflect their profound respect for God, and operate within the boundaries of righteousness and justice. The wise know how to succeed God's way. They know how to superbly achieve their goals, and they enjoy good things as the days of their lives progress.

Jesus Christ is God's wisdom, both the way to God and the way to live in the world. To follow Jesus is to walk in the way of wisdom. However, following Jesus involves more detail than many people imagine.

Think About It

Consider a couple of questions. Do your strategies bring you what you really want? If they do, do you like living with what you get?

For example, think about your strategy for relating to your supervisor or the authority over your at work. Does it bring you what you really want? If it does, do you *like* living with what you get?

You might extend this into other areas of life: dating, marital relationship, decision-making, etc.

IF THE RESULTS OF YOUR ACTIONS KEEP TURNING OUT DIFFERENTLY FROM WHAT YOU WANTED, YOU MAY HAVE BOUGHT INTO COUNTERFEIT WISDOM!
IF SO, YOU NEED TO UNLOAD IT
AND GET THE GENUINE ARTICLE!
WHAT IS COUNTERFEIT WISDOM? READ ON!

Chapter 4

COUNTERFEIT WISDOM

Wisdom's Seductive Look-Alike

We have looked at the basic use of the words "wise" and "wisdom" in English. Then, we surveyed Biblical wisdom, which offers phenomenal advantages and blessings. We saw that Biblical wisdom begins when a person decides to "fear the LORD."

The question naturally arises: If the blessings of wisdom are so highly attractive, and wisdom turns out to be so crucial to life, *why aren't people flocking to the fear of the LORD?* While Jesus Christ has exerted considerable influence down through history, currently there doesn't appear to be a stampede in His direction! What's wrong?

The problems have to do with the human preference for independent autonomy and the presence of wisdom's seductive look-alike. To understand these, we will look at the human quest for "wisdom."

THE SEDUCTIVE FANTASY

There is a *kind* of "wisdom" that human beings long for and seek to develop. Eve felt its tug as she stood under the forbidden fruit tree thinking that the fruit would make her wise "like God." She saw what *she thought* was the opportunity to obtain a knowledge base and mental powers that would enable her to function effectively in the universe without needing to rely on or having to obey God. With such "wisdom," she would be self-sufficient. She could rely on her own understanding and discernment, make excellent choices, and chart her *own* course in the life ahead of her (Gen 3:5-7).

Her hopes were dashed when she rebelled against God and found not the beginning of self-sufficiency, but the *end of intimacy* with the only self-sufficient person, God (Gen 3:22-24). The vision of a God-like wisdom available apart from God turned out to be a tantalizing mirage dancing in the bare desert wasteland of human autonomy, a mirage skillfully projected into human hearts by the Father of Lies (Rev 12:9).

Down through the history of mankind, the tantalizing mirage of such incredibly powerful, autonomy-generating wisdom has remained. As we noted in chapter one, people have turned to different sources to find such wisdom: religions, traditional wise people, the occult, and reason and philosophy. The various sources, except for the occult, have provided some helpful insights into life.

Traditional Wisdom. Tribal societies have often compiled a "wisdom" that lives on through wise men, who pass on the "tradition of the elders" to a new generation. These wise men are a sort of living library of tribal "wisdom." Ancient urban societies wrote down such wisdom and deposited it in kings' libraries.

Because human life *does* have patterns of cause and effect within it, such "observational wisdom" has contained much that has been helpful in different societies, but it has always fallen short of being able to liberate and make one self-sufficient. Indeed, much of the "wisdom of the elders" usually turns out to be a way to keep society intact and to reinforce the harmony of the group while severely limiting the individual.

Reason. The ancient Greeks wanted to couple *observations about life* with *logical reasoning* in order to come up with an adequate wisdom. Because of the mental power God has given to humans, the Greek efforts at reason helped them learn much about life. But Greek wisdom was inadequate to curb either legendary Greek debauchery or the rise of tyrannical despots. Both Greek problems were epitomized in the most famous student of the great Greek philosopher, Aristotle. Alexander the "Great," student of Aristotle, conquered most of the known world in three years and died about age thirty, probably by poisoning, some scholars say, as the result of an intrigue between his female and his male harems. The Greek approach to wisdom also failed to discover God's plan for bringing mankind back to God (1 Cor 1:21). It did generate the rise of philosophy as the sophisticate's path to wisdom.

The Occult. Others have turned (and some still turn) to revelations from supernatural spirits, seeking hidden (occult) wisdom that could not be known by mere observation and reason (e.g. Job 4:12-17). Such revelations—and the records of them in "hermetic" literature—are a brew of truth and error, and lead to engagement with demonic spirits, which are spiritual predators capable of enslaving and damaging human beings.

The information gained by direct demonic encounter or revelation is unlike information gained from observation of life. Insight gained from observation might be checked by observing several cases of it in the external world or by debating it with other observers. But insight gained by direct encounter with the demonic has to be taken completely by faith. There are no corroborating witness or debates. One essentially accumulates a "wisdom" that cannot be verified as true. The "blind faith" in demonic sources opens one up to deception by the demons, leading to enslavement and possibly insanity. You might want to read a letter from C. S. Lewis, English scholar, to a friend involved in revelations from the occult. See John Warwick Montgomery's *Principalities and Powers* (see pages 159-164). *The Beautiful Side of Evil* by Johanna Michaelsen is a true account of someone caught up in demonic activity masquerading as the work of God.

Modern Science. In the tradition of the ancient Greeks, the western world of the past three hundred years has hoped in "science," a more studied, tedious and statistically confirmed way to generate observations of life and nature. Science, it has been thought, coupled with human reason would provide the keys to a technology that would make life less burdensome. And, it would provide a basis for constructing societal values, laws, and governments that would lead human communities into a paradise on earth.

However, by the late 1800's, it began to dawn on perceptive philosophers (such as that fascinating mixture of insight and depravity, Nietzsche) that, without the existence of God, life had no ultimate meaning or purpose. Without a god to tell us what had value or what was moral, or which sentiments were noble and which depraved, the subjects of ultimate values, morals and noble ideals, which had been so important in the past, were only empty categories. They become only personal or societal preferences without a reality beyond their popularity. Reason, based on scientific observation, could lead to effective control and manipulation of the environment and people, but it could not construct the principles by which one could create liberating governments. Paradise was going to be lost. A hundred years later, nearly all other atheistic philosophers have finally agreed with Nietzsche.

As Eve did with her fantasy fruit, western society has trusted and bitten into science. And, science has helped in many wonderful arenas: technology, medicine, education, etc. But it has also empowered the most devastating wars in human history, poised mankind on the brink of its own nuclear annihilation, and poisoned the environment. And, it has never solved the problem of how to make the best choices with one's life. (See Appendix 1.)

Indeed, science, by its very nature, *cannot* deal with the great issues of life: discerning our meaning and purpose, establishing morals that bless the world, pointing us to the values we should pursue, embrace, and emulate. You might want to read *The Limitations Of Science* by J. W. N. Sullivan or *Science & Its Limits* by Del Ratzsch. Again, *by its very nature, science cannot solve the problems* of finding the meaning and purpose of life, or of discovering the ultimate values and morals on which individual lives and societies can be built.

This has been the curse of relying on the sciences of psychology and forms of sociology to come up with the keys to living life well apart from God. Psychology and sociology, as sciences, can only "*de*scribe" what they observe in life. Once either begins to "*pre*scribe" what people *ought to* do, it is no longer just science; it has stepped from the realm of science into the realm of philosophy, a very different arena from science.

In our own day, philosophy has been generally recognized as bankrupt of true aims and ideals (purposes of life, meanings of life, ways to make ultimate value choices and moral decisions). You might want to read *The Universe Next Door* by James Sire and *Lifeviews* by R. C. Sproul.

Again and again, mankind has bitten into what it hoped would be the source of liberating wisdom only to find a depressing awareness that such wisdom was not in the fruit/source of choice. Wisdom in the full, rich, sense of *ability to deal with the many facets of life* dwells with God alone. It can be found in *no other source*. The God of the Bible is "God only wise" (Rom 16:27 KJV), "God, who alone is wise" (NLT).

Those who would find *more than* mere technical know-how, those who want to understand how to handle the complexities of life and society, must turn to the one source of such wisdom: God.

WHY DON'T PEOPLE FLOCK TO GOD?

When our original parents chose to find wisdom apart from God, they chose to separate themselves from the only source of real wisdom, God (Isa 53:6; 59:2).

Eve was led to believe that wisdom was a route to *independence* from God. And, she thought, the path to wisdom danced before her eyes, the fruit of the forbidden tree. All that was needed to obtain wisdom would be the bold exertion of her will.

The lie that deceived Eve had several facets.

First, it is a lie that something can make one like or equal to God. There is *nothing* that can make one like or equal with God. God is unique and self-sufficient (Isa 40:25; Acts 17:25); all the rest of the universe depends on Him (Heb 1:3; Col 1:17; Acts 17:28). Nothing which *depends on* God (such as, a human being) can become fully *independent* as is God.

Second, while wisdom does offer the possibility of a better life, it *does not lead to independence* from God. Indeed, true wisdom comes *only from* God as one *walks with* God in trust and obedience. Contrary to what Eve was led to believe, wisdom does not offer the possibility of independence; rather, *dependence offers the possibility of wisdom.* Wisdom does not allow one to create an excellent life apart from obedience and dependence on God. Rather, *wisdom begins* as one makes the decision to *obey God and depend on God* to come through for him. (See chapter five on the fear of the LORD.).

THE SPREADING DECEPTION

The deception/rebellion of our original parents, has been passed on to all their descendants (Rom 5:12). Romans 1 charts the downward spiral into which the human race locked. As human beings down through history have beheld nature, they have seen, heard, tasted, smelled and touched *fully adequate* evidence that there is a Being of incredible wisdom and power who has created the fabulous things around us (Rom 1:18-20). However, most people do not immediately begin to search for such an incredibly superior and wise God. In fact, we humans hesitate to even admit our conclusion that there exists a vastly superior being.

Following our original parents, we want to be in control of our own lives. To admit the existence of such a vastly superior God would be for us to admit that we are not in final control of our lives and to admit that we probably ought to connect with such a great God and serve Him. We prefer to believe that we can be adequately in control and serve *ourselves* in life. So, down inside of us, we resist the awareness of God's vastness and refuse to admit it (Rom 1:18).

If we will not admit to the great God's existence, we certainly will not thank and worship Him (Rom 1:21). With internal spiritual shivers still upon us from grasping the magnitude of God, we reject the idea of such a great God as "defective." That is, we need to find a "better" explanation of life and the universe. Because we use our minds to reject His existence as a defective concept, God gives us a mind (perceptive ability) that is "defective" (Rom 1:28). So, since we have suppressed the obvious truth about the real God, our preferred illusions begin to seem quite real to us, and we build our lives upon them.

God has built into humans the need to worship. So, we set about to create our own scaled-down, less threatening, less demanding ideas of God, and images of God (Rom 1:22-23). Some have reconstructed God to be much more like humankind, as in Greco-Roman mythology. Others have gone even further, and scaled God down to the subhuman level: birds, cattle, reptiles, etc.

And, societal morals have tracked after the gods we have created (Rom 1:26-32). An extramarital affair? Why worry? Didn't Jupiter, the king of the Gods, have many affairs? Or, worried about human sacrifice? Doesn't the jaguar god eat human flesh?

ATHEISTIC NATURE WORSHIPPERS

In the contemporary Western world, we have reduced the concept of god to *"no god at all."* We do not want to bow our knee to any god. So, we have concocted a mixture of science and pseudo-science to explain how everything came into being without any god behind it. Morally, we have decided that we human beings can be and do *whatever we want.*

But, when contemporary atheists face the beauties and complexities of creation, their God-given, innate religious sense begins to seep into their discussions, and they begin to speak of nature and its majesty and complexity with a sense of awe. They personify it and attribute intelligence and ability to it, saying things like: "But nature is too smart for that." And, they spell nature with a capital "N," Nature, as though it were a person, a god. Theoretically, they may be atheists, but at a practical level, many atheists and agnostics give their devotion and worship to "Nature."

Claiming to be wise (perhaps, "scientific") we actually have become fools. Having a vague awareness of the great and powerful God behind the universe, we humans prefer to bow down before less intimidating gods and god-ideas that only reflect our spiritually deprived humanness or even the subhuman. Our idolatry has achieved one thing we have desperately wanted. The gods/god-ideas we have created *do* allow us to *gratify our desires* (get what we want) (Rom 1:22-23). So, disconnected from the only real God, we indulge our passions until we are enslaved by them. And, society is torn by our hatred of those who have used us and by our treachery as we try to figure out how to use others to get what we want (Eph 2:3; Titus 3:3-4, James 4:1-4). In time, society deteriorates until disgusting ways of behaving become the norms, and the heroes become, not the noble, but the depraved (Rom 1:26-32).

And yet, amid such a sophomoric (Greek: sophos = wise; moros = fool) world, a world claiming to be wise but immersed in folly, it is *still* possible to find non-Biblical sources that have of some true insights about life.

GOD'S COMMON GRACE:
Why Not Only Christians Have Good Ideas

Theologians talk about God's "common grace" and "special grace." Special grace is the favor of God given to God's people, a special empowering to recognize spiritual truth and do the works associated with the Gospel of Jesus Christ. Without God's special grace, the world would remain spiritually in darkness.

God's *common grace* is His grace still operating upon all creation. God still provides for and governs the world, restraining the effects of sin, and keeping the effects from being as bad as they could be.

For example, God made humans in His "image." We were intended to reflect the characteristics of our creator in a special way. Human rebellion against God has marred the extent to which we reflect our Creator, that is, marred the image of God in human beings. But, by the grace and mercy of God, it has *not* totally *eradicated* it. We remain with some ability to observe and think.

Also, sin has brought deception upon the human race. We do not perceive life as accurately as our original parents once did. By ourselves we construct inadequate and skewed views of God and the universe and live depraved moral lives. However, though the judgment of God has brought a "defective perception" upon us (Rom 1:28), He has still left us able to perceive truly enough to be able to investigate the world, do science and create technologies and societies. So, one does not have to be a follower of Jesus Christ in order to be a good student of chemistry, an excellent engineer, or effective surgeon.

In the "hard sciences" (physics, chemistry, biology), one mainly deals with "hard data," observable events upon which a theory of the science is built. Philosophy—opinions about how reality is structured and life should work—*remains mostly on the sidelines* of the hard sciences and is rarely called into play. Philosophy mainly gets involved in the discussion of the origins or fate of the universe and of life—events that no one has actually observed.

However, in the "soft sciences," like psychology and sociology, the data that is used tends to be much more open to a variety of interpretations. The philosophical preference of the psychologist or sociologist is usually very active in the interpretation placed on the data. The way a psychologist structures his view of psychology usually depends far more on his philosophical preferences and his ethical biases than on his actual research. The various schools of psychology tend to be just the different schools of atheistic philosophical thought draped with rather thin scientific research that has been interpreted so as to bolster the philosophy and make it appear more acceptable.

In the "soft sciences," unlike the "hard sciences," *philosophy constantly remains on the playing field.* Indeed, philosophy is the game's quarterback, calling and running the plays, directing the conclusions. A Hindu or Christian or Atheist engineer might design *quite similar* bridges to span the same river. But, Hindu and Christian and Atheist psychologists tend to produce *very different* approaches to the personal problems addressed by psychology.

Because of the kindness and grace of God, even rebellious humans are still able to make some observations about the world and life that have a degree of truth to them. Thus, some of the ancient philosophers have made amazingly accurate statements about how life works.

However, no philosopher or scientist, operating upon the information derived from observation of this world alone, or with the speculative ability of the unaided human mind, would have ever been able to conceive how God would bring about our redemption through Jesus Christ (1 Cor 1:20-25). Even with the common grace of God, the human ability to think and conceive still has its limits.

One day, near the end of this age, as the Anti-Christ arises, sin will be revealed for just how devastating it really is, and its effects will increase dramatically. Delusion, now restrained to an extent, will be released upon the human race (2 Thes 2:5-12). Until that time, humans will have a defective mind, but not a totally deluded perception of things.

This means that as societies observe life and put together their traditional wisdom, they will discover and include some helpful things.

And, some of their insights may *not* be that helpful. As contemporary science attempts to study the universe and draw conclusions, it will discover some helpful things. Others of its insights, shaped more by its philosophical preferences, will not be that helpful. Whether the approach is traditional or scientific, the "wisdom" so created will yet have shallow roots and not reach down far enough to deal with the core of the human problem, which is our rebellion against the God of the universe, the God described in the Bible.

To find the deepest wisdom for dealing with life, one has to go all the way to its source, the God of the universe, to His nature, His goals, and His ways of dealing with the universe and how He governs life. To fail to go that deep leaves one with an inadequate foundation for life. So, Jesus warns those who listen to Him that to put His teachings into practice is like building on unmovable rock. But, to fail to implement His teachings is like building on easily shifted sands. The difference between the two is the ability to withstand the pressures and ups and downs of life (Matt 7:24-27)—prosperity or pain!

REAL WISDOM? START AT THE SOURCE

Wisdom can answer the question, "How can I pick goals that are really good for me?" It can also answer the follow-up question: "What course of action should I take to make sure I accomplish my goals?" And, it knows the answer to an even greater question: "How can I live the best life?"

God grants a wisdom that can accomplish goals. And, godly wisdom not only accomplishes its goals, it brings blessing as it unfolds. The person who has genuine wisdom is quite successful in achieving his goals. That person has a remarkable sense of the proper timing and procedures (Ecc 8:5).

However, not all that is effective in accomplishing its goals is actually genuine wisdom from God. Some ungodly people also are capable of setting their sights on a goal and attaining it by the strategies they develop. Their *other kind* of "wisdom" accomplishes its goals amid foul things happening.

James, the brother of Jesus, wrote to believers describing these two different approaches to wisdom (Jas 3:14-17). We will look at their characteristics in chapter six.

To find wisdom, one must begin at the source: God. God is wise (Rom 16:27); He created the whole matter of wisdom (Pro 8:22-36). Only God possesses wisdom in the absolute sense (Job 12:13). His wisdom enabled the creation of all that exists outside of Him (Ps 104:24). His wisdom set up the way for mankind to reconnect with God after its rebellion against Him (1 Cor 1:20-25). Indeed, His wisdom is so upside-down to the world's preferred ideas that the world never could have reasoned out in advance how God would reconcile the whole mess human beings had made of life (Luke 16:15; 1 Cor 1:21).

Godly wisdom cannot be derived by human intelligence alone (Job 28:1, Ecc. 7:23; Job 2:21). To attempt to do so only results in frustration and grief.

Wisdom is bestowed by God (Pro 2:6). Out of His grace, He grants the creative wisdom of an artist (Ex 31:1-6) the governmental wisdom of a king (Pro 8:15-16), or, to those who bow to the LORD, the broadest wisdom in dealing with life (2 Chr 1:11-12). God, whose attribute is wisdom (1 Kg 3:28, Dan 2:20), freely gives it to those who seek it (Pro 2:6; Ecc 2:26; James 1:5). The special agent in bestowing wisdom is the Holy Spirit, who is the Spirit of Wisdom (Isa 11:2; Eph 1:17). The one who possesses the Holy Spirit has an incredible edge in gaining wisdom—if he capitalizes on it.

A WARNING

You will *not* find genuine wisdom if you insist on starting with your ideas about life and try to fit God and His ways into them. One must start with God and let God transform one's viewpoints about life and reality (Rom 12:2). You may discover that many of your opinions about God, morality, society and life have to be redone to fit what the word of God says.

Out of common grace, other religions contain some insight on life. However, we cannot start with another religion and find the wisdom of the God of the Bible. We must start with God as He has revealed Himself in the Bible.

We cannot start with science and try to fit God into its categories. We must start with God and discover how science fits into God's categories.

We must never "check our brains at the door." However, we must use the reasoning power of our brains by starting with the proposition that the God of the Bible is real.

If you are not sure of the reality of the God of the Bible, you might want to read Josh McDowell's books, especially *Evidence That Demands A Verdict.*

Think About It

What people or sources have you turned to for help or guidance in making significant decisions?

Can you think of some illustrations of how people try to use their own insight to run their lives without having to consult God?

IT IS IMPORTANT TO REALIZE THAT SOMETHING COMES BEFORE WISDOM. FIRST THE SOMETHING ARRIVES, THEN WISDOM COMES.

WHAT IS THE SOMETHING?
YOU MIGHT BE SURPRISED!
READ ON!

Chapter 5

WISDOM'S PREREQUISITES

Like the envoys of a great eastern prince arrive much before him to make all arrangements ready for him, wisdom has two envoys that arrive before wisdom and set the stage for it. Their names are Humility and The Fear of the LORD.

PREREQUISITE #1: HUMILITY

When pride comes, then comes disgrace, but with humility comes wisdom (Pro 11:2)

When one gets into pride, shame results. First pride comes, then shame shows up. Pride is antecedent to shame. And, as pride precedes shame, humility precedes wisdom. First comes humility, then like the cars behind the engine of a train, wisdom follows (Pro 11:2).

Humility is the great precursor to wisdom (Pro 11:2). Without its presence, wisdom will not arrive. Humility arrives before wisdom and sets the atmosphere for wisdom's entrance.

Interestingly, humility is not merely a *precondition* for the arrival of wisdom, it is also both a *product* of wisdom and the *continuing condition* of the one in whom wisdom is growing (Jas 3:13).

In contemporary usage, "humble" tends to have the edge of "mousiness," a timidity and lack of strength of character that leaves one without the ability to confront conflict and to take aggressive action to have one's rightful place in life. Actually, the word "humble" has more to do with one's perspective and values than with one's timidity. In reality, a very powerful and aggressive person can be humble (see Phil 2:5-11).

To be "humble" is to rank low in a hierarchy or scale, or to operate with a spirit of deference or submission. The Hebrew term indicates "forcing" or "depressing" (pushing down), and can indicate affliction (humility is the goal when God afflicts us). The usual Greek New Testament verb indicates a similar depressing, a making or bringing low.

Related to humility, the frequent command in Scripture is to "humble *yourself,*" either before God or before others (Ex 10:3; Pro 6:3; James 4:10; 1 Pet 5:5-6). It is up to human beings to *assign to themselves* a lower rank in the hierarchy of God and man (Jas 4:10), or in the society of believers (Phil 2:3-4), or in social situations (as, Luke 14:7-11). God wants us to walk humbly with Him (Amos 6:8). That means we are to *defer to God's judgments and preferences* for our lives and submit to Him. (See "honor" in *Webster's Dictionary.*)

To be humble is to recognize *one's position before God* as a *dependent* creature unable to make demands of the Creator. Pride prefers to act self-sufficiently.

Pride prefers to pretend, that though we were sinful and "needy," we weren't really *that* bad! Humility before God admits our sinfulness and our need of God's action to redeem us. Humility is also willing to admit that we *still* struggle with sin.

Humility acknowledges our need for the grace of God and deeply appreciates grace given. Pride likes to pretend that it can adequately handle the challenges before it. Humility quickly cries out for the help and favor of God.

To be humble before God also means to take one's place as the servant of God, not the director of God, not the adviser to God, not the scheduler and arranger for God and His plans. Pride prefers to tell God how to run the universe, especially in those matters that affect our own lives. Pride also resents God bringing inconvenience into our lives. Humility bows before the infinitely wise Sovereign of the universe and trusts Him with the things we don't understand.

To be humble also means to recognize one's *position relative to other people.* A humble person realizes that God is the creator of every human being. He also knows that God values each person impartially. The humble person thus entertains no secret fantasies about how excellent or deserving he is of God's favor.

Seeing all people as of *equal worth*, especially in the Kingdom of God, *the humble person refuses to*

- *Choose honor for Himself* at public functions. Rather, he will choose a "lower rank" seat and leave the decision with his host as to whether he should be honored or not (Luke 14:7-11). Refusing to "cut in line" is a contemporary way to take you proper rank. "Cutting in line" is done by people who feel they are more deserving than those already in line.

- *Play favorites.* That is, he will not treat people unjustly because of their possession or lack of political power and money. Rather, he will treat all with respect (Jas 2:1-7). There is an additional respect to be given to those who have "office" (parents, the aged, officials, etc.), but everyone is to be treated with respect, whether billionaire or street person (Ex 20:12; Eph 6:2; Lev 19:32; 1 Pet 2:17; Gal 3:28; Col 3:11).
- *Swagger or abuse others.* Even if he is master to one who is a slave, he knows that God has made each person, is impartial in His dealings with people, and so will take offense at unjust treatment of others (Job 31:13-33; Eph 6:9, 1 Pet 5:3).
- *Rebel against God-ordained authorities.* Instead, he will choose to work out a way to cooperate with them. Humility turns out to be a requirement for both leaders and followers (1 Pet 5:5-7). While there is a point at which authority should be opposed, rebellion is the humble person's last resort.
- *Selfishly focus entirely on his concerns and ignore others.* Rather, he will take care of his responsibilities in a way that also looks to the interests of others (Phil 2:3-4).
- *Resist instruction and correction.* He realizes that God is trying to teach him through human teachers and challenging circumstances (Pro 3:11-12; Heb 12:5-11). Rather than despise God's discipline, he will rather focus his attention to learn and heed rebuke (Pro 8:33), knowing that wise correction is really the doorway into life itself (Pro 6:23). Indeed, in the Old Testament, corrective instruction (Hebrew—muwcar [moo-sawr']) is a major vehicle through which one gains wisdom (Pro 8:33).

The opposite of being humble is to be proud or haughty, arrogant or assertive.

There is a *right* kind of *pride*, in the sense of appropriate self-respect. However, there is also a wrong kind. The Hebrew words indicating a proud spirit use the image of "lifting up" or being on high. The Greek terms indicate a person who is "inflated" or appears to be "above" others. The proud person is "high on himself." As a horse rider sits higher than pedestrians, the proud person sees himself as of a higher quality, nature or condition than those around him, and therefore as *more deserving* than they. To use an English phrase, he is "on his high horse." The wrong pride has an unwarranted sense of superiority to others.

To be *haughty* means to look down on others as of less worth or value. To be *arrogant* is to be demanding of more importance or consideration for oneself than is really warranted. The arrogant one feels that he simply deserves more and better than others. "Assertive" is what the arrogant person quickly becomes, asserting his own will in order to get what he feels he deserves more than others.

HUMILITY AND PERSPECTIVE

In a sense, the genuinely humble person has a realistic perspective on himself, his role in life, and how God deals with people. His humility enables him to *see life as it really is*. Pride skews our sense of proportions, creating a kind of spiritual astigmatism, leading us to distorted strategies that do not fit reality—in other words, to failure, to "a fall" (Pro 16:18).

Indeed, if one continues in pride, he *cannot* attain to wisdom. Pride causes a person to react angrily to advice and get involved in quarrels. It leads to scoffing at the suggested ways and mocking the person who suggested them. The proud person is *wise in his own eyes*—he thinks he is smart enough all by himself without the input of others (Pro 3:7; 28:26). Sometimes laziness is the driving force behind the cocky, know-it-all attitude. A lazy person does not want to have to exert energy to improve his situation; if he can convince himself that he is sufficiently wise, he does not have to listen to others and make changes in his life (Pro 26:16). Caught up in pride, and perhaps also in laziness, the proud person does foolish things (Pro 26:12).

MOCKING

Actually, taking advice is one of the major ways we learn wisdom (Pro 13:10). The proud person who resists advice, or feels that he needs none, is actually rejecting one of the key instructors in the wisdom school.

Many of the proud go further and mock at, or make fun of, the advice or ways of wisdom. Mockers may one day seek wisdom but, as long as they are mockers, they will not find it (Pro 14:6).

Instead, the Lord mocks the mockers, but gives grace to the humble (Pro 3:34). That is, God works life out such that those who mock at what is right and wrongly deride people ultimately find themselves the object of ridicule. In contrast, God guides the humble in what is right and teaches them His way (Ps 25:9).

GOD AND HUMILITY

Humility is extremely important to God, for God, Himself, is humble. Jesus was fully God, and as God, Sovereign of the universe. But He was also humble (Matt 11:29). Though He had every right to "get on his high horse," He was of a humble spirit. It was this humility that led to His refusal to grasp and hold onto His glory as deity and choose the humble form of a human peasant and become a servant of the Father, even to the point of death on the cross (Phil 2:5-8). His humility enabled Him to take the right road to the greatest honor in the history of the universe, being given by the Father the name at which all else will bow (Phil 2:9-11).

When we yield our lives to Jesus Christ, His Holy Spirit enters us. From this root within us, the qualities that are characteristic of God begin to grow in our lives. One of these "fruit of the Spirit" is humility (Gal 5:21-22).

God, being humble, desires that we walk humbly with Him (Micah 6:8). God highly regards a humble person whose spirit is contrite. God will hear his prayers and bring blessing upon him (Isa 66:2).

Indeed, humility is the *precursor to the rewards* that God grants to human beings, such as honor, a long life, and enduring wealth (Pro 22:4). If a person will humble himself and play well the role in life that God has given him, especially his role under authority, God will exalt and honor that person in due time (Matt 23:1-12; Luke 14:7-11; Luke 18:9-14; 1 Pet 5:5-7).

The twofold promise of God stands: if one exalts himself, God *will humble* him; if one humbles himself under the mighty hand of God, God *will exalt* him.

HUMILITY AND STRATEGY

Realizing and accepting my true, humble position in the universe allows me to clearly see the life situations around me and assess accurately what is occurring. It creates the possibility of good judgment based on accurate discernment, resulting in good decisions.

In the Scriptures humility is not simply a theoretical concept, it is a way of living practically as the minutes of the day tick away and you face hundreds of different situations. To get a further grasp of how it affects daily life, read Appendix 2, Actualized Humility.

At the bottom of it, humility is a spirit of deference and submission to the Lord, intending to honor Him and operate based on His judgments and opinions. That spirit of deference precedes wisdom.

Humility is the departure platform for the train of wisdom. You won't make it onto the train until you get onto the platform. Once on the platform, access to the train is possible.

To get a more practical grasp of humility, read Appendix 2, Actualized Humility.

PREREQUISITE #2: THE FEAR OF THE LORD

Several verses in the Old Testament make it clear that wisdom has a starting point—a beginning point, a breakthrough point—and a key that unlocks its treasures.

"The fear of the LORD is the <u>beginning</u> of wisdom, and knowledge of the Holy One is understanding. Proverbs 9:10 NIV

In this verse, "beginning" translates the Hebrew "techillah" (tekh-il-law') coming from a word meaning to bore or to break. Techillah is the breakthrough point in the process of boring through something. In that sense, it is a commencement of things. Here, the fear of the LORD is the point at which one breaks through into the realm of wisdom. When the one who has been searching for wisdom finally arrives at the point of the fear of the LORD, the breakthrough occurs! Lo and behold! The darkness that has surrounded him as he tunneled along has suddenly given way! A whole new and shining realm now stands open to him!

The fear of the LORD is the <u>beginning</u> of wisdom; all who follow His precepts have good understanding. To Him belongs eternal praise. (Psalms 111:10 NIV)

The fear of the LORD is the <u>beginning</u> of knowledge, but fools despise wisdom and discipline. (Pro 1:7 NIV)

In these verses, "beginning" translates the Hebrew "re'shiyth" (ray-sheeth'), a term indicating the first in place, time, order or rank. Here, the fear of the LORD comes first, and at that point—at the point of the fear of the LORD—knowledge and wisdom begin to unfold. The one who decides to fear the LORD has just taken his first wisdom-step. Like a toddler, his first step may be awkward, and he later will learn much more about walking in wisdom, but he has *taken his first step!*

The fear of the LORD is the first step in the march to explore wisdom's domain. It is the first note of wisdom's symphony. Without the first step, there are no other steps!

The one who has yet to reach the point of the fear of the LORD cannot find wisdom, for the breakthrough point has not yet been reached. The first step of the march into wisdom has not been taken. Without the first step, the march has not yet begun. The first note of the symphony has not yet sounded. Without the first sound, the symphony has not started. For that person, wisdom is *not yet.*

Jesus agrees with this viewpoint. Jesus says that the wise are those who hear His teaching and *put it into practice* (Matt 7:24). Fools will refuse to do what Christ says and suffer for it (Matt 7:26-27). Indeed, only if one has already decided to do God's will does he have the capacity to discern between spiritual truth and error (John 7:17). After one has decided to obey, he receives the understanding of what he needs to do.

James, the brother of Jesus, reflects the same idea. We can ask God for wisdom, but we will get it only after we have decided to obey. The double-minded person is unstable, not having really decided what he is going to do ("I will; I won't; I will; I won't"). Because of his indecision, he will receive nothing from God (Jas 1:5-8)

The Bible also says that the fear of the LORD is the key to all God's treasures of salvation, wisdom, and knowledge.

He (The LORD) will be the sure foundation for your times, a rich store of salvation and wisdom and knowledge; <u>the fear of the LORD is the key</u> to this treasure. Isa 33:6 NIV

Salvation, wisdom, and knowledge remain locked up beyond the reach of the person who does not fear the LORD. But the one who fears the LORD has come upon the key to unlock all the treasures that God has for humankind.

The fear of the Lord is the *breakthrough point* into wisdom's realm. It is the first step in the wisdom expedition. It is the key to unlocking God's treasure of wisdom, knowledge, and salvation.

The fear of the LORD is also a major *teacher of wisdom.* In a sense, the fear of the LORD *is* wisdom.

The fear of the LORD teaches a man wisdom, and humility comes before honor. Pro 15:33 NIV

And He said to man, 'The fear of the Lord-that is wisdom, *and to shun evil is understanding.'" (Job 28:28 NIV)*

The one who operates within the fear of the LORD will be under constant instruction on the "ins and outs" of wisdom. One cannot acquire adequate information with which to construct genuine wisdom apart from the fear of the LORD acting as his instructor. Those who live outside of the fear of the Lord never encounter the teacher, and so, must remain ignorant.

DEFINING THE FEAR OF THE LORD

In Hebrew, "yare" is the word we translate "fear." In the New Testament Greek "phobos" (from which we get "phobia") is the word. Both terms, like their English translation, can have the sense of "fright" and/or the sense of "respect" or "reverence." Both the sense of "fright" and "reverence" apply to the fear of the LORD.

The words "fear of the LORD" indicate a reverential respect for a *certain* god. "The LORD" (all caps) is the English translation of the name of the God of the Covenant in the Old Testament: Yahweh, meaning "I am who I am" (Ex 3:14). It was the name by which Abraham, Isaac and Jacob had known God. The entry into wisdom is not upon reverential respect for *deity* in general, or a reverential respect for all gods, but respect for a *very specific* god: the God of the Bible

The God of the Bible is the God who, by His great power and incredible intelligence, created everything outside Himself for His purposes (Isa 40:26; Jer 32:17; Ps 104:24; Rev 4:11). He possesses more power than all things in creation summed up together. He is aware of all things and has limitless wisdom to be able to deal with them (Rom 11:33-34). He is good and desires good for people. He is also holy and will judge wrongdoing and reward righteousness (Pro 24:12; Rom 2:5-11; 1 Pet 3:12; Rev 14:6-7). He is Sovereign; no facet of the created realm escapes His sovereign will (Eph 1:11). He is involved in the course of nations (Acts 17:24-27) and in the lives of individuals (Luke 12:22-31). See also Ps 33:8-11.

Before such a God, this planet is tiny in scope; its powerful governments are merely a drop in a bucket (Isa 40:10-26). We are well advised to *take this God into account* as we develop our strategies for living (Pro 20:30-31; Isa 8:9-10). We ought to love, respect and reverence Him. His character deserves it, and His power commands it. It is wise to take seriously His commandments and the ways He tells us to live—and to fear the consequences should we violate His will

God wants us to fear Him—in both senses of the word: reverence (1 Pet 2:17) and dread (1 Pet 1:17). He displayed His power to Israel in order to drive home their need to fear Him (Ex 20:18-20; Josh 4:22-24)

And now, O Israel, what does the LORD your God ask of you but to fear the LORD your God, to walk in all His ways, to love Him, to serve the LORD your God with all your heart and with all your soul, and to observe the LORD's commands and decrees that I am giving you today for your own good? (Deu 10:12-13 NIV)

To fear the LORD is practically equivalent to understanding and doing His will.

Assemble the people--men, women and children, and the aliens living in your towns--so they can listen and learn to fear the LORD your God and follow carefully all the words of this law. Their children, who do not know this law, must hear it and learn to fear the LORD your God." (Deu 31:12-13 NIV)

Trust in the LORD with all your heart and lean not on your own understanding;
in all your ways acknowledge Him, and He will make your paths straight.
Do not be wise in your own eyes; fear the LORD and shun evil.
This will bring health to your body and nourishment to your bones.
(Pro 3:5-8 NIV)

The one who fears the LORD is the one who takes the God of the Bible seriously enough to *not* pretend before Him, or to try to "con" Him, or to sneak past the commands of God. The one who fears the LORD genuinely desires to live in a way that pleases God, the God of the Bible, and shows respect for Him.

Sometimes people are scared of God, but do not really want to respect Him. This was the case with the Egyptian Pharaoh who was under severe punishment from God for his disobedience and feared things could get worse. Pharaoh would appear to relent until the devastation from God stopped. Then, with the scary stuff behind him, Pharaoh would go back to Plan A, doing what Pharaoh wanted no matter what God said—or what Pharaoh had promised God under pressure. Moses realized that the leaders of Egypt were scared of God but did not really intend to do what God wanted. Moses said to the scared Pharaoh,

...I know that you and your officials still do not fear the LORD God." (Ex 9:30 NIV)

People who are only scared of God fall short of the fear of the LORD and miss the breakthrough into wisdom.

THE NATURE OF THE FEAR OF THE LORD

The fear of the LORD is not merely a general concept. It has a certain content. The Bible notes several facts about the fear of the LORD. The fear of the LORD:

- **Demands fidelity**. One must give up his other gods and fear the LORD only. No one can serve the LORD and another god also (Josh 24:14; Matt 6:24). Those who go back and forth between Jesus Christ and another god, such as possessions or greed, have not yet landed on the fear of the LORD.
- **Sets boundaries.** Those upon whom the fear of God comes do such things as refusing to attack God's people (Deu 25:18; 2 Chr 17:10; 20:29) and making sure they judge impartially (2 Chr 19:7, 9). Those who do not fear God have no such restraints (Psalm 55:19ff). Those who transgress God's boundaries are outside the fear of the LORD.
- **Is associated with bringing God glory.** (Rev 15:4) People concerned to pursue their interests regardless the impact on God's reputation are outside the fear of the LORD.
- **Is concerned to please God.** And that includes persuading others to follow God (2 Cor 5:9-11). People stubborn about their own will are outside the fear of the LORD.
- **Is pure.** The Hebrew word comes from a root word meaning to be bright. It means pure or clean in a chemical, physical, ceremonial or moral sense. The fear of the LORD operates with pure and genuinely good motives. It cannot be pursued with mixed motives nor does it's practice involve mixed

(bad and good) motives in dealing with people (Pro 19:9)

- **Is identified with righteousness.** (See 2 Sam 23:3). The Hebrew word can be rendered "justice." Cheats, con men, and people who play favorites rather than justly treating others are outside the fear of the LORD.
- **Involves the hatred of evil.** Evil includes such things as pride, arrogance, evil ways/behavior and perverse speech (Pro 8:13). The fear of the LORD:
  - o *Refuses to speak lies and evil* (Ps 34:11,13). Liars, frauds, slanderers and gossips are outside the fear of the LORD.
  - o *Turns from evil and positively does good* (Ps 34:11, 14; Pro 3:7). Like Jesus, the one who fears the LORD does not merely cease doing bad; he goes around doing good (Acts 10:38; Gal 6:9).
  - o *Aggressively seeks peace.* The Hebrew of the verse implies searching for peace by any means possible and chasing after it when it is sighted. (Ps 34:11, 14). An angry, contentious person is outside the fear of the LORD.
- **Endures forever.** Not merely a matter for time only; it will last for eternity (Pro 19:9).

One could say that the fear of the LORD is "taking God seriously enough that we respect Him and stay within the boundaries He has set for us," or "reverencing God enough to want to please Him." Another way to say it is "a profound reverence for the God of the Bible."

One has to focus on staying within the fear of the LORD. The Hebrew of Proverbs 23:17 literally says to be in the fear of the LORD *all day long*. One's zest for the fear of the LORD can flag if he begins to envy sinners (Pro 23:17 RSV; see Ps 73). And, it is so easy to rely on our own insight and opinions rather than to take God's word at face value and simply do as God says (Pro 3:4-8). So, one needs intentionally to *keep his zeal* for the fear of the LORD alive and not let it run down (see Rom 12:11).

THE CONSEQUENCES OF THE FEAR OF THE LORD

God blesses those who fear Him (Ps 39:9-10; 115:13). The fear of the LORD is such a priority that it is to be chosen with poverty rather than choosing great wealth with confusion and uproar (Pro 15:16). Life will go better for the God-fearing person (Ecc 8:12-13), allowing success to his labor, blessing on his family (Ps 128:1-4), and health to his body (Pro 3:7-8). The fear of the LORD:

- **Keeps one from sin.** It turns a man from evil, keeping him from sin and out of hurtful things (Pro 14:27, 16:6; Ex 20:20).
- **Gives life.** It is a fountain of life; it keeps on producing a flow of refreshment for us (Pro 14:27).
- **Gives peace.** It leads us into a contented rest without fear of trouble (Pro 19:23).
- **Lengthens life.** See Pro 16:6.
- **Leads to wealth, honor and life.** (Pro 22:4) To do so, it must be coupled with humility.

Fools refuse to fear the LORD. They reject the idea that He is involved in daily life, handing out reward and punishment, and feel that they can pursue ungodly strategies and prosper (Ps 53:1; 92:6-7; 94:4-10; 73:3, 8-11 [KJV]; Jer 5:21-25). Since they have hated knowledge and did not choose to fear the LORD, there will be a point at which they are "stuffed to the gills" with the disastrous results of their path in life (Pro 1:29-31).

The hand of God is against those who will not fear and obey Him (1 Sam 12:14-15). Even though a wicked person lives a long time and has what looks like a blessed life, he will not do as well as those who fear the LORD (Ecc 8:12-13). Like a powerful earthly king, God is capable of sending sudden destruction upon rebels who will not fear Him (Pro 24:21-22).

A NEW TESTAMENT CONCEPT

Some feel that the fear of the LORD is just an Old Testament concept. However, it is a New Testament concept also. The fear of the LORD is characteristic of the Holy Spirit. The coming Messiah, upon whom the Holy Spirit would rest, would delight in the fear of the LORD (Isa 11:2-3). Indeed, the early church in Judea, Galilee, and Samaria lived in the fear of the Lord (Acts 9:31). Paul is motivated by the fear of the Lord to please the Lord both in the way he lives and the way he pursues his ministry (2 Cor 5:9-11). Peter urges us to fear God (1 Pet 2:17), and since God judges each man's work impartially, we are to live our lives as strangers here in reverent fear (1 Pet 1:17). Hebrews challenges to worship God with reverence and awe, for He is a consuming fire (Heb 12:25, 28-29). In the Revelation, John sees an angel calling all on earth to fear God (Rev 14:6-7).

Using Christian terminology, the "fear of the LORD" is living under the lordship of Christ, letting Christ "call the shots." Christ rebuked people who wanted to claim a relationship with Him, but did not obey Him:

"Why do you call me, 'Lord, Lord,' and do not do what I say?
(Luke 6:46 NIV)

At one point Jesus told a story about the men who built houses, one on rock, the other on sand. When storms broke against the houses, the rock-based house endured; the sand-based one collapsed.

Jesus identifies the *wise* man as the person who *accepts His teachings and puts them into practice.* The foolish man is the one who does not put Jesus' teachings into practice. He may know *about* the teachings or even *know* the teachings, but until he starts to *practice* the teachings, he is a *fool.* The wise man was able to keep and continue to enjoy the fruit of his labor. The foolish man lost everything for which he had labored.

Jesus was driving home the point that His teachings, as the word of God, are the only adequate foundation upon which to build a life, that is, the only adequate foundation for emotional health, enjoying relationships, marriage, parenting, career, etc. His teachings were to be obeyed. The man who obeyed His teachings was the wise one.

Until a person bows the knee to Jesus Christ as Lord, he or she will never enter into the realm of genuine wisdom. Self-ruling rebels will continue with a skewed perspective on life and continue to damage themselves by the choices they make—as do so many contemporary people who claim to have accepted Jesus as Savior but refuse to bow the knee to Him as Lord. Living outside the fear of the Lord, they fail to find wisdom and damage themselves (Pro 8:36). 'Round and 'round they go on the merry-go-round:

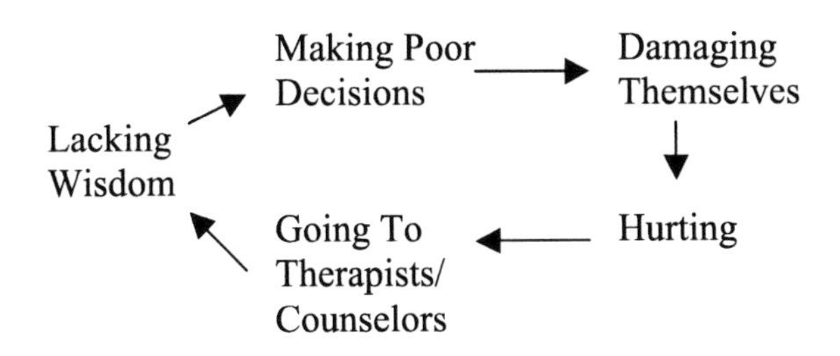

THE MOCKER'S MERRY-GO-ROUND

THE MOCKER'S MERRY-GO-ROUND

One can get off the merry-go-round when one decides to live life God's way, that is, according to the way laid out by God in His word, the Bible. That person has entered into the "fear of the LORD." He has tunneled out of the "Realm of Mocking." And, he has just broken through into the Realm of Wisdom. Now the self-damage may stop—if he moves further into wisdom.

HOW THE FEAR OF THE LORD IMPACTS STRATEGY

Remember our example of the situation at the campsite: lost in the woods, hungry, discovering a campsite with food—and maybe a bear? We saw that four things shape our choice of a course of action: what we really want (value structure), our discernment, our understanding, and our sense of judgment. Deciding to walk in the fear of the LORD impacts all four of these.

Value Structure. The person who has decided to live in the fear of the LORD has just decided to *radically rearrange his value structure.* The things important to God will now rank *high* in his value system. The things of little consequence to God will now rank *low.* The things which are offensive to God are *dropped* from the value system completely. Time will bring up situations which will challenge the ranking of specific values. And, the Christ-follower will struggle with gaining understanding, and wrestle with his emotions until he works through the process of *demoting* or *promoting* the specific value. As he places it in the proper order, he wins the struggle.

Remember the impact of our *value system* on the strategies we choose (see chapter two)? We tend to set our course of action to get what we *want most of all.* The person who begins to walk in the fear of the LORD has made a commitment to want, more than all else, the honor and glory of God to come out of the situations he faces. As a result, his choices change.

Discernment. Remember the role of discernment in shaping one's choice of a strategy to achieve his goals?

Christ promised freedom to those who would, not only continue to learn His teachings, but *remain* (abide) within the boundaries of them (John 8:31-32). Those who remain in His word come to know the *truth.*

As the follower of Christ begins to learn the teachings of Christ and stays within their boundaries, he begins to grasp the real truth about life and the situations he faces. He begins to see the components of life's problems from a different perspective. His *discernment grows more accurate.*

Some things that he earlier would never have thought to be a major problem turn out to be horrific sources of pain in life (such as, a hot temper)—and, he sees it now! Other things he thought rather inconsequential turn out to be sources of great blessing (such as, kindness).

Understanding. By learning from and obeying Christ, we can begin to grasp the truth, and that truth begins to set us free from the bondage and frustration so common in merely cultural approaches to handling life. One not only sees life more clearly, he has a more accurate grasp of the nature of the items that he or she discerns.

For example the media pushes the idea of a "hot babe" to guys. In the eyes of men in the society, a "hot babe" (attractive, sexily dressed and probably promiscuous) represents potential sexual prey. In the view of Scripture, her nature is not that of "prey" but "powerful predator," one who can conquer the mighty (Pro 7:24-27). Currently in the news is a very famous basketball player who is in court over his experience with a "hot babe." He is learning the difference between "prey" and "predator."

As one's discernment and understanding grow, one begins to be able to create successful strategies for handling problems and capitalizing on opportunities.

Such enabling and freeing truth is *only* available to those who decide to learn and obey Jesus' teachings. To say it another way, such truth and freedom come to those who walk in the fear of the LORD, who obey God's will.

Many want to *understand* God's will *first,* and *then decide* whether or not to act in line with it. However, Jesus indicated that *willingness* to obey *precedes* understanding.

Anyone who <u>wants to do the will of God will know</u> whether my teaching is from God or is merely my own. (John 7:17 NLT)

Without a willingness to obey, people see things around them, but do not really *interpret* them correctly. They may hear the teachings of God, but they do not really *grasp* how they fit into practical, real life situations. If they were willing to obey, they would begin to see and correctly interpret what is going on around them. They would hear, and insight would pop into their heads about how to implement God's word practically. Being aware of what is really truly going on in their life and in the world around them, they would turn to God and he would heal their ripped, torn and blasted lives (Matt 13:14-45).

But, without a willingness to obey, one's eyes are mostly closed; the ears are hard of hearing; the heart remains calloused and hard, and the healing never comes.

HUMILITY, THE FEAR OF THE LORD AND WISDOM

The Lewis and Clark expedition charted the northwestern wilderness of early America. The expedition pulled all its resources together in St. Louis, Missouri, at the edge of the uncharted territory. After months of preparation, on May 14, 1804, the group set out in boats on its great journey of exploration.

Humility is the "St. Louis" for a person's expedition into the fabulous territory of wisdom. It is the staging ground at the edge of the great realm; it is the "get ready" place.

"The Fear Of The Lord" is the moment of departure for the expedition. From that moment of decision, the great adventure unfolds.

Think About It

What are some situations in which you have consciously chosen to humble yourself? Scan Appendix Two. Are there some new ways you need to humble yourself? What?

How would you describe your own position related to the fear of the Lord? Outside it? Tunneling toward it? Already broken through?

How would a person who lives in the fear of the Lord go about dating? Or, how would they go about handling their marriage?

SO, IF A PERSON STARTS ON THE WISDOM JOURNEY,
HOW WILL HIS LIFE CHANGE?
DOES HE GET A FARAWAY LOOK IN HIS EYE AND GO AROUND SPOUTING PLATITUDES? DOES HE MERELY BECOME BORING AND UNINTERESTING?
HOW DO YOU RECOGNIZE WISE PEOPLE?
WHAT ARE THEY LIKE? HOW DO WISE PEOPLE ACT?
ACTUALLY, THEY DON'T ACT WEIRD AT ALL.
BUT, THEY ARE DIFFERENT!
READ ON!

Chapter 6

THE PROFILE OF THE WISE

How would you describe a wise person? Or, to ask a similar question, what would convince you that a certain person qualified as *wise*?

Or, suppose that you have decided on a particular course of action to take. How could you tell if it were a wise course of action?

Some businesses, before starting to interview candidates for a particular job, prepare a "profile" of the kind of person they are seeking. The profile may include the training level preferred, prior experience, skill levels in certain areas, and perhaps personality factors. They intend that the profile would enable the interviewers to identify a suitable candidate.

One could potentially identify a wise person in a similar manner. By studying the Scriptures for the characteristics of a wise person and listing them, we can produce a "profile of the wise person." With such a profile, we may be better able to identify a wise person if we encounter one. And, we get some idea of the characteristics that need to grow in our own lives as we are "careful how we *live*, not as unwise but as *wise*" (Eph 5:15).

We can do a similar profile of the "wise" strategy or course of action. Having constructed the profile, we can use it to measure our execution of our own strategies to see if they remain within the realm of Wisdom. We can also identify strategies that are going out of bounds.

In this chapter we will discover the Biblical characteristics of the wise person and the wise strategy.

PROFILE OF THE WISE PERSON

The concept of wisdom appears in the first book of the Bible, Genesis, and flows through the Bible into the last book, Revelation. Similarly, the concept of the wise person begins with Genesis and flows through the New Testament. Many individual traits characterize the wise. We will try to fit them together, like the pieces of a puzzle in order to see the picture that emerges.

We have already seen **two characteristics of the wise**. Since they have entered into the realm of Wisdom, they already possess ***humility*** and the ***fear of the LORD***. These two shape the way a wise person handles life.

A wise person also possesses and exhibits the capacities of wisdom, such as knowledge, understanding, discretion, prudence, and the ability to give wise counsel.

However, as the wise person conducts his life, several other things stand out about him. The wise exhibit the following characteristics:

1. HUMBLY DOES GOOD

Fruit And Root

Perhaps the easiest ways to tell the difference between an apple tree and a peach tree is to see which one has apples hanging on it and which has peaches. This means, of course, that one has to wait for fruit to grow in order for the distinction to be made.

There are other ways to distinguish the trees, such as the kind of bark and the shape of the leaves. Someone quite familiar with trees might make the distinction even before the fruit season. However, most of us can tell the difference between apples and peaches!

The nature of the tree determines the kind of fruit it bears. As the root, so the fruit.

Jesus tells us that the same principle applies to people. Who they really are on the inside shows up in how they act on the outside.

"Make a tree good and its fruit will be good, or make a tree bad and its fruit will be bad, for a tree is recognized by its fruit. The good man brings good things out of the good stored up in him, and the evil man brings evil things out of the evil stored up in him. (Matt 12:33, 35 NIV).

One's word patterns indicate what fills the person's heart. When the person speaks, his/her tongue simply dips down into the owner's heart, loads itself, and dumps out into the world what is covert in the heart. If the pattern of words over time is good, the heart is good. If the words over time are evil, the heart contains the same stuff. What is in the heart shows up on the tongue.

...out of the overflow of the heart the mouth speaks (Matt 12:34 NIV).

In the same way, a person's behavioral patterns indicate who he or she really is on the inside. Good actions over a period of time indicate a good heart. Other actions over a period of time indicate another kind of heart. What is in the heart shows up in the actions.

Even a child is known by his actions, by whether his conduct is pure and right (Pro 20:11 NIV).

Tiny budding apples and tiny budding peaches may not look much different. With time, however, they will be quite distinct. So it is with words and deeds. Early on, the fruit (words and actions) may not be of adequate size (quantity) to indicate the manner of person with whom we are dealing. But, as time goes on, what is really going on inside the person cannot be kept hidden. If it is sin, it will come out; if it is good, it will show up—just give it time (1 Tim 5:24-25)!

James says that internal wisdom is indicated by certain things that show up externally in a person's life.

Who is wise and understanding among you? Let him show it by his good life,...(Jas 3:13 NIV)

According to James, the major indicator of wisdom is a good life. A good life is one characterized by a good attitude, good values, good words, and good deeds. One might do good deeds ostentatiously (see Matt 6:1-6; 23:5-7), or for the purpose of boasting (Luke 9-14). So, James adds a phrase to make sure his readers grasp what he is talking about.

Who is wise and understanding among you? Let him show it by his good life, by deeds done in the humility that comes from wisdom. (Jas 3:13 NIV)

Humility not only *precedes* wisdom, it is *produced* by wisdom. The good life involves good deeds and must be done in a *spirit of humility.* Deeds that are technically good but done in a spirit of arrogance, haughtiness, resentment or manipulation, (anticipating a returned favor), indicate that something *other than* wisdom is at work in the heart of the doer.

The Crucial Importance Of Good Deeds

In an age that despises "do-gooders," and laughs at the attempts of Boy Scouts to do a good deed each day, we need a clear understanding of the importance of good deeds for those who follow Christ. We run the danger, especially in America, of a Christian "privatism" (concern for me and my immediate interests only) that focuses only on how Jesus helps me solve my problems with a minimal awareness of any desire on the part of God for me to be of help to others.

Good and doing good are quite important to God. The LORD Himself is good and does good (Ps 119:68). Indeed, only God is *completely* good (Luke 18:19, Rom 7:18). When Jesus came to earth, He went around "doing good" (Acts 10:38). Those who became followers of Jesus imitated Him (Acts 9:36). They understood that one of the major ways they could bring honor to God was good deeds to others, prompting people to praise God (Matt 5:16). They knew Christ wanted them to bear much fruit and so bring glory to God (John 15:8), and one way to do so was through doing good things in the world (Col 1:10).

God wants us to do good to others. He is really pleased when we do good to others and share what we have with others (Heb 13:16). We were actually created by God in Christ to do good works that God had, in advance, prepared for us to do (Eph 2:10). So, we are to *positively seek the good* of others (1 Cor 10:24). We ought to give ourselves to good purposes, which God can empower and bring to pass (2 Thes 1:11). Indeed, God is willing to strengthen us in every good deed we do and every good word we say (2 Thes 2:17). As we have opportunity we are to do good to *all people*, especially to those who follow Christ (Gal 6:10).

As a matter of fact, this is the very reason Jesus gave Himself. He wanted to create a people of His own who would be like Him, *eager to do what is good* (Titus 2:14, 1 Pet 3:13). So, if we really want to follow Christ, we have to not just turn from evil, but *positively do good* (1 Pet 3:11). For that reason, once we have trusted Christ, we should be *careful* (the Greek word means "exercise thought") to *maintain* (keep ourselves occupied with) good works—that is, *keep on doing them* (Titus 3:8, 14)! If we are aware of the good we ought to do, and don't do it, we sin (Pro 3:27; James 4:17).

"Good deeds" are defined by *what God thinks is good.* They involve the things that are right, just, and fair to others (Pro 2:29) and treating others impartially (Pro 28:21). And they include doing the kinds of things that are *excellent and are profitable.* The Greek words imply that such deeds are valuable and helpful to other people, especially to people in need (Titus 3:8, 14; 1 John 3:16).

So, Christ followers are to keep in a state of readiness to act, to go into "good works mode" at the slightest opportunity (Titus 3:1). When it comes to doing good things, we are to be like "God's Marines"—the first to serve!

In order to stay ready and fit for God's use in good things, we need to keep ourselves spiritually clean (2 Tim 2:21). A growing awareness of Scripture will help equip us for any good thing God wants to do through us (2 Tim 3:17). And, we need to be in regular fellowship with other believers who are stirring each other up to keep on with doing good to others (Heb 10:24-25).

Doing good to others is to be our way of life. Even if we are unjustly accused or punished, we commit ourselves to our faithful Creator and continue to do good (1 Pet 3:19). Rather than being overcome by evil, we overcome evil with good (by doing good) (Rom 12:21). Indeed, the way we seek the glory, honor, and immortality that come with eternal life it is by persistence in doing good (Rom 2:7).

Good deeds are for *all* Christians to do. Wealthy followers of Christ are to make sure they are rich in good deeds (1 Tim 6:18-19). The overseer in the church is to be one who loves what is good (Titus 1:8). Christian leaders are to set an example of doing what is good (Titus 2:7). The best adornment for a Christian woman is not expensive clothes, jewelry and coiffure, but good deeds (1 Tim 2:9-10)—that is to say, the focus of her life needs not to be her clothing and appearance, but good deeds. The thing which qualifies an older widow for support by the church is not merely her age, but her track record of a life doing good deeds (1 Tim 5:9-10). Indeed, the best wife sees to it that she does only good to her husband, never harm (Pro 31:12).

Some resent having to do good to others. They pose a theological excuse, that even though they have no works/deeds (that is, they are doing little or nothing), they *still* have faith in Christ. James, the brother of Jesus, challenges their idea as worthless. Good deeds include meeting the needs of brothers and sisters who are lacking clothes and food. If one has the ability to meet their needs and will not, but simply wishes them well, his "faith" is *no good.* It won't save him. Faith that is not accompanied by works is dead. One shows his faith, not apart from his deeds, but *through* his deeds (Jas 2:14-19). Christian "privatism" is disobedience to Christ.

Doing good blesses the doer. As Jesus said, it really is more blessed to give than to receive (Acts 20:35). Doing good has always been part of the formula for having the best life (Ecc 3:12). The one who does good is favored by God (Pro 12:22) who will reward him (Pro 14:14). The one who seeks good will keep finding good will around him (Pro 11:27). As he plans good, he keeps discovering that love and faithfulness surround him (Pro 14:22). When he dies, he leaves a heritage and inheritance for his grandchildren (Pro 13:22).

Doing good is not some minor appendix to the life of God's people. It is at the very core of what God wants. Therefore, it is not surprising that good shows up in the life of the wise person. The wise one:

A. Lives A Good Life. (Jas 3:13) The wise person is a source of good, not evil. If a person engages in negative behavior, he is not wise.

B. Acts In Humility. (Jas 3:13) A spirit of deference and submission surrounds and permeates the good deeds of the wise one. Arrogance or haughtiness indicate the presence of a fool. A spirit of bitter envy or selfish ambition indicates the actor is not wise (see James 3:14-17).

2. *PRACTICES* THE WORD OF GOD

Jesus says that the wise are those who hear His teachings and then put them into practice, using them as the basis for the way they build their lives. Those who base their lives on anything other than the teachings of the Scripture are foolish (Matt 7:24-27). The wise person not only *learns* the teachings of Jesus, he *practices* them.

Since the wise person fears the LORD, he is concerned to make sure his life is consistent with God's directions in the Scriptures. The Scriptures make one wise for salvation through faith in Christ (2 Tim 3:15).

One can drift into living like an unwise person. Effort has to be made to live *wisely*. Living wisely means paying close attention to see that one's manner of life aligns with God's will (Eph 5:15-17). Rather than operating in a mindless, foolish fashion, the wise person seeks to *understand* God's will—and then he does God's will.

3. IS SELF-CONTROLLED

Self-control is also a significant concern for believers in the New Testament. In presenting the Gospel to the ruler Felix, Paul discourses on major Christian teachings. Self-control is one of the three major topics Paul covers (Acts 24:25). It is one of the fruit that grow out of the Holy Spirit as we walk in Him (Gal 5:22-23). Self-control is a major need for both older and younger men in the church (Titus 2:2, 6) and for younger wives (Titus 2:5). It turns out to be one of the major themes of the Christian life:

(The grace of God)...teaches us to say "No" to ungodliness and worldly passions, and to live self-controlled, upright and godly lives in this present age, (Titus 2:11-12 NIV).

Self-control is also a qualification for overseers in the church (Titus 1:8). Two Greek words describe the qualified overseer: sophron (so'-frone), curbing one's desires and impulses, and egkrates (eng-krat-ace'), meaning to be strong in a matter and implying self-mastery, especially control of one's appetites.

Respect is the practical basis for leadership in the church. Since the church is made up of "volunteers" and there is no way to compel people to follow, the only real authority church leaders have is due to the respect members have for them. Therefore, to qualify for leadership, a person must live a respectable life in many categories. Self–control is one of the categories in which leaders must set the example for others and by which they win their respect. Paul is aware of this. He considers it necessary for him to aggressively exercise self-control over his own body. A lack of self-control might disqualify him from the ministry (1 Cor 9:25-27).

The wise person is a self-controlled person. He controls both his passions and his speech.

A. Controlled Passions. In the normal course of this world, people simply follow the desires of their bodies and minds, and gratify their cravings (Eph 2:3). The result is addiction/enslavement to their passions and pleasures, and a life of malice and envy. Envy grows as we become aware of others more gratified than we are. Malice, mutual hatred, and bitterness grow as people use one another (Titus 3:3). God's grace teaches us to say no to ungodliness and worldly passions and to live self-controlled, upright, and godly lives (Titus 2:12).

God does not let His emotions and urges rule over Him. Instead he rules over them. Like the Lord, the wise person refuses to let his urges and impulses have control of his life. Instead, he restrains and controls his:

1. Impulses. Human beings occasionally experience sudden surges of emotion or impulses to act. The wise person resists the surges and controls his:

a. Anger. Fools have hot tempers and vent their anger. But the wise person calms himself, overlooks offenses, blesses those who curse him, and attempts to help others calm down (Pro 29:8, 11; 19:11; Luke 6:27-28). A hot-tempered, easily angered person has not yet attained wisdom.

b. Recklessness. Fools are not only short-tempered, they are also reckless (Pro 14:16). A reckless person lacks proper caution and is careless about consequences. He exposes himself more to danger than good sense requires. When the reckless impulse strikes, the fool is off and away (Pro 14:16). The words of a reckless person can wound others like a sword (Pro 12:18). The reckless person simply does not understand and value what is really important in life.

The fear of the LORD stops the wise person short of reckless behavior, especially as that behavior moves toward evil (Pro 14:16). Rather than being reckless, the wise "walk exactly," the literal understanding of the Greek in Eph 5:15. They check their actions to make sure they conform exactly to the will and word of God. The wise think through their actions before they start out on a course (Pro 14:8, 18). They are especially concerned to look for trouble ahead (Pro 27:12). They may have a reckless impulse, but they think through before they take their next step (Pro 15:14).

In order to qualify as an overseer in the church, one is to live an "orderly" life, not a chaotic and reckless ones (1 Tim 3:2). And, he is to conduct himself with dignity and gravity, living with a sense of the important in life—not throw caution to the wind with a disregard for what matters (1 Tim 3:4, Titus 2:7).

2. Appetites. The wise person reins in his appetite for:

a. Drink. He refuses to be led astray into drunkenness, mocking and brawling by wine or beer (Pro 20:1). Top level leadership in the church must not "hang out near the wine; linger over the wine." (1 Tim 3:3; Titus 1:7).

b. Food. He restrains his appetite for food (Pro 21:20; 23:20-21). Gluttony leads one to drowsiness, laziness, and ultimately to poverty (Pro 23:21).

c. Sex. He keeps his thought life and his sexual drive channeled within God's will (Pro 6:32; Matt 5:28). The overseer in the church is to be a "one woman man" (1 Tim 3:2; Titus 1:6), not a guy with a roving eye. As a godly person, he keeps his affections set on his own wife (Pro 5:19-21). And, he treats other women as he would his mother or sister, in absolute purity (1 Tim 5:2). Those who become immorally involved are outside the will of God, and face serious trouble from God (1 Thes 4:3-8, Pro 5:8-14, 21-23).

3. Greed. The love of money is the seedbed of all kinds of evil (1 Tim 6:8-10). And, it is addictive. The one who loves money never has money enough (Ecc 5:10). Indeed, the drive for "mammon" (material goods, possessions, money) competes in the hearts of people for the loyalty that is due only to God. One will serve God or Mammon; he can't serve both (Matt 6:24). While money is "uncertain" (it can be suddenly lost) (Pro 23:5; 1 Tim 6:17), it appears to be the answer for every problem in life (Ecc 10:19). So, this rebellious world loves it and the things it can buy (the lust of the eyes). And, the world can set its hooks in us who follow Christ (1 John 2:14-15).

Actually, greed (being eager for more) is idolatry (Col 3:5). The greedy one has decided to serve Mammon, not God. Greed is one of the hallmarks of illegitimate leadership in the church (2 Pet 2:3). Church overseers are to keep their lives free from a love of money or greed (1 Tim 3:3; 1 Pet 5:2), and from pursuing "dishonest money" (Titus 1:7).

The wise person refuses to let his desire for material things get out of hand. Though he has an appreciation for the value and power of money, he will not wear himself out in order to get rich (Pro 23:4-5). Neither will he fall into the love of money (1 Tim 6:8-10). He knows the desire to get rich will cause the growth of other foolish desires that will bring him deep pain, not prosperity (1 Tim 6:9).

B. Crafted Words. Fools tend to "run off at the mouth," whether the style is gushing out foolish things without thinking (Pro 12:23; 15:2), a constant flow of drivel (Pro 10:8), verbosity about the future (Ecc 10:12-14), or pompous posturing (Ps 73:3, 8-9 KJV). As a result, the fool's own words result in severe trouble for him (Pro 18:6; Ecc 10:12).

The wise weigh their words and choose them carefully for the impact they will make. The wise choose words that are:

1. Prudent. The wise show skill and good judgment in the way they use words. Their words demonstrate:

• **Restraint.** They prefer fewer words. Fools prefer to multiply words (Pro 10:19; 17:28; Ecc 10:14).

• **Forethought.** They consider the impact of their words, both as they speak (Pro 16:23), and especially as they instruct. They prefer words that will engage the minds of hearers and stimulate them to thought and learning (Pro 1:6; Ecc 12:9).

• **Discretion.** They have a cautious reserve in their speech (Pro 26:16) that protects them (Pro 14:3) and allows them to deal verbally with fools (Pro 26:4).

2. Pleasant. Their words are quiet, calm (Ecc 9:17), gracious (Ecc 10:12), and pleasant (Pro 16:21). "Pleasant" indicates that their words are pleasing and agreeable rather than harsh or irritating.

3. Persuasive. The verbal persuasiveness of the wise comes from their forethought and their pleasantness. Their forethought makes their speech judicious, which increases their persuasiveness (Pro 16:23). And, the pleasant nature of their words adds to their persuasiveness (Pro 16:21). As a result, the wise are able to motivate and goad others into helpful paths in life (Ecc 12:9, 11).

4. Profitable. The wise choose words that are profitable to others. Even though their words are quiet, they should be heeded (Ecc 9:17), for they benefit others. The wise select words that:

• **Heal.** Reckless words wound (Pro 12:18). The wise choose healing words.

• **Change perspective.** They help people toward knowledge, the information that shapes spiritual perspective to be more like God's. The wise commend knowledge (spiritual perspective) and spread it (Pro 15:2, 7).

• **Reorient.** They help people change direction, turning people from death to life (Pro 13:14). Even their rebuke adds attractiveness to the life of those who will heed it (Pro 25:12). Given the benefit, the rebuke of the wise is to be preferred to songs in one's own honor sung by fools (Ecc 7:5).

5. Edifying. All the above traits add up to "edification" and help define it. A godly person will let *no unwholesome* communication come from their mouths. Rather, they select only those words that will *benefit the hearer* according to the hearer's needs in the situation (Eph 4:29).

Note that the fear of the LORD (discussed earlier) provides incentive to rein in oneself. Gratitude to God for His grace (Titus 2:11) and an understanding of the consequences God can bring lead to a profound respect for God that motivates us to self-control.

Therefore, since we are receiving a kingdom that cannot be shaken, let us be thankful, and so worship God acceptably with reverence and awe, for our "God is a consuming fire." (Heb 12:28-29 NIV)

4. AGGRESSIVELY SUBMITS

God has instituted authority in the human realm (Rom 13:1-2), in the state (Rom 13:1-5), in the home (Eph 5:23-24, 33; Col 3:20), in business (Col

3:22-25), and in the church (Heb 13:17; 1 Cor 16:15-16). God works in an unseen way through those in authority (Pro 21:1). While there is a time to refuse to obey those in authority (Acts 4:19-20), God desires that those under authority follow the authority's direction (1 Pet 2:13-14)—in the state, in the home, in business, and in the church. Those who humble themselves under God's hand by submitting to their leaders will find God's grace and help. And, later God will exalt (promote) them (1 Pet 5:5-6, Matt 23:12). Rebels find God opposing them (1 Pet 5:5), and pay a dear price for their rebellion (Pro 24:21-22).

A wise person follows valid authority. And, he follows with his mind engaged and his creativity operational.

A. Heeds Instructions. Fools tend to be inattentive or chattering when instructions or commands are given out (Pro 10:8). Rather than ignore directions and commands, the wise person receives and heeds them, especially when given by a boss who follows Christ (Pro 10:8; 1 Tim 6:1-2; Luke 12:42-48).

B. Thinks Ahead Creatively. Some carry out a leader's direction mindlessly and minimally, like the crass and lazy servant in the story of the "talents" (Matt 25:18, 26-30). The wise person engages his mind and creativity to give forethought to both proper timing and procedures for carrying out his leader's wishes (Ecc 8:5). He frequently will earn the accolade, "Well done, my good and faithful servant!" (Matt 25:23)

C. Calms The Anger Of Leaders. The boss's anger portends severe damage to the offender (Pro 16:14; 20:2). A wise person appeases the boss's anger. Likely, he will give a soft answer in the situation, which turns away wrath (Pro 15:1; 14:9). He finds out what he did wrong and rectifies it. He doesn't simply ask forgiveness without making amends (Pro 14:35; Matt 5:23-24; Acts 24:16). And—he doesn't repeat the offense (Pro 17:9; 26:11).

Again, the fear of the LORD helps motivate submission to valid leadership. The desire to honor God by doing his will, even when it is mediated through human leaders, prompts our submission.

And, having previously come to a point of humility removes much of the emotional struggle from the heart of the wise. Rather than struggle with the question of whether the *leader deserves* to have his obedience, the wise one has already learned to humble himself (that is, assign himself a lower rank in the scheme of things), and can focus his energies on carrying out the assignment, not emotionally stewing over having to lower himself to serve.

5. LEARNS AGGRESSIVELY AND APPRECIATIVELY

A. Takes initiative to learn. Fools despise wisdom and helpful corrective instruction (Pro 1:7). They resist advice and see no need for improvement in their plans or their lives (Pro 12:15). The wise actively seek, acquire, and retain knowledge (Pro 18:15; 10:14).

B. Is Teachable. When instructed, the wise person learns. When advised, the wise listen (Pro 9:9; 12:15; 13:10; 21:11). One correction will sink more deeply into a person of discernment than a hundred lashes with a whip do into a fool (Pro 17:10).

C. Is Appreciative. Mockers hate and abuse those who try to correct them (Pro 9:7-9). The wise person heeds and loves those who correct him (Pro 13:1; 9:8).

Note that for the wise, humility has already opened the door to learning. To accept the posture of a learner, one has to admit his need of instruction (ignorance), and admit that the one who is attempting to instruct him actually possesses information or insight that the learner does not. However, the humble one has already admitted to his neediness and to the possible excellence of others. He does not have to defend an inflated ego. So, the wise one can spend his time understanding the one who would correct or teach him, rather than emotionally stewing over his situation and feeling judged (to be ignorant) by the other person. Without humility, it is difficult for people to learn from others. Pride keeps getting in the way and blocking the opportunity to learn.

The fear of the LORD also enables learning. Since the learner already wants to honor God with his life, he wants to bring any and all areas of his life into conformity with God's will. Those who would teach him or correct him are actually doing him a favor, enabling him to be more like Christ. He is not naïve enough to accept just any instruction or advice; he will check it out to make sure it is true and accurate (Acts 17:11). But his motive in checking is not to resist the instruction. Nor is it to prove that he has a greater grasp of the Scripture than the one attempting to teach him. He simply wants to be like Christ. Therefore, he will learn even from a jackass, if the jackass is telling the truth (Num 22:21-33).

6. HAS *"GUMPTION"*

Gumption is a term little-used today. It combines two wonderful qualities: initiative and good sense. Gumption is *initiative in using good judgment* to direct one's actions.

In bygone days of raccoon hunting, a well-known pastor defined gumption as *that which, if a small quantity were rubbed on the nose of a hunting dog, would cause him to bark up a tree with a raccoon in it, not just any tree.* Gumption causes a person to rise above minimal performance and mumbled excuses. Its combination of initiative and good sense take people to higher levels in life.

Five characteristics of the wise person add up in different ways to initiative in using good judgment to direct his/her actions. The wise person has gumption. He:

A. Asks The Right Questions. The wise person recognizes that some questions are not worth considering. He takes initiative to focus on helpful matters.

1. **He doesn't waste time on useless questions.** Such questions do not have real answers (Pro 20:24). It is not wise to ask such questions (Ecc 7:20). Examples would be:
   - "Why were the former days better than these?" (Ecc 7:10). This particular question not only does not have an answer, it may also mask a complaint against the Lord. And, the wise do not complain against God (Eze 18:25, Pro 19:3, 20:24).
   - "What will my life be like tomorrow?" (Ecc 8:7, 7:14, Mt 6:33-34)
   - "How can I tell in advance which of my efforts/projects will prosper so that I can avoid all risk, for I want to invest only in the definitely profitable ones?" (Pro 27:12, Ecc 11:1-6)
   - The list of useless questions could go on, such as, "What if I...were to die,, ...lose my job, ...get married, ...had never gotten married?
2. **He ponders profitable questions.** Examples might be:
   - What must I do to be saved? (Pro 16:31)
   - What is my current financial condition? (Pro 27:23-24)
   - What promises have I made that I need to keep, especially promises of gifts, services or loyalty? (Pro 25:14; 20:6)
   - How is God viewing this situation right now?
   - What really is right and just and fair in this situation? (Pro 2:9)
   - What are my responsibilities in this situation—and which things are not my responsibilities?
   - What is God trying to say to me through this situation right now?
   - What does the Scripture say about this? (Acts 17:11)

- What is really going on in the heart of the person I am dealing with right now? (Pro 20:5)
- In this situation I am facing, how can I seek first God's kingdom and His righteousness? (Matt 6:33-34)

B. Lays Up Resources For The Future. The foolish person takes little thought to the future. He tends to consume all his resources in the moment (Pro 21:20).

The wise person, however, while trusting God for provision daily (Matt 6:33-34), takes initiative to lay up resources for the future (Pro 30:24-25).

This is the lesson of the ants: they lay up resources for future times of short supply. It is also the lesson of the wise maidens in the story told by Jesus (Matt 25:1-12).

C. Takes Cover In Danger. Most people don't look ahead to see danger coming. The prudent person does, and hides himself (Pro 27:12). Also, many people are too proud to admit their inability to handle a more powerful opponent. Humility helps one take a wiser course.

The wise person is not a fearful person for he is righteous, and the righteous are as bold as a lion (Pro 28:1). But, he has the good sense to take refuge amid danger. This is the lesson of the coney. The little hamster-like animal, in a sense, has a "proper assessment of himself." He grasps that he is weak. He does not mistake his inability to survive an encounter with an eagle or a lion. He accepts his vulnerability and so takes appropriate action. When predators appear, he squeezes into cracks in the rocky crags where he lives (Pro 30:24, 26). There he is safe until the danger passes.

In a similar vein, we are to have an accurate self-estimate (Rom 12:3), so that we do not get into pride and tackle things inappropriate for us: things too large, too dangerous or too "exalted" for us (Ps 131:1-3).

The gumption to admit one's weakness and to seek sanctuary is not cowardly; it is wise. This principle applies not only to situations of physical danger, but also to taking safety measures and to running to Christ amid spiritual danger (Ps 18:2, 31, 46; 31:2,3). One might battle for what is right against impossible odds, even risking death. But it is not courageous to go to certain death against impossible odds for the sake of sin (pride, vengeance, greed, etc.); it is merely foolish.

D. Aggressively Cooperates. Most people are focused on their own agendas. They spend their time, energy and money *almost entirely* on their own interests with, at best, minimal concern for the interests of others. In order to freely pursue their selfish agenda, they become *loners* They separate themselves from the group. In so doing, they *defy* all "sound judgment" (Pro 18:1). "Sound judgment" translates a Hebrew word that speaks of an ability to bring projects to completion or to take ideas and make them become a reality. Becoming a loner *flies in the face of* what it *really takes* to make one's dreams come true. By selfishly withdrawing from others to work on his own agenda, the loner violates the way reality works, and does the very thing that will prevent his agenda from coming to fruition.

The wise person values teamwork and voluntarily cooperates; he has a volunteer spirit. He or she takes the initiative to voluntarily (without command by a leader) and aggressively fit in with others and work together for the common good. This is the lesson of the locusts. Without a king to make them do so, they advance together in ranks (Pro 30:24, 27) across the countryside—and succeed in stripping it clean of vegetation!

The need to take one's place as part of a team and work cooperatively with others is:

- **A fact of life.** If one is going to succeed in life, he or she must learn cooperative teamwork—it is simply the way reality works (Pro 18:1).
- **The preferred way**. The Scriptures prefer it, for it provides a much greater comfort (as warmth), protection, production/reward, and chance for success (Ecc 4:9-12). Thus, the one who isolates himself from others lives with greater discomforts (as, enduring the cold by himself), exposes himself to risks he can hardly handle by himself (a fall or an attack), multiplies his labor, and reduces the increased return (good reward) that could come through a team effort. Overall, he decreases his chances for success. He acts against all sound judgment (Pro 18:1).
- **Essential to the Body of Christ**. No single person possesses all the gifts needed to make the Body of Christ fully functional (Rom 12:4-6). The healthy functioning of the Body requires that people with different gifts voluntarily choose to work cooperatively for the greater good without division but with compassion and concern for one another (1 Cor 12:7,12, 14-21, 25, 27; 1 Pet 4:10-11).

E. Diligent. Sluggards find any excuse, no matter how fantastic, to avoid responsibility and work (Pro 26:13). A lazy person never finds an appropriate moment to work.

Fools may work, but quickly tire of it (Ecc 10:15). And, fools tend to design their work poorly for they tend to operate out of their weakness—which grinds them down even faster (Ecc 10:2). The failure to work hard means that the fool will profit little from his efforts (Pro 14:23), and the sluggard will have to drown in his own desires, for desire is all he will ever have (Pro 21:25).

Diligent work brings tremendous benefit: the accomplishment of goals and a sense of satisfaction (Pro 13:4; 21:25), rising to leadership (Pro 12:24), making profit (Pro 21:5), and gaining wealth (Pro 10:4).

The diligence to develop high skill in one's work will lead one into a higher realm of service. Such skilled people have kings, not commoners, as their clients (Pro 22:29).

The wise person takes initiative to be diligent so that he may advance in life. This is the lesson of the lizard (or in some translations, spider). Though rather common and neither impressive nor intimidating, some manage to live in king's palaces (Pro 30:24, 28).

For example, to be a secretary is not an exceptionally impressive career. Secretaries serve all over the world. However, CEO's of multinational corporations need secretaries. While many get a job as a secretary, it is possible to become secretary to the wealthy and powerful, and to enjoy the privileges of functioning in their elite and luxurious environment—like a lizard living in a king's castle. However, the rich and powerful don't choose lazy, sloppy people to be their secretaries. They look for the skilled and diligent.

The wise person operates in such a way that, even though he is a rather ordinary person, he gets to work with top-level leadership, and experience the benefits and privileges (the king's palace) of those who live in the top echelons of society.

How does he do it? He does it by diligence and skill, on the job and across life.

Diligence is essentially persevering effort, an effort that is:

- **Steady** (Persistent)—not off and on, but consistent (1 Cor 15:58 NLT).
- **Earnest** (Energetic)—not lackadaisical, but intense, making the most of the opportunity (Eph 5:15-17); working, not halfheartedly, but with all the heart (Eph 6:6-7; Col 3:22-23).

• **Thorough**—It does not miss or skip parts of the job to be done. See the story of judgment upon a man who did part of his job but not all of it in 1 Kings 20:37-41.

The crucial factor in job promotions is not brilliance, but diligence and skill in one's work. Diligence requires skill in the *whole job*, however, not just in one's technical skill, but also skill in dealing with people. The one who develops great skill in his work will serve top officials; he will not remain at the bottom of the ladder (Pro 22:29).

The wise person is diligent, not just on the job, but all across life. In the view of Scripture, God is frequently sending us seasons of opportunity that can be exploited for the good of God and for ourselves. Amid a world of inconvenience and opposition, wise people remain focused on the will of God, and make the most of the opportunities that God sends. We need to be diligent with the opportunities he gives us (Eph 5:15-17).

The diligent person is self-motivated. A Christian is to have such self-motivation, desiring to work and to respond to the opportunities of life in such a way that, not only is his human supervisor pleased, but Jesus Christ, the one for whom he is really living and working, is pleased (Eph 6:7-8; Col 3:23-24).

I once heard a saying: "When the required minimum becomes your chosen maximum, the sum of your life is mediocrity." Mediocre lizards don't live in the king's palace. The diligent, self-motivated, skilled, high-performance lizards do.

7. STRATEGIZES EFFECTIVELY

A. **Uses Proper Timing And Procedures.** The wise person knows both how to create an effective plan for achieving his goals, and he has an accurate sense of timing as to when to execute his plans (Ecc 8:5-6). The result is repeated success.

B. **Produces The Right Results.** His ability to produce the results he intended proves his wisdom. Wisdom is proven right by her children (results) (Luke 7:35).

C. **Employs Only Godly Strategies (Jas 3:13-18).** The wise person chooses to achieve his goals in a manner that is in line with the values and character of God Himself. Indeed, these characteristics not only mark the wise strategy, but they also mark the wise person. See the Profile of the Wise Strategy below.

8. IS HIGHLY SUCCESSFUL

Fools rise to shame, not honor (Pro 3:35). In the best scenario for fools, the financial dreams of the fool arrive, but only to be later destroyed by the Lord (Ps 73:3, 18-20 KJV).

Over time, the wisdom of the wise person brings to himself recognition, honor, and leadership as well as wealth and the other blessings of wisdom (listed in chapter one) (Pro 3:35; 4:7-9; 8:14, 17-19, 21; 14::24).

PROFILE OF THE WISE STRATEGY

James, the brother of Jesus, distinguishes between two approaches to the wisdom/strategy one uses to get what one wants. He identifies one as being from heaven, that is, characteristic of God and proceeding from Him. The other strategy/wisdom has nothing to do with heaven.

THE UNGODLY STRATEGY

According to James, the ungodly strategy is:

- **Unspiritual or "soulish."** It is just like what unregenerate humanity cooks up, and has nothing to do with the Holy Spirit.
- **Earthly.** It has no taste to it of the grace and joy of God's dominion. The citizens of this world would recognize it quickly enough for the governments of the world, the businesses of the world, and the people of the world usually operate in just this sorry manner. This kind of strategy is only the ways/wisdom of this world warmed over.
- **Demonic.** It is just the kind of strategy/wisdom used in Satan's realm, in which it has its roots.

When people really want something—*especially* when they want it for the wrong reasons—and they are not getting it, they generate conflict in an attempt to secure their desires (Jas 4:1-4). Rooted in the demonic, widely practiced in the world, and appealing to unregenerate hearts, this type of strategizing is capable of achieving its goals, but it has nothing to do with God.

Many times the motives behind the strategies people create are two ugly things:

- **Bitter Envy.** Someone gets angry and hurt because another person is enjoying some advantage. The envious person may want to enjoy the advantage the other person has or may not really want the advantage—they just don't want the other person to have it! Amid their jealousy, they develop an angry, hurt, bitter attitude toward the other person. Jealousy is part and parcel of this world (Rom 13:13; 1 Cor 3:3; Gal 5:20). It tends to be far more destructive than anger or rage (Pro 27:4).

Jealousy costs terribly. It has driven deep bitterness and sorrow into families (Gen 30:1; 37:11; Acts 7:9). It also is the motive behind competition for achievement (Ecc 4:4), much religious conflict (Ps 106:16; Matt 27:18; Acts 5:17; 13:45; 17:5), and, often, ministry zeal (Phil 1:15). Envy actually can generate a wasting disease in the envier (Pro 14:30).

- **Selfish Ambition.** Someone decides to have his way at the expense of others. He has a goal (ambition) and will hurt others to achieve it (selfish). The Greek term implies "pushing forward for personal ends; partisanship" (see *Robertson's Word Pictures*). It brings up images of under-the-table strategizing, contentious politicking, and the intent to have victory at the expense of the health of the group or church.

This stubborn determination to have what one wants is much the same as *'ivveleth (iv-veh'-leth)*, Hebrew for the stubborn, adversarial determination to have one's own way (see p. 150). The willingness to hurt others is an expression of *ra' (rah)*, Hebrew for the willingness to harm that is born into the hearts of all people (see p. 151).

Selfish ambition is actually forbidden to Christians. They are commanded to look to the interests of others, not just themselves (Phil 2:3-4). Rather than getting into selfish ambition and exalting themselves, Christians should adopt the humility that Christ had when He left heaven to live as a peasant and die a horrible unjust death on earth (Phil 2:5-11).

Sometimes those who are into bitter envy or selfish ambition will boast to their confidantes about the intensity and vehemence of their desire ("I won't rest until…;" "I will die before I let them…;" "How I will enjoy the look on their faces when…;" etc.). Faced with their opponents, they may try to hide their motivations with lies ("How could you think that of me? I would never…;" "We are only out for the good of the whole organization;" etc.) James warns them to do neither (Jas 3:14). Rather, he urges them to realize the ungodliness of their strategy and recognize its corrupt, earthly, demonic, source (Jas 3:15).

When envy and selfish ambition are the driving forces, the chosen strategy will have predictable results:

- **Disorder.** The Greek word implies confusion, instability and disorder, like a crowd starting to panic. Where envy and selfish ambition take root, the organization starts to shred, to disintegrate, as damage spreads among its members.

• **Every evil practice.** All kinds of flawed, disgusting and harmful deeds are done. People are not only hurt, but others become disgusted and disillusioned with the organization because of the foul things done.

What goes on could be pictured as

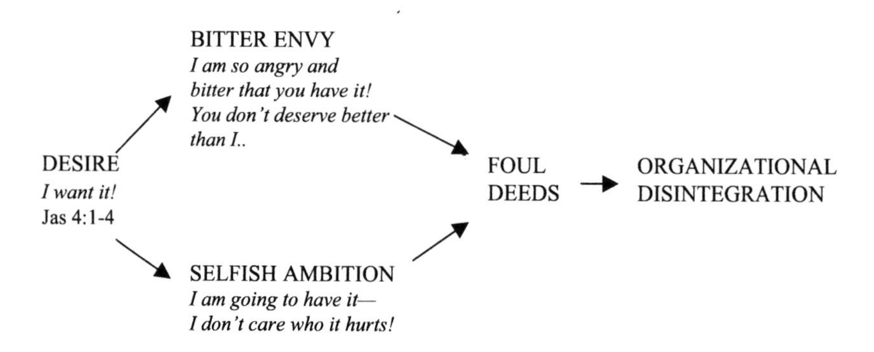

THE TRULY WISE STRATEGY

There is a different strategy/wisdom, a wisdom that is actually from the Lord. It bears the marks of the character of God upon its attitudes and approaches. This divine type of strategy is used by the wise as they seek, in a spirit of humility, to do good.

James uses several Greek words to describe the godly strategy. We will use English terms in the light of the meaning of the Greek words used by James. He says that the strategy with its source in heaven is:

Pure. The Greek word is hagnos (hag-nos') meaning clean, "innocent." This word is related to the Greek word we translate as "holy." It implies pure from fault; it is all good, not half good, half bad. In order to please themselves, the ungodly operate with impure or mixed motives. God, Himself, is pure (holy), and wants us to be holy (1 Pet 1:16). So, the wisdom that comes from Him is pure. Godly strategies are driven by pure, holy motives. Especially, they intend to do what is pleasing to God.

Peaceable or peace-loving. Fools are quickly ready to fight in order to get their way. But, God is a God of peace (Rom 16:20). The wisdom He bestows reflects His character. It prefers to make peace, not war, and tries to find ways to do what is needed without conflict.

Considerate. The Greek word is somewhat difficult to translate into English. It means "seemly, fitting, appropriate," and carries the idea of doing what is considerate or fitting rather than being rude, harsh or shocking. It implies being equitable, fair, moderate, forbearing, not insisting on the letter of the law (see *Vine's Word Studies of the New Testament*).

Fools are rough and demanding with others (Pro 14:3 NKJ). As the wise person pursues his goals, he is considerate of people. He is mild of spirit rather than rough, equitable in approach not selfish and demanding, and does what is appropriate rather than being rude or shocking. The same thought is captured in Paul's writings about how Christians are to treat one another considerately (Eph 4:2; 1 Thes 2:7, 1 Tim 3:3).

Reasonable and Submissive. The Greek word implies "ready to obey," "compliant." Fools resist correction and redirection (Pro 15:12). And, the ungodly tend to be defensive lest covert motives be uncovered (Pro 28:1). Many people feel that the only way to protect their interests is to be rebellious and demanding. Such an approach has no place in a godly game plan.

God Himself experiences submission. Submission is right in the heart of the Godhead, as the Son submits to the Father (John 8:28-29) and the Spirit submits to both Father and Son (John 14:26; 15:26). The wisdom that comes from God is not rooted in rebellion. As it pursues its goals, it is easy to approach and engage in discussion for it has no secret rebellions to protect.

The godly strategy is open to reason. Since its ultimate desire is to please God, it has no fear of finding better ways to please God. Questions can be raised about the current strategy without hackles also being raised. Rather than being defensive, the wise person is willing to yield to better methods.

Merciful. The implication of the Greek word is kindness or good will toward the miserable and afflicted, joined with a desire to relieve them (see *Thayer's Greek Lexicon*). Foolish and ungodly people tend to become hard-hearted and vindictive toward their opponents—and toward those who may be hurt by their strategies. Along the path to victory, the ungodly are ruthless.

Godly wisdom is not ruthless, achieving its goals at any cost to others. Like the Lord Jesus, it will not build its success by crushing the weak or afflicted (Isa 42:3). Instead, it moves to do them good and relieve their troubles. Many have no mercy (Isa 32:5-6). God, however, is merciful (Luke 6:36). Thus, the path chosen by the wise person contains mercy for people accidentally hurt or for hurting opponents.

Replete with Good Results. When the foolish or ungodly implement their devilish plans, all kinds of foul things begin to happen to people. Then, the organization begins to unravel as hurt and animosity build.

However, God is good (Luke 18:19), and desires that good be done on planet earth (Acts 10:38). As time goes on and the results of the godly strategy start coming in, the constant report is of good things happening *to* people and *for* people. Time passes, effort is expended, and people are increasingly blessed and edified as a result. The wisdom from above is full of good fruit.

Impartial. The Greek term implies both "undistinguishing"—not being partial in judgment—and unhesitating, refusing to place a premium on doubt (see Robertson's *Word Pictures of the NT*). The ungodly play favorites and will pervert justice for the sake of their cronies.

But, God Himself is impartial (1 Pet 1:17). The wise person refuses to play favorites, and to, thereby, treat people unjustly. Like the Lord, the wise person will give honor where honor is due, and reward where reward is due (Rom 13:7; Rev 22:12). The plans of the wise operate justly and impartially, giving to others what is due them.

Straightforward. The Greek word implies "un-pretended," without false pretences; sincere. The fool is full of deceit (Pro 12:20; 14:8).

God, however, does not lie (Num 23:19). Godly wisdom "puts things out on the table." It does no double-dealing. The wise person is sincere and genuine. The wisdom from above contains no hypocrisy, fraud, deceit or hidden traps. Such sincerity, operating as it does "in the light," protects the fellowship of the church or other organization (1 John 1:7).

SUMMARY OF THE WISE

The above characteristics serve as a check-list to distinguish the wise person and the strategy used by the wise—a very different strategy from that rooted in the shrewdness of this world and the demonic.

These characteristics of the wise strategy are also additional earmarks of the person in whom God's wisdom is active. They could be added to the above Profile of the Wise Person.

The divine wisdom, that is, the deep wisdom that God gives, is able to select and achieve excellent goals. It will not merely accomplish *goals* pleasing to God, it will also always operate in line within the *ways of God* and *keep the word of God*, his commandments, testimonies, statutes, etc. (Pro 4:11). The divine wisdom operates in line with the fear of the LORD (Job 28:8; Pro 9:10), and is characterized by humility (Pro 10:8), knowledge and understanding (Pro 2:6-7), discernment (Pro 14:8), and prudence (Pro 8:12). Such wisdom is of inestimable value (Job 28:13ff). It is not to be found apart from God.

It may be apparent now that, at the level of "strategy," *genuine wisdom is doing things God's way*: doing my work in the manner pleasing to God, spending my money in a manner pleasing to God, handling my marriage in a manner pleasing to God, or setting and achieving goals in a manner pleasing to God.

The characteristics of the wise person and the wise strategy (heavenly wisdom) have many overlaps with the list of the fruit of the Holy Spirit (Gal 5:22-23), the keys to a fruitful life (2 Pet 1:5-7) and the qualifications of the elder/overseer/pastor (1 Tim 3:1-7; Titus 1:5-9). These great and wonderful statements about the important things to be put into a life are not *merely* "noble ideals." They are statements about how life really works.

Many kids in youth ministries across the nation wonder about how to make life work. And, tugged between the persuasive images of the culture and the pious talk of the church, they are uncertain about the specifics of the kind of person they need to become.

The Scriptures have concrete answers. "Wisdom" is not merely an abstract concept; it is actually quite practical. And, "wise" is not a mystical, misty term—it gets down to the nitty-gritty, practical attitudes and actions that shape how we deal with people as we try to move ahead in life.

Many troubled marriages will continue to have problems because the partners want to *solve their problems while hanging on to a foolish approach* to life. Until they move beyond selfishness (selfish ambition) and resentment, and begin to humbly seek to do good to their partner, they will continue to ride the "Mocker's Merry-Go-Round," for wisdom will evade them.

A *wise* person uses a *wise* approach to life—*God's way.*

Think About It

Which characteristics of the wise most describe you right now?

Which characteristics of the wise do you most need to develop in your life? In what ways do you need to grow in them? Can you think of any steps you need to take to develop these?

Which characteristics of the "wise strategy" have you normally used in going about getting what you want?

Can you identify any ploys or techniques that you use to get what you want that violate the concerns of the "wise strategy?"

Which of the earmarks of wise strategy do you need to grow in? How?

EARLIER, WE SAID THAT THE STRATEGIES WE CHOOSE ARE
SHAPED BY OUR GOD-CONCEPT.
EXACTLY WHAT ARE THE GOD-CONCEPTS
BEHIND WISDOM'S STRATEGIES?
WHAT IS WISDOM'S GOD LIKE?
HOW DOES THIS GOD OPERATE?
WANT TO KNOW?
READ ON!

Chapter 7

THE GOD WHO IS THERE

Wisdom's God-Concept

GOD-CONCEPT AND STRATEGY

We have already seen that one's god-concept shapes the way he makes his decisions in the world. This brings up a set of questions that need to be answered. Who is, or what is, the nature of the God of the Bible? How does the God of the Bible act in relation to the world? What kinds of "ways" are pleasing and honorable to Him? How does He want us to act in relation to Him and in the way we handle life?

We have looked at the wise person and the wise strategy. Both have some strong moral characteristics. Those moral ways of acting flow out of the wise one's understanding of the God behind the universe.

In 1970 I was trying to understand how God fit into daily life. A friend suggested that I read a book entitled *The God Who Is There* by Francis Schaeffer. Schaeffer laid out the connection between philosophy, art and the development of popular culture beginning with the middle ages and ending with the rise of the Beatles. I had never realized the extent to which the "god-concept" behind the emerging philosophy in one generation shaped the culture of succeeding generations.

What is true of "god-concepts" on a *cultural level* is also true of god-concepts on a personal level—except that, at a *personal level*, the impact of the god-concept doesn't take generations to develop. One's god-concept (that is, the ideas about God he considers to be *real*, not merely *true*) impacts his *own immediate* strategy for living out his life and for pursuing his desires. Whether the god-concept is positive or negative, strong or weak, theistic, deistic, Christian, atheistic or Hindu, it shapes a person's approach to life.

Ultimately, one's god-concept will impact his/her children as they grow up under parental influence. They will absorb from parental *example* what is really important in life and how one *actually* goes about solving problems and getting what he wants.

According to the Bible, *fools* prefer certain types of god–concepts. That is why they mock the things that are important to the LORD, the God of the Bible (see Ps 92:6-7; 94:3-11; 73:3, 8-11 [KJV]; 53:1-3).

The Wise buy into different concepts about God and live their lives out of profound respect for Him.

The long-term difference between the mockers and the wise is this: pain and prosperity! While everyone will encounter difficult problems in life, in the long run—over time and eternity—the result with be that *mockers will suffer* and *the wise will be rewarded* (Pro 9:12).

Why? Because there is a certain God *who is really there*, who *really runs the universe in the way He wants.*

Wisdom has certain assumptions about who God is, what is important to Him, and how He relates to the universe of things and people. Therefore, wisdom is able to see more accurately how life really works. And, it is able to choose courses of action that will succeed, not just in the short-term, but also in the long-term.

WISDOM'S KEY ASSUMPTIONS

All of us operate from assumptions, from things we assume to be true. Most of us do not sit down and investigate our assumptions, we just make them and act based on them. How many times have you heard people say, usually after a problem has emerged, "But I *thought* that..." What we *assume* affects what we *do*, the course we take in life. And, what we *do* impacts what *happens to us*, our personal life history.

The way chosen and advocated by Wisdom is based on certain truth/realities about the *real* God and how that God relates to the lives of human beings.

Four important assumptions underlie Wisdom's approach to life:

1. The God of the Bible is the Creator. The Bible says that there is one (not many) "personal" (not an "it") God, revealed as masculine—"He," not she. God has made everything that is outside of Himself. And, everything that God has created reflects its Creator, His intelligence, design, power and character. Just as a work of art reflects the ability, techniques and preferences of the artist who created it, the created universe has patterns within it that reflect its Creator.

Rom 1:18-20
18 The wrath of God is being revealed from heaven against all the godlessness and wickedness of men who suppress the truth by their wickedness,
19 since what may be known about God is plain to them, because God has made it plain to them.
20 For since the creation of the world God's invisible qualities-- His eternal power and divine nature-- have been clearly seen, being understood from what has been made, so that men are without excuse (NIV).

These statements have tremendous **implications:**

First, there *is* a reality outside ourselves. Philosophy has tried different ways to prove that there is an outside world, a reality that exists beyond the thoughts in our minds, but philosophy keeps getting stuck.

Actually, in order to begin discussing, we have to assume that some things exist—like me, my mouth, the words I hear as I speak, you, the expression on your face, whether bored or interested (actually I would be also assuming that I know adequately enough what a bored expression looks like), etc. Philosophy has tried to prove different ways that something exists, but can't.

Perhaps you have heard the old conundrum: "I am sitting and contemplating a beautiful butterfly. How do I know for sure that reality is *I am thinking of the butterfly* and not actually *the butterfly is thinking of me contemplating it?"* A student of philosophy could work on that problem all day long and have difficulty establishing which is the accurate version of reality. However, about dinner time, with hunger pains increasing, the student would become less concerned whether *he has hunger pains* or *the butterfly thinks he has hunger pains*. Putting away his books, he would go get something to eat! Under pressure from necessity, preoccupation with theory can be postponed!

Every time a philosopher has come up with a way to prove that reality exists or to prove that he has a way to know reality for certain, a later philosopher finds a problem with the earlier person's theory. In the mean time, many philosophers have been born, educated, been hungry many times, eaten a lot of meals and died.

Reality rolls on, whether or not we have figured it out theoretically. In contrast to philosophy, the Bible does not start with merely human reason and observation alone and attempt to come up with an explanation of the world. It is much more matter-of-fact in its approach to the world. It announces to us who the Creator is, and tells us that the world in which we find ourselves was created by the Creator.

And, it presents a world/universe that exists *independently* of our perception of it. That is, *regardless what we think*, the Creation really is there. Rather than getting stuck on the issue or proving something exists or that we can know for certain that something exists, we can move on to more important questions about the life we need to live.

Because the universe exists independently of our perception of it, we will have to deal with the realities that exist in the world. The universe will not change itself to suit our opinions. We can study it to discover more about it, but it *really* is there and will not go away because we don't like something about it.

A second implication is that **reality will have *patterns* to it, patterns that we may discover.** Made by an intelligent designer, it will reflect His creativity and the principles of design He has used.

Science becomes a possibility, because the Creator-Designer is intelligent, and has produced a designed and ordered reality. Like a computer chip manufacturing company studies the new chips created by a sophisticated competitor in order to figure out how to design similar things, science can investigate reality and discover some of the principles by which the Sophisticated Designer put together reality. And, it can use those same principles to improve its own inventions.

We will find the "fingerprints" of God in the work He has created.

Reality exists and has patterns to it—patterns that may be discovered.

2. The God of the Bible is Holy and Sovereign. He rewards righteousness and punishes sin.

Holy means that God is pure and zealous for what is right and good. Unlike human beings, God is not "willy-nilly" about these things. He is decidedly *for* what is right. And, He is decidedly *against* evil. He is repulsed by the ways we hurt others, and the suffering brought into the world through human rebellion and cruelty. Not just the *results* of evil, but the very *existence* of it is an affront and a grief to Him.

That God is sovereign means that He is in absolute control of the universe and all that occurs in it. The Bible is not fully clear about exactly *how* God's sovereignty works together with human responsibility. It is clear that God's control does not overrule the human ability to make genuine, real, personal choices. Nor does God's sovereignty make God the author of sin (Jas 1:13). Within the sovereign plan and rule of God, we make real, genuine, personal choices, but even those choices fit ultimately into the outworking of God's plan (see Eph 1:11; Pro 16:4).

Putting together the holiness of God with the sovereignty of God leads to a highly significant conclusion: God, who runs the universe, will run it in a way *directed by His holiness.* The God who hates wickedness wants wickedness punished. And the God who is sovereign is *fully capable* of doing the punishment.

But because of your stubbornness and your unrepentant heart, you are storing up wrath against yourself for the day of God's wrath, when His righteous judgment will be revealed. God "will give to each person according to what he has done."

To those who by persistence in doing good seek glory, honor and immortality, He will give eternal life. But for those who are self-seeking and who reject the truth and follow evil, there will be wrath and anger.

There will be trouble and distress for every human being who does evil: first for the Jew, then for the Gentile; but glory, honor and peace for everyone who does good: first for the Jew, then for the Gentile. For God does not show favoritism. (Rom 2:5-11 NIV)

The *implication* of God's holiness and sovereignty is this: *Morality figures into our success in this world.* It will be a key part or a key hindrance to our ability to find or generate success and happiness in this world, and in the world to come.

3. The God of the Bible is not far off, but close at hand. He is very much aware of what we do and intervenes in detail in our lives.

God is quite aware of the minute details or all that is going on, whether it is the location and needs of each of billions of tiny birds in nature (Luke 6:26; 12:6) or the physical details (Luke 12:7), whispered secrets (Luke 12:2-3) or hidden motives of each human being (Luke 16:15; 1 Cor 4:5).

God also intervenes in the lives of individual human beings. He does so by His management of large scale matters such as weather patterns which affect crops, and thereby, individual human lives (Jer 5:24-25; Acts 14:17) and direct action. His intervention can impact our ability to grasp what He is doing (so, Paul *prayed* for converts Col 1:9). God can also affect individuals physically (Jas 5:14-15; Acts 12:23).

God's awareness and intervention have a key implication for us: *Our moral relationship to God will dramatically affect our well-being in life.*

Know therefore that the LORD your God is God; He is the faithful God, keeping His covenant of love to a thousand generations of those who love Him and keep His commands. But those who hate Him He will repay to their face by destruction; He will not be slow to repay to their face those who hate Him.

Therefore, take care to follow the commands, decrees and laws I give you today.

If you pay attention to these laws and are careful to follow them, then the LORD your God will keep His covenant of love with you, as He swore to your forefathers (Deu 7:9-12 NIV).

Do not be deceived: God cannot be mocked. A man reaps what he sows. The one who sows to please his sinful nature, from that nature will reap destruction; the one who sows to please the Spirit, from the Spirit will reap eternal life (Gal 6:7-8 NIV).

4. The right, moral relationship to God involves love.

The writings of the New Testament make it abundantly clear that God wants His people actively involved in agape-love, a love that sacrifices for the good of others, not based just on affection, but based on the principle that such is right; it is the way God operates. Jesus summarized the two greatest commands of the Old Testament. First, *love God* with all one's heart, soul and mind, and second, *love one's neighbor* as oneself (Matt 22:37-40). We are to do what is pleasing to God (Eph 5:10). And, a part of what is pleasing is us imitating our Father: as He has loved us, we ought to live a life of love (Eph 5:1-2; 1 John 3:16).

Indeed, this is the *aim* of all Christian instruction: a love that grows out of a pure heart, a good conscience, and a sincere faith (1 Tim 1:5 RSV). The core of Christianity is not ceremonies, nor is it ideologies. Worship services are important, but not the core. Orthodoxy is important, but not the core. Rather, the core is simply faith (trusting God) that expresses itself through love to God and people (Gal 5:6). Without such love showing up in practical deeds done to meet the real needs of people, faith is pointless. Actually, a claim to faith without such works is invalid (Jas 2:18-19, 26; 1 John 3:17).

The Law, the first section of the Bible (Genesis-Deuteronomy), had the same concerns. Laying the foundation for the nation of Israel and its legal and religious culture, it used a different verbal style from that of the stories of the Gospels or the letters of the New Testament. Yet, under it all, the concern of God is the same: the wholehearted love of God and the love of oné's neighbor as one loved himself.

Know therefore that the LORD your God is God; He is the faithful God, keeping His covenant of love to a thousand generations of those who love Him and keep His commands. (Deu 7:9 NIV)

Love the LORD your God with all your heart and with all your soul and with all your strength. (Deu 6:5 NIV)

"'Do not seek revenge or bear a grudge against one of your people, but love your neighbor as yourself. I am the LORD. (Lev 19:18 NIV)

And you are to love those who are aliens, for you yourselves were aliens in Egypt. (Deu 10:19 NIV)

Keil and Delitzsch, scholars who produced a commentary on the Old Testament, talk about the "twin hinges upon which the teachings of Wisdom turn" on page 42 of their book on Proverbs. The "hinges" are:

• **Living in the fear of the LORD,** the God of the Bible, who is omniscient (Pro 15:3, 11; 16:2; 21:2; 24:11-12), who ultimately orders life (Pro 20:12, 24; 22:2; 14:31), whose overarching plan all will ultimately serve (Pro 16:4; 19:21; 21:30).
• **Active pure love to man,** with its goodness (Pro 12:2; 15:9), its kind acts (Pro 28:27; 10:12), and its forbearance (Pro 24:28-29; 20:22) even toward enemies (Pro 25:21-22; Pro 24:28-29), a love that commits even its most difficult ways to God (Pro 20:22).

The spirit of the Wisdom Writings in Proverbs is the same as the spirit of the Gospels and the Letters of the New Testament.

If your enemy is hungry, give him bread to eat; and if he is thirsty, give him water to drink; For so you will heap coals of fire on his head, and the LORD will reward you. (Pro 25:21-22 NKJ)

"But I tell you who hear me: Love your enemies, do good to those who hate you...

But love your enemies, do good to them, and lend to them without expecting to get anything back. Then your reward will be great, and you will be sons of the Most High, because He is kind to the ungrateful and wicked. (Luke 6:27, 35 NIV)

On the contrary: "If your enemy is hungry, feed him; if he is thirsty, give him something to drink. In doing this, you will heap burning coals on his head." (Rom 12:20 NIV)

The similarity really should not be surprising. The One who spoke through the Proverbs to the hearts of His people was the One who spoke in person as He walked the hills of first century Galilee and Judea, and the same One Who spoke through Paul to the churches of the Lord.

The *implication is that a genuinely wise person will take a humble and loving approach to life and to other people* (Jas 3:13-18).

GOD-CONCEPT *PLUS*

Having the right set of assumptions (about what is *real* versus merely *true*) is *one* key to "prosperity—versus pain," the difference between a life spent in wisdom or in mockery.

Wisdom, however, is somewhat like a safe-deposit box. My wife and I have rented a safe deposit box at our bank When I go to the bank to place something in the box or take it out, I must use our key to the box. But, one key is not enough. To make doubly sure of the safety of the box, I must sign into the bank's record book, and then a bank official will accompany me to the secure area. I place my key in the lock. Then, the official places her key in an accompanying lock. When both keys have been engaged, the door guarding the box opens.

Wisdom requires two keys:

• One key is the *correct set of assumptions* about the God who is there and the way He relates to His universe of things and people. An adequate orthodoxy is one key.

• The other key is a *heart willing to trust and obey* the God who is there, a heart willing to live in the fear of the LORD. Without the second key, the door that guards wisdom never opens. While truth is crucial to living a wise life, academic orthodoxy alone is not enough to retrieve wisdom's deposit.

But, with both keys, the door to wisdom swings open.

ISSUES RAISED BY THE BIBLICAL UNDERSTANDING OF GOD

The Bible doesn't tell us *everything* about how God relates to the world. Actually, *no* religion (or philosophy) has ever come up with *completely* satisfactory answers to certain questions human beings have raised. From my own investigations, the Bible contains better answers than the other systems. However, the Bible gives us *adequate* information for us to know how to trust God, but *not exhaustive* information. It leaves some questions not fully answered, some information hidden.

Understand that it is perfectly *okay* to ask difficult questions and seek answers to them. That quest has brought tremendous benefits as science has pursued it related to the physical universe. As science hits the limits on human scientific knowledge, it presses further with research using a logical structure called the *scientific method.* Scientists keep collecting and analyzing newer data, wrestling with the barriers to further knowledge. The barriers finally give way, and more is learned.

Science works on knowledge about the *physical universe.* Theology, however, works on the *mind and thought of God.* God is not subject to further testing by the theologians. Logical principles can be used for interpreting what God has revealed in the Bible, but they do not make God give us additional data. When we hit the limits on theological knowledge, we can re-investigate the Scriptures looking for things we have missed, and we can pray for better understanding. But we cannot pry new information out of God. There is a point at which we *finally hit the limits* on what the Bible says. After that point, we need to focus on what we *do* know, and *obey* it, rather than continuing to try to pry up the edges of the hidden things so we can peek underneath (see Deu 29:29). The occult bent (trying to peek into the hidden things) is *not* healthy.

We will briefly survey certain questions in order to see the angle of approach we need to take as we deal with the issues in daily life.

These questions are legitimate, and the Bible does give *some direction* on them, but again, it is not exhaustive. The Bible gives information up to a point, and beyond that point is *speculation,* merely guessing. Further information is not forthcoming. Like mountain climbers, we can labor up the mountain of inquiry so far, then we hit a fog. We do well to camp at the edge of the fog. Those who insist on going further into it will only lose their way.

God reveals only so much insight in these difficult areas. Beyond what He has revealed lies impenetrable mystery. We do well to go as far as the fog. At that point, we should stop and worship the God who is greater than all that we know. To try to explain further than the Scriptures do about God and His ways is to risk heresy and incur judgment from the LORD (Job 42:7-8).

It could be, that our human brains do not have the *capacity* to fathom the answers that lie cloaked in the fog. We humans tend to be very confident of our capacity to understand. But our minds have a limit. It may be that, were God to share the full, comprehensive answer to the questions below, we simply would not have the capacity to grasp the final answers. We may be like ants attempting algebra!

If God is completely sovereign, how can human beings make real choices?

It would seem that, if God is actually in charge, humans can't make real choices. If they make real choices, then God can't be really, fully in charge.

The Bible doesn't solve this puzzle. It affirms that God is sovereign, an absolute ruler. It also affirms that we make real, responsible choices. We are not mere robots; nor is the universe out of God's control. God's sovereignty means that, regardless the hard time that comes our way, God can use it to bless us (Rom 8:28). We can also pray for protection against hard times (Luke 11:4). However, God's ability to use hard things to bless us should keep us from discouragement when difficulties arise, for we know that God will use them to develop His character in us (Rom 5:3; James 1:2-4).

God's sovereignty also means that all *will ultimately* have to deal with God. No one will be able to evade Him and avoid dealing with Him, either in time, as Jonah discovered (Jonah 1:2-3; 2:10; 3:1-2), or in eternity when all knees bow before God (Phil 2:9-11; Rev 20:11-13).

If God is sovereign, why pray?

Won't whatever He wants to happen, happen anyway?

We pray because God told us to pray. He is sovereign. And, He is good. And He knows what we need. Jesus says as much and uses that as a reason to not babble on and on in our prayers (Matt 6:7-8). God knows what we need, but as one famous author wrote, He likes to be asked!

Actually, God gives us a chance to participate in the shaping of history through prayer. He prompts us to pray. We pray, and He responds—and we receive part of the blessing as His participants in creating what occurred. We get the privilege of helping bring into being the things that God desires (1 Tim 2:1).

Can prayers change the course of history? Yes—but even the change will turn out to be within the plan of God (Eph 1:11). Rather than getting stuck on things about which you cannot know more, just get busy with doing what you know you are supposed to: pray! (Matt 6:9; Eph 6:18; 1 Thes 5:17)

If God is sovereign, how can He be good?

If He were good and sovereign, as the argument goes, He would wipe out evil and suffering from the world. So, if He is good, He must *not be able* to wipe it out, that is, He must not be *sovereign.* Or, if He is letting suffering and evil continue, and He actually is sovereign, He must enjoy evil and *not be good!*

One person made the arrogant statement that, if there is a god (implying a sovereign god), then He is the devil. The truth is, if God is sovereign, we are *stuck with Him,* and had better *hope* He is *not* the devil.

The Bible affirms that God is both powerful and good (e.g., Ps 62:11-12).

The Scripture sees evil arising from rebellious choices made in the angelic realm and consequent choices by our original parents to rebel. The original human sin—and all the human sins since then—has resulted in a fractured universe in bondage to decay (Rom 8:18-22). Sin has produced a race of people (humans) capable of nobility and cruelty, but driven by selfish determination to have what they want, when they want it (Pro 22:15). They feel that they deserve to get what they want, and are willing to hurt others in order to get it (Ecc 9:3). Our human history of murder, theft, oppression, adultery, and other forms of using people is something *created by our race,* not God (Rom 1:28-32). The birth of deformed babies, the ravages of nature, the horrors of disease, war and famine—these are the legacy the human race has bequeathed to itself. They all go back to our decision, first as a race and later as individuals, to rebel against God and have our own way.

God has, in His kindness, through His own sacrifice, worked out a way for some to be saved out of the mess. But, the human race plunges ahead in rebellion against the ways of God. Were God to remove all evil from the universe at this point in time, He would immediately *erase each of us* from the stage of history, for we are all infected with the rebellion. In His patience, God is yet granting time for people to come to Him (2 Pet 3:15). In due time, He will create a world in which righteousness alone will live, a world without tears (Rev 21:1-5). It will arrive *after He* has dealt with the wickedness of the human race (Rev 20:11-15).

Actually, many of the issues regarding God's sovereignty that are difficult to figure out *theoretically* can be dealt with *practically*, especially amid crisis. If our house catches on fire, we do not debate whether we should grab a water hose to try to put out the fire or submit to God's sovereign will. We do not sit in a quandary wondering whether our prayers will be significant. We don't debate whether fire is evil and if, since God allowed this fire to happen, we should let it burn, lest we be fighting God.

No. Instead we *pray like mad*—because we know God can help. And we *work like mad*, because we know our actions are important if the damage is to be restrained.

Does God work through miracles or through natural processes?

Do we really see the hand of God *only* in His intervention in the world (crossing the Red Sea, turning water to wine, the resurrection of Christ, etc.)? Or, is God at work behind the scenes also, working in and through "historical processes" or "natural processes?" That is, is His hand also involved in things like allowing the rise of Rome in order to create a peaceful and well-connected world that would allow the Gospel to travel swiftly across international borders in the first century?

Theologians refer to God's ability to work in and through natural processes as the "immanence" of God. His ability to intervene in the normal flow of events and do the miraculous is referred to as God's "transcendence."

In reality, God works through both means as He sees fit. Sometimes God intervenes and heals a withered leg. Other times He works through medication and doctors to do it. God is involved in the very process of growing the grass on which animals on the African savannah graze. He is the one who feeds the predatory animals their prey through their hunts at night. And He is the one that feeds human beings through the jobs that they have (Ps 104:14, 20-23; 147:8-9). At the same time, He can feed 5,000 people with five small loaves of bread and two fishes (Matt 14:18-21).

God is also the one superintending and aggressively guiding history (Acts 17:24-27; Amos 9:7). He can punish a nation through the shifting affairs of international politics and aggression (2 Kings 24:1-2). He can also eliminate a cultural cesspool by immediate destruction (Gen 19:24-25).

We need to pray for God to *do more than we* can while we handle the responsibilities that He has given us. Planning is important to any enterprise (Pro 14:15). God works through it (immanence). He can also show us plans we never thought of—if he wants to (transcendence) (see Acts 16:9-10).

To say it another way, God has an *ordinary* way of working, the way things usually happen. He also has *extraordinary ways*. We make a mistake if we want to try to keep Him locked into either pattern. We are merely God's servants, we are not His managing directors.

We rejoice when the miraculous shows up, as with the healing in Acts 28:7-10. At the same time, we are not naïve; we also check to make sure the supernatural source is the Lord and not the demonic (1 John 4:1-4).

We are also willing to be faithful and do hard, diligent work if God chooses the more ordinary means, as when Paul left a co-laborer sick, or God did not choose to heal Paul (2 Tim 4:20; 2 Cor 12:7-10).

TO WHAT EXTENT CAN YOU TRUST GOD?

The vast majority of people in our society will affirm a belief in a god. The greater number of them will affirm the God of the Bible.

However, they do not consider that god to be engaged sufficiently with the ordinary flow of their everyday lives to make a crucial difference in what happens to them. So, they rely on *something other* than that god to "get them through"—their own brains, force, friends, personality, money, deceit, etc. They will obey their god *in general*, but in specific situations, they are not concerned to do what their god wants. Their god can get them into heaven, but it doesn't deal with specific situations.

They think their god is not really *able* to take care of them in a given situation. So, rather than being concerned about how God would want them to respond, they do what they think will "get them through." They rely on, not the God of the Bible, but their own insight. To them, it is *true* that God is there, but this is the *real* world!

As Jesus was winding up His stay on earth, He knew the challenging future His disciples faced. And, He knew how people think. So, He addressed the extent to which He could take care of His followers and challenged them to live their daily lives out of concerns for God's great plans.

Then Jesus came to them and said, "All authority in heaven and on earth has been given to me. Therefore go... (Matt 28:18-19 NIV)

He has all authority in heaven and earth—nothing, no matter how great or how small, is beyond His control. The God of the Bible is both true *and* real. Because He is real, we stake our lives on Him. He is in charge of all and can take care of us.

Our preoccupation in life becomes to walk with God and *do what is pleasing to Him.* As we please Him in situation after situation, over time it turns out that we are functioning *in line with the very way the universe really works*—for God runs the universe in a manner that is also *pleasing* to Him. Our devoted approach to life meshes with His divine governance of life.

The assumptions of wisdom are not mere ideas; they are a key to unlocking the best kind of life. When used with the other key, the heart willing to trust and honor God, the treasures of wisdom *are unlocked.* They are not yet unpacked, but they are unlocked.

Trust in the LORD with all your heart and lean not on your own understanding;
in all your ways acknowledge Him, and He will make your paths straight.
Do not be wise in your own eyes; fear the LORD and shun evil. (Pro 3:5-7 NIV)

Think About It

What do your ways of handling life say about your god-concepts? For example:

• If you are single, what does your approach to dating say about your God-concepts (the ones you believe are *real*, not just true)? How should the Biblical God-concepts impact your strategies for dating?

• If you are married, what does the way you handle your marriage say about the god you believe is real? How should the Biblical God-concepts shape the way you handle your marriage?

WANT TO KNOW HOW TO UNPACK WISDOM'S TREASURES?
WE ARE GOING TO CHECK IT OUT.
BEFORE WE GO THERE, HOWEVER,
IT WILL HELP TO UNDERSTAND THE CAPACITIES OF WISDOM.
WE WANT TO INVESTIGATE WHAT WISDOM CAN DO
AND THE LEVELS TO WHICH IT CAN RISE.
THE PERSON WHO TAPS INTO WISDOM
HAS BEGUN AN EXPANDING SET OF ABILITIES.
WHAT THEY INCLUDE IS QUITE INTERESTING!

Chapter 8

THE COMPONENTS OF WISDOM

In its broadest sense, wisdom is a remarkable skill in dealing successfully with life. Biblical wisdom begins with a profound respect for the LORD (the fear of the LORD), a respect that wants to conduct all of life in a manner that is pleasing to God. Biblical wisdom is eminently successful, but it always achieves its successes within the boundaries of *righteousness and justice.*

Wisdom has several *components* to it. It is compounded of certain things and has increasing capacities in decision-making. It also needs to be operative over the different arenas of life. In this chapter, we will look at several facets and levels of Biblical wisdom. Then we will summarize its behavior in key arenas of life.

The first component of wisdom is *knowledge.* Because of the crucial, foundational nature of knowledge, we will give it extensive attention. We will deal with the other aspects of wisdom more quickly.

KNOWLEDGE

The primary Hebrew word translated "knowledge" is *da'ath* (dah'-ath). It comes from a verb *yada'* (yaw-dah), meaning to ascertain by seeing, to know by experience.

In English, knowledge is facts or ideas (information) acquired by study, investigation, observation or experience. The Hebrew term can be used for such "bare information." Used related to wisdom, however, *da'ath* indicates *more than bare information.* According to Proverbs, there can be an "information" exchange without a "knowledge" exchange.

Stay away from a foolish man, for you will <u>not find knowledge</u> on his lips. (Pro 14:7 NIV)

Fools are usually replete with facts and ideas. It is not a lack of information that one will find on the fool's lips, but the lack of a *certain kind* of information. The foolish person may possess information (his name, address, who won the NBA championship, etc.), but there is a *kind of knowledge* that will never appear on his lips. *Da'ath* is especially used for that *certain type of knowledge.*

Da'ath, in this sense, is *information that shapes how one sees life, information that increases spiritual understanding of, and perspective on, life.* *Da'ath* is essentially the *"What"* from God's perspective, the information (facts and ideas) that allows us to see the situations we face from God's perspective.

"Perspective" is the capacity to view things in their *true relations* or *relative importance.* A person with accurate perspective on a situation is in much better position to deal with it. They can see how the factors in the situation really relate to one another, and can pick out what is most important among the factors.

In the stock market, "insider trading" is illegal. It provides some people (insiders) with information that gives a much *more accurate perspective* on a company's immediate future than the general public possesses. Insiders can use their knowledge to reap a fortune or to avoid devastating loss—contrary to the fate suffered by the general public. Those who are privy to the right kind of perspective-shaping information have a tremendous advantage over others.

The kind of knowledge that lets one *see things as they really are* is an extremely valuable resource. Indeed, it is the knowledge resource accumulated and guarded by the highly successful "prudent" person (Pro 12:23, 13:16). It is his key to gaining wealth and honor (Pro 14:18).

Da'ath knowledge is information that *lets me know how life works.* It helps one to *see how* the facets of life are *related to one another* and their *importance* relative to one another. Such information would enable one to know:

- How the facets of life are *connected* to one another, the *relationships* between them and the *flow of cause and effect* between the different facets of life. A person with knowledge "knows the flow."
- The *relative importance* of the facets of life (which is more important than the other) so that, as one makes decisions, one does not mistake the more important for the less important or sacrifice the more valuable for the less valuable.

To grasp the difference between ordinary knowledge and *da'ath*-knowledge we will look at some examples. First, consider *ordinary knowledge*, mere facts, mere bald information:

• *The world is approximately 25,000 miles around.*

• *The square of the length of the hypotenuse of a right triangle is equal to the sum of the squares of the lengths of the other two sides (a2 + b2 = c2) (the Pythagorean Theorem).*

• *Babe Ruth's home-runs- in-a season-record stood for decades.*

This type of information (facts and ideas) is *not unhelpful.* Indeed, while some of this information is "trivia," other parts (like the Pythagorean Theorem) can help one solve certain types of problems in the world.

Now, consider the following examples of *da'ath*, the perspective-shaping information:

• *"The fear of the Lord is the beginning of wisdom..." (Pro 9:10)*

• *"If you are wise, your wisdom will reward you; if you are a mocker, you alone will suffer" (Pro 9:12)*

• *Listen to advice and accept instruction, and in the end you will be wise. (Pro 19:20 NIV)*

Bare information is not unhelpful. With bare information, I can understand how to pass a test in a course at college, or perhaps I can impress my friends with my knowledge.

But the *da'ath*-type information, is crucial. With da'ath-information, I begin to understand *how life works!* For example, based on the above verses, I now know that wisdom will reward me in life! If I want a good life, I need to start acquiring wisdom! And, I know *where to start* prospecting for wisdom. I must begin with the fear of the LORD. In addition, I realize that I need to change the way I have responded to advice. In the past, I have resisted both advice and instruction. In the future, if I will begin to receive input, I can become wise.

Out of *da'ath*-knowledge I can do more than pass tests and look impressive! I can start to create intelligent strategies for succeeding in the world!

The Importance Of Categories

"Categories" are the concepts we use to understand life. They are the divisions within our system of classifying life. We are able to grasp and deal with life only as well as our categories allow.

In a hilarious comedic skit on Saturday Night Live, one of the regular cast played a medieval barber. Barbers were also the physicians of the middle ages. A lady brings her sick teenage daughter to the barber. The daughter is very nauseated. The barber announces that the daughter is fortunate to live in an age of modern medicine, for once people thought such conditions were caused by evil spirits. He announces that modern medicine now knows, however, that such conditions are actually caused by a dwarf or toad living in the child's stomach. As the skit progresses, the daughter dies from the prescribed treatment.

While the comedic sketch was hilarious, the impact of our *categories* on our ability to analyze life is quite serious. A "primitive" society, unfamiliar with germs, might observe a horrible headache, assume it was caused by demonic attack, and call the shaman. A western doctor might recognize the symptoms of a sinus infection, and prescribe antibiotics. Having the category of "germs" or "viruses" affects how we analyze illnesses and the response we make to them.

Our categories help us sort out life. One unfamiliar with the city might walk through a crowd on the streets and see only "men and women." An experienced urbanite might see business people, tourists, potential pick-pockets or muggers, and "marks," people the criminals are likely to target.

We use our categories to determine *"what is there,"* and, depending on what we think is the *nature* of what is there, to decide *"what to do about it."* Remember the campsite illustration: we observe the categories *tent, table* and *food.* If those were all we observed, we would rush to eat! However, if we hear sounds that convince us the category of *grizzly bear* is also present, because we *know the nature* of the things in the category of grizzlies (that is the nature of grizzly bears), we decide on a *different course* of action.

Our categories are *extremely powerful* in shaping what we can do in life. We *can't even discuss* things for which we have no category. If someone gives us a category name, and we don't know the nature of the things in it, we *still* can't discuss the category.

For example, suppose that I tell you that I think the Levant has a dramatic impact on the future of Europe, the United States and the world. You may be impressed, but if you don't know that the Levant is a term for the countries bordering on the eastern end of the Mediterranean, you will not be able to discuss the matter with me. Without the category, you cannot really participate.

Knowing categories and the nature of the things that go in them dramatically affects our ability to solve problems, to seize opportunities and to be creative.

For example, suppose you and I decide to create an *innovative zoo.* Rather than the traditional groupings of animals in exhibits, we are going to arrange our exhibits based on the *number of legs* the animals have.

It takes some time to get the exhibit spaces built, but finally the animals are turned into their new homes, and we go out for lunch to celebrate. We are so excited over the "no-legged" exhibit (fish, shellfish, whales, sea cucumbers, snakes and the like), the two-legged exhibit (kangaroo mice, kiwis, and large, non-flying birds), the three-legged-exhibit (kangaroos and wallabies—we decided that the tail really counts as a third leg), the four-legged exhibit (antelope, buffalo, rabbits, elephants, rhinos, hippos, wild dogs, lions, tigers, etc), the five-legged (star-fish), six-legged (insects), seven-legged (more starfish), eight-legged (arachnids and some starfish), and the multi-legged exhibits (some starfish, jelly fish, centipedes, etc). What a creative job we have done!

After an extended lunch-time celebration, we return to the zoo to discover spreading devastation. In many of the exhibits, some of the animals have devoured the others! Our zoo is a mess! How could such a creative idea go so wrong?

The answer is, of course, it went wrong because we did not use adequate categories to separate the animals. Besides merely noting the number of legs, we should have also studied the nature (including behavior) of the different animals in each of our "legged" categories. Closer study of the things in our categories may have caused us to realize we needed to also divide them by *what they ate.* A deeper acquaintance with their nature may have suggested the additional divisions: prey and predator.

I admit this example is a bit silly, but it drives home a point. Attempts at problem-solving, at exploiting opportunities, or at innovation can fail due to using inadequate categories.

Our categories enable or hinder our ability to recognize and deal with our surroundings. Indeed, our categories shape our very approach to life.

Manipulated Categories

The power of categories to shape our lives was discovered sometime back by "social engineers," those who wanted to remodel society through manipulation. Such people have exerted tremendous pressure through the media and the educational system to alter the categories ordinary Americans use to understand the life around them, discuss it, and decide how to deal with it.

For example, in education, major historical facts have been repressed in order to remove the understanding that America had distinctly Christian roots. For example, George Washington's farewell speech was considered to be significant for understanding how the framers of our government designed the system to work. So, it was published for 150 years in history texts. About fifty years ago it was dropped for it had too much Christianity in it. Ignorance of the speech would promote the secular agenda of emerging educational power brokers.

Indeed, the very events involved in the founding our nation have largely been ignored in many newer elementary and high school history texts. Those who do not know the events of the past cannot discuss them. Events that are forgotten have no active effect on the future.

Another example of the manipulation of categories to control social outcomes has been the media reporting on the controversy over abortion. In the early 70's the news media reported on the conflict between the "pro-abortion forces" and the "pro-life forces" in the U.S. Wanting to promote abortion, the media began changing the terminology. The conflict became between the "pro-abortion" and "anti-abortion" forces ("anti" carries a nasty, closed-minded connotation). Later the terms changed to "pro-choice" versus "anti-abortion." The American who uses these terms in a discussion has already been emotionally committed to view the pro-abortion movement from a noble standpoint, and the anti-abortion (pro-life) movement from a negative one.

"Homo-phobic" has been invented to pejoratively categorize people who oppose the movement to legitimize homosexuality. In reality, I know very few people who "fear homosexuals," as the term indicates. I know a great many who think homosexuality is an unwise strategy for life and for society. However, heavy but inaccurate use of the term "homophobe" in the media has effectively browbeaten dissenters.

"Sexist" and "racist" are categories promoted as the way to recognize problem people and to indicate a strategy for dealing with them: make them "non-sexist" or "non-racist." Public browbeating to keep people from expressing their opinions has not converted sexists or racists, nor has it created respectful relationships between men and women or race and race. To create respectful relationships would require the use of other categories.

Such politically and socially charged categories are aggressively promoted through the media in order to shape the political and social outcomes preferred by power brokers. And, the average American chooses the predicated outcomes because he has been brow-beaten (he doesn't want to look un-cool), or because he knows no better.

Our categories enable us to discern what we call a "problem" and what we call an "opportunity." And our categories impact the "prescriptions" we write for ourselves and for others.

Consider one more example. I once led a ministry to "street people," a term of the seventies and eighties, indicating where the people lived: on the streets. Over time I realized there were different kinds of people on the street: bums, out to live minimally and preferring that life, people down on their luck who needed help re-establishing themselves in society, druggies and drug dealers, prostitutes, and petty criminals, etc. Each group had different reasons they were on the street. And, they needed different approaches to helping them.

In the 1980's, the media decided to change the term from "street people" to "homeless." "Homeless" has, already built into the term, a prescription for how to deal with the people: provide them a home. Much emotion and many dollars have been spent on trying to provide for the "homeless." Some (the down-on-their-luck) have needed homes. The others, however, need very different approaches to their problems. "Homeless" changes what we perceive to be the prescription to deal with the problem.

Da'ath: Revised Categories

Da'ath is information that revises one's categories.

Da'ath gives us categories for interpreting life. For example, the usual political agenda in the western world involves "improving education." Certainly education can help. But, the most educated nations in the world fought World War II—it was not the ignorant, backward nations who were destroying each other.

Based on Proverbs, the great factor that decides whether people suffer or prosper in life is *not* the divide between the "educated" and the "uneducated," *but* between the "wise" and the "mockers." The transformation that will help the world most is not simply to change people from "ignorant" to "educated," but to go *further* and change them from "mockers" to "wise."

Da'ath also lets one know the *characteristics of the things* which go in the categories. Our creative zoo above would have profited from a more accurate knowledge of the nature of the individual items in our categories. For example, it would have been good to know that, in the 4-legged category, lions and tigers are *meat eaters;* antelope and buffalo are *grass eaters.* So, *da'ath* gives us the key information about, not only which categories to use to analyze life, but also the nature and tendencies of the things in the categories.

For example, the Old Testament English term "fool" is actually used for people with five different types of integrated lifestyles, all of which exercise poor judgment, but do it in rather *different* styles (See, *Fools and Follies,* also *Self-Defeating Strategies* by the author). To understand the category of "fools" is good; to have more detail about the types of fools is even more helpful.

Da'ath can also give one a grasp of how the different things in our categories *impact one another.* Knowing how the things interact, we can better anticipate problems as we strategize for the future. For example, in our creative zoo, it would have been helpful to realize that meat-eaters impact grass-eaters negatively: they eat them. Again, among the five fools, one type especially preys on one other type. The two frequently appear in the news as a couple living together. Knowing how the different things in a category interact helps one succeed in analysis and strategizing—such as putting meat-eaters and plant-eaters in separate exhibits. Knowing how the different major categories interact with each other also helps.

Da'ath provides *categories, contents* (the nature of the stuff in the categories) and *connections* (how the items and categories tend to interact). It provides not merely data, but accurate *perspective.*

The Categorical Challenge

Most of our categories for handling life today are shaped by psychology, politics and marketing, primarily through the media and secondarily through public education. The rampant *un-success* of our times in dealing with personal, marital, parental, business, social, financial, and moral problems indicates our need of *more accurate categories* than the ones we have been provided in order to better grasp *how life really is.* And, we need *clearer and truer insight* on *how the flow of life occurs*—what causes what, how the stuff inside the categories interacts.

Where psychology and sociology have been more related to common sense, they have been more helpful. However, due to their political and philosophical biases, much of psychology and sociology has chosen categories that preclude the real solution to most problems. They have been about as effective as the "medieval barber" trying to drive the dwarf or toad out of the nauseated girl's stomach. To this point in time, they have induced much emotional and social "vomiting," but healed little of our disease.

Christian higher education faces a tremendous challenge, for it tends to use many of the same categories as secular education, adding on Bible information, more positive role models on the part of the professors and a less corrosive environment. Some progress has been made in redefining the categories by which students are taught to interpret and evaluate life. However, much education in Christian colleges still tends to utilize the culture's scientific, psychological, and other categories for evaluating life. So, usually against its wishes, it tends to set students ultimately in the same direction as the culture. Though it may provide a more positive educational experience and produce "nicer" people, many of its graduates tend to move on with the non-Christian flow of the culture.

Christian counseling faces a similar challenge. Most problems are analyzed from the same perspective (knowledge) used by secular psychology. The use of secular psychological categories results in secular psychological prescriptions and results—perhaps somewhat improved by the grace of God because of prayer. Until different categories are used, until problems are seen from a superior perspective, we will continue to identify problems using the same grid that secularists do, write similar prescriptions for dealing with the problems, and keep on being surprised that our success rate is not that much better than the secularists.

Da'ath can supply the critical information we need. One of the purposes of Christ was to supply accurate, adequate information about how life *really is.* He brought us the truth that would set us free (John 8:31-32). However, *da'ath,* like wisdom, begins with the fear of the LORD (Pro 1:7). It is those who *abide* in Jesus' teaching that come to know the truth and are set free.

The Great Knowledge

According to the Scripture, the great knowledge to attain is the knowledge *(da'ath) of* God, a grasp of God which shapes spiritual perspective on life

(Pro 2:5). It is not merely information acquired *about* God, but information *gained by experience of God,* by practice in walking with Him. It is the stuff from which the strategies of wisdom are constructed and the framework within which the strategies of wisdom must operate. The knowledge of God opens up to the one who fears the LORD. It is a quest of both the Old and New Testaments.

Then you will understand the fear of the LORD and find the knowledge of God. (Pro 2:5 NIV)

We demolish arguments and every pretension that sets itself up against the knowledge of God, and we take captive every thought to make it obedient to Christ. (2 Cor 10:5 NIV)

And we pray this in order that you may live a life worthy of the Lord and may please Him in every way: bearing fruit in every good work, growing in the knowledge of God, (Col 1:10 NIV)

Da'ath is occasionally used as a synonym for Wisdom, as in the following verse:

For wisdom will enter your heart, and knowledge will be pleasant to your soul. (Pro 2:10 NIV)

Da'ath can also be viewed as more a component of Wisdom, along with understanding:

For the LORD gives wisdom, and from His mouth come knowledge and understanding. (Pro 2:6 NIV)

"Knowledge" *(da'ath)* is the lowest level of wisdom. With knowledge, one arrives at *accurate perspective.* The other abilities of wisdom are constructed out of its fund of *da'ath*-knowledge. At this point, you may find it helpful to read Appendix Five, Interpreting Wisdom Passages.

UNDERSTANDING

The primary Hebrew word translated understanding is *biynah* (bee-naw'). It comes from a verb, *biyn (bene),* meaning to mentally separate, distinguish or understand.

The one who is skilled at *biyn* is able to "mentally separate" situations into their component parts. He is also able to see how specific things happening in the situation are related to general principles or to the nature and tendencies of the components in the situation. He can also see into people and discern motives and other things going on in their hearts.

Thus, the *person of understanding* has the ability to *accurately analyze* people, situations, events or ideas from God's perspective. A person of understanding is able to separate things into component parts, grasp the relationship between generals and particulars, principles and applications, items and implications. Understanding can take complex situations and break them down into underlying issues, components and influences, and point out the flow of cause and effect in the situation.

In effect, understanding can take the information supplied by knowledge and use it to grasp and then explain what is going on in complex life situations. Note that the most gifted analyst will still fail in his analysis if he is using the wrong categories to guide his analysis. Adequate understanding (analysis) is built on adequate knowledge, on *da'ath.*

A person of understanding knows how life works from God's viewpoint. So, he can look at a specific situation and identify what "behind-the-scenes" matters are causing the situation to shape up as it is. Or, he/she can discern people and detect what factors or concerns are driving their behavior. Because of their ability to accurately analyze, the persons of understanding usually have a reputation for being able to explain situations to others.

"Discern" would be a good translation of many of the uses of *biyn.*

The Great Understanding

The great understanding *(biynah)* to achieve is the "knowledge *(da'ath)* of the Holy."

The fear of the LORD is the beginning of wisdom: and the knowledge of the holy is understanding. (Pro 9:10 KJV)

All translations, other than the King James Version, use the phrase "knowledge of the Holy One." The Hebrew, however, *does not have* a term for "one' in the text. The phrase in Hebrew is simply "knowledge of the holy."

The author of the verse could be referring to the Holy One. In that case, the verse would be saying that understanding *(biynah)* is defined as the accumulated experiential knowledge of God.

However, the author may be referring to the "holy" in the sense of "what is important and sacred to God." The "holy" would be "all that is wrapped up in holiness," that is, "God, His values and His prescriptions for how life ought to flow in line with His character and purposes." The verse would be saying that to achieve understanding is to be able to look at the world and the situations going on in it, and see them from the angle of what is *important* to God, what is holy before Him. When one knows God and knows His values, intents and manners of governing life, that person has arrived at "understanding." He possesses the true categories for evaluating life and an accurate grasp of the relationships between them—and a grasp of how cause and effect flows from the hand of God. He will now be able to effectively read and analyze what is going on in the complex situations of life.

So, on his journey to understanding, a person would do well to ask such questions as:

- In the world, what is of high value and holy according to God? What is of low value?
- In this situation before me right now, what is of high value to God? What is of low value to Him?
- Of the responses I am considering, which are of high value to God? Which are of low value to Him? Which things in this situation or its possible outcomes, because they are of high value to God, ought to drive my response?

Two other words occasionally translated "understanding" are *"tabuwn"* and *"sekel."* We will look at them below.

Understanding is the second level of Wisdom. With it, one has moved from accurate perspective to *accurate discernment.*

WISDOM

Biblical wisdom is a skilled ability to deal with life and to successfully achieve one's goals in a way that is pleasing to God, within the boundaries of righteousness and justice. Different Hebrew words are translated "wisdom." They share the common core meaning of "skilled ability to achieve desired results." However, they have different shades of meaning. Some seem to indicate greater levels of skill/wisdom.

We will survey the terms starting with the ones indicating a more basic ability in making good decisions and proceeding to ones apparently representing greater skills.

Sensible. *Leb* (labe) is a Hebrew word often translated "judgment," but that can be translated as wisdom or understanding. The focus of this term is *making decisions about the direction to choose.*

The word literally means "heart." It refers to the inner person as seen from the angle of making decisions. In the Scriptures, the heart is something like "guidance central" for the life, the central guidance system of a person. One needs to develop a central guidance system wrapped around wisdom, not around folly.

Leb is the ability to make good decisions, or good "judgment calls." The simple person is *chacer leb (khaw'-ser labe)* (Hebrew meaning "without heart/judgment"). He lacks judgment and gets trapped in damaging situations before discerning the danger (see Pro 7:7, 22-23).

But a man who commits adultery lacks judgment; whoever does so destroys himself. (Pro 6:32 NIV)

The lips of the righteous nourish many, but fools die for lack of judgment. (Pro 10:21 NIV)

The person with *leb* has good sense and makes good decisions. He has a reliable ability to form conclusions that are sound and prudent.

Someone with good judgment is able to accurately *discern* the realities of a situation and the factors influencing the realities. Good judgment next *compares* the relative strength of the different factors. Then, based on its assessment of which factors are stronger and which are weaker, it *draws conclusions* about how the situation is likely to turn out. Based on how it thinks things will likely turn out, it *decides how to respond* in the situation in order to accomplish its goals.

Leb is extremely valuable. It is the dividing line between the naïve, and the fools on one side, and those who succeed in life on the other. The one who acquires *leb* is doing good to himself!

He who gets wisdom (leb) loves his own soul; he who cherishes understanding prospers. (Pro 19:8 NIV)

Such a valuable ability is developed by practice with the help of people who can coach the learner as he begins making decisions. The word for "discipline" in Hebrew is a term meaning corrective instruction, instruction with an edge to it—like that of a coach, informing then correcting. If a person won't listen to serious correction, he is going to hurt himself. But, if he is willing to learn under correction, he will gain leb.

He who ignores discipline despises himself, but whoever heeds correction gains understanding (leb). (Pro 15:32 NIV)

Tasteful. *Ta'am* (tah'-am) comes from a Hebrew word meaning to taste or perceive.

Ta'am is "taste" and is used in a figurative sense for perception. The one with *ta'am* possesses a degree of intelligence and shows it in his "taste" in situations. He possesses the knowledge of what is appropriate behavior and speech along with the ability to choose the appropriate in varying settings.

The focus of the term is on "appropriateness." The possession of *ta'am* enables a person to choose the appropriate, tasteful response to people. Helpful though it is, *ta'am* is unimpressive to a sluggard (Pro 26:16).

The sluggard is wiser in his own eyes than seven men who answer discreetly (ta'am). (Pro 26:16 NIV)

Interestingly, one of the characteristics of the *wise plan* is its "appropriateness". The wise plan is "considerate" (see p. 103) or fitting, doing what is tasteful, rather than being rude, harsh or shocking (Jas 3:17). The refusal to be rude is one of the marks of genuine agape love (1 Cor 13:5).

Good taste *(ta'am)* can be learned from the LORD, especially through his commands.

Teach me knowledge and good judgment (ta'am), for I believe in your commands. (Ps 119:66 NIV)

The lack of *ta'am* is something that even exceptional beauty cannot overcome.

Like a gold ring in a pig's snout is a beautiful woman who shows no discretion (ta'am). *(Pro 11:22 NIV)*

Scheming. *Mezimmah* (mez-im-maw') is usually translated as "discretion."

It comes from a verb *zammam* (zaw-mam') meaning "to press together" and referring to mental concentration. *Zamam* basically means "to plan," and is *usually* used in a *bad* sense of wicked plotting and scheming, though it could refer to a plan for good.

The wicked plot (zamam) against the righteous and gnash their teeth at them; (Ps 37:12 NIV)

A related word, zimmah (zim-maw') or zammah (zam-maw') indicates a plan, especially a plan for evil.

One of wisdom's capacities is of the ability to uncover or arrive at knowledge of *"mezimmah"* (Pro 8:12). The KJV translates the term "witty inventions." Wisdom has the ability to discern *plots in process* and the discreet actions used to implement them.

Mezimmah, used in the sense of *discretion,* is the capacity of "well-considered action." It implies an awareness of how scheming is done, both how to plan and also how the wicked lay plots—an awareness that keeps one from stepping into traps laid by the wicked. Mezimmah is a procedural kind of wisdom. *Mezimmah* uses intense mental concentration to come up with the right goals and to choose the right methods for advancing the right plans. Then, a person with *mezimmah* is *very careful* about what he says and does so that his plans will go forward. One needs to learn such discretion—and also learn to detect its use when a plot is afoot.

Discretion will protect you, and understanding will guard you. (Pro 2:11 NIV)

Savvy. *Sakal* (saw-kal') means to be circumspect, and thus, intelligent. One who is circumspect is careful to consider all circumstances and all possible consequences before acting or deciding.

The Hebrew words related to *sakal* are variously translated as "wisdom," "understanding," "discernment," and "prosper." The reference point for *sakal* is the *situation.* In the situation, the person who *sakals* is savvy; he has practical know-how; he knows what to do.

The one who *"sakals"* looks around at his situation and reads what is going on correctly. He decides where things need to go. Then he constructs an *effective, successful response* to the situation that will allow him to achieve his goals—and, thus, he prospers in the situation. Judgment (leb) tends to focus on particular decisions, while *sakal* focuses more on situations, which involves several decisions coming together.

Sekel (seh'-kel) is the noun related to *sakal. Sekel* is the ability to analyze a situation and come up with the right way to handle it. It is a situational prudence, a wisdom that is *"situationally effective."* It uses:
• *Judgment* to read and evaluate the influences in a situation;
• *Prudence* to assess risk, align resources, and exercise restraint.

Abigail, the wife of the fool, Nabal, was a woman of "good counsel" (literally, good *sekel*) (1 Sam 25:3). She was able, therefore, to effectively intervene in the nasty situation created by her husband and keep her household from being destroyed (1 Sam 25:14-27). The person of *"sekel"* can create effective strategies for success in a given situation. They make wise counselors (1 Chr 26:14).

Sekel provides continuing refreshment to those who have it, like a refreshing fountain of life. It is also recognized by others and draws praise for its possessor.

Understanding is a fountain of life to those who have it, but folly brings punishment to fools. (Pro 16:22 NIV)

A man is praised according to his wisdom, but men with warped minds are despised. (Pro 12:8 NIV)

However, *sekel* isn't always appreciated. Advice on how to respond in situations is *"sekel."* Fools resent it.

Do not speak to a fool, for he will scorn the wisdom (sekel) of your words. (Pro 23:9 NIV)

Sekel appears to be somewhat like "street wisdom," more "intuitive" than trained.

Effective. *Tuwshiyah* (too-shee-yaw') is from a Hebrew word meaning "to substantiate," implying to give substance to, or to support.

The word can be used to imply *ability.* Directed toward a goal, it could mean "an undertaking," *"an enterprise."* It is a *sound wisdom* and can designate the results of sound wisdom: *"abiding success."*

Tuwshiyah is basically an *ability to take ideas or plans and turn them into reality*, the ability to go from "concept to concrete," intent to reality, idea to substance, goal to accomplishment, and to create *enduring* successes.

The reference point for *tuwshiyah* is accomplishment, the bringing of what was once theoretical into firmly established and enduring reality, whether it be a victory or a success. *Tuwshiyah* is a wisdom that *works*, a wisdom that effects *results*, an effective wisdom. It is a "sound wisdom," a wise ability to effectively bring to substance/reality the intentions of those who use it to design their enterprises.

Those with the capacity of *tuwshiyah* are "highly effective people." They do not merely dream up or start projects. They bring them to solid success.

My son, let not them depart from thine eyes: keep sound wisdom (tuwshiyah) and discretion (Mezimmah). (Pro 3:21 KJV)

Tuwshiyah is the practical insight that enables one to be highly effective in his undertakings. Sometimes it is translated "victory" (Pro 2:7).

God hoards this kind of effective wisdom for His people. He stores it up for them, desiring to give it to them.

He holds victory (tuwshiyah) in store for the upright, He is a shield to those whose walk is blameless. (Pro 2:7 NIV)

Since success usually requires the help of many people, those unfriendly people who become loners in order to pursue their own selfish agendas are actually acting against all principles of *tuwshiyah*. They will not be able to establish enduring success (Pro 18:1). (See p. 96 on cooperation)

Shrewd. *`Aram* (aw-ram') is Hebrew meaning to be (or make) bare. It is used to mean *be cunning* (usually in a bad sense), shrewd, crafty or prudent. Just as fresh limb that has been stripped of bark is slick and difficult to hold without slipping, the person who "arams" is "slick."

To "*'aram*" is to think through and plan one's way, consider all contingencies, and then to execute the plan successfully without giving crafty people the opportunity for advantage. The focus point of the term is the *shrewd execution.*

`Ormah (or-maw') designates the activity of the person who does "*'aram.*" It can be translated trickery; or (in a good sense) discretion, prudence. It is the ability to conceive and manage a plan effectively, a managerial wisdom. The *prudent person* in Proverbs has this type of wisdom/ability.

Prudence is the ability to govern and discipline oneself and one's affairs by the use of reason. Prudence implies a self-imposed restraint that comes from accurate discernment. Prudence keeps the decisions made by wisdom within appropriate boundaries. The prudent one is a sensible person.

The person who has this capability is the *'aruwm* (aw-room'), the prudent one. The prudent one:

- *Aggressively acquires knowledge,* the perspective shaping *da'ath*, to enable his planning (Pro 13:16). Because he values accurate perspective, he will heed reproof (Pro 15:5). His exceptional knowledge and the perspective it gives him is a key component in his success (Pro 14:18).
- *Notes his assumptions* about facts or persons, and double-checks to make sure they are true before he relies on them. He doesn't believe just anyone or anything; he requires proof and data (Pro 14:15).
- *Thinks his plans through in detail* before he ever takes action (Pro 14:8).
- Conceals his assets and his emotional responses as he executes his plans (Pro 12:23).
- Is continually checking ahead for contingencies, and when they strike he is ready for them (Pro 27:12).
- Manages himself and his resources extremely well so that he is able to complete his plans and bring in the success he desires.
- Possesses *tuwshiyah*, the effective wisdom.
- Once he has completed his project, it is difficult for adversaries to find mistakes that they can capitalize on or use to damage him. This is a part of his slickness.

The naïve (usually adolescents) need to learn prudence, how to shrewdly make decisions and manage themselves. They tend to believe too easily (Pro 14:15) and don't look ahead (Pro 27:12). They might learn prudence from the Proverbs (1:4). Often the simple one learns it as he watches mockers punished (Pro 19:25).

No matter how slick one is, no one can out-maneuver God. Those who try to cleverly out-maneuver God are caught by Him in their own cleverness (Job 5:121-13).

The New Testament Greek word *phronimos (fron'-ee-mos)*, implying a cautious character, corresponds to the Hebrew *'aruwm.* The *phronimos* person is the who is thoughtful, sagacious, discreet, cautious. Such persons govern their affairs by the use of their minds.

Expert. *Tabuwn (taw-boon')* or *tebuwnah (teb-oo-naw')* is a noun coming from *biyn* (bene) meaning to understand, distinguish, separate. In some ways, it is a synonym to *biynah*, the fund of understanding that results from and enables *biyn*. At the same time, it appears to involve the spiritual understandings and perspectives that are contained in the discussions of the wise (Pro 18:2), especially as they are more practically applied. It appears to be the application of *biynah* to setting direction and making decisions in life, a sharpened *biynah*, understanding focused and distilled for dealing with specific issues in life.

The reference point for *tabuwn is breadth of understanding.*

My own study suggests that *tabuwn* utilizes trained, refined judgment coupled with an intentional and intelligent application of principles derived from broad knowledge. It is not just:

- Being aware of the broad categories and principles (which is *biynah*)
- Creating strategy out of a practical read of the circumstances *(sekel)*
- Creating success by bringing an idea into reality *(tuwshiyah)*
- Shrewdly planning and executing *('ormah)*

Tabuwn seems to add to the others the intentional and intelligent application of *principles* in creating the process and executing the leadership that brings success.

The greater awareness of principle and the judgment in application is due to training under the wise. *Tabuwn* is concerned with practical success. However, it creates its successful strategies from a breadth of understanding brought to bear on the practical situation. It is a trained, wise, practical intelligence. *Tabuwn* is something like "street smarts with an MBA." It has both the intuition and the trained intelligence to plan and execute with eminent success.

The Greek word *sunetos* (soon-et'-os) implies mental acquirement, and indicates someone who "mentally puts it together." The sunetos person goes back and forth to learn, first learning, then processing their understanding, and then adding more. It could be an equivalent of *"biyn"* or perhaps *"tabuwn"* from its tabuwn's practice of moving back and forth from learned principle to practical application.

Eminent. *Hakam* (khaw-kam') is a Hebrew verb meaning to be skilled. The skill could apply to a specific field, such as art or politics. Used in a broad sense, it refers to a great breadth of understanding and broad ability to be *eminently successful* in life, doing what is pleasing to God and creating success in this world in the process. *Hakam* is the word most often translated as "wise" or "to be wise."

The *hakam* are those who understand how legitimate and illegitimate impacts are made on people and life. And, they are able to effect the impact they want in a way that is right before God and just and merciful toward people.

Hokma (khok-maw') is the noun related to "be wise" *(hakam). Hokma* is the knowledge of things in the essence of their being and the reality of their existence; knowing things as they really are. It denotes at the same time, the use of reason and the acceptance of God's will. *Hokma* has the knowledge and ability to make the right choices at the right time. Maturity and development in *hokma* are indicated by consistent right choices.

Those who are wise stand out eminently above others in their knowledge, understanding, judgment and success.

The Greek term *sophos* (sof-os'), meaning skill and implying the ability to create the strategically best plans, equates to *hakam* in Hebrew.

RELATIONSHIP BETWEEN THE TERMS

How do these wisdom terms relate?

In some passages, they appear synonymous to one or more of the other terms. Indeed, they all share a common core: making good decisions.

In other ways, they appear to involve increasingly complex skills. Several of the skills seem somewhat like the differences in capability for example, in the field of construction. *Leb* involves skill in a simpler arena, somewhat like that of a trades-person, a plumber or electrician. *Sekel* can deal with situations, like an excellent remodeler can come into a home, survey the situation, and given the goals the owner has, put things together excellently. *Tuwshiyah* is the ability to take a plan and bring it to completion, like a custom builder can take a floor plan and create a house where there was none. *'Ormah* is able to a manage a complex plan excellently, marshalling resources and anticipating contingencies, somewhat like the construction manager of a mall construction project. *Tabuwnah* is able to start from principles and choose excellent goals, create innovative plans and bring them to completion like an architect.

WISDOM IN THE ARENAS OF LIFE

There is a "way of wisdom," a way to live that engages wisdom in all arenas of life. Spiritually, a wise person is committed to the holy and sovereign Creator God. Morally, wisdom calls one to do what is right and avoid wrong. Practically, wisdom pursues skill in various arenas, uses prudence in actions, and builds strong relationships. Wisdom enables us to adapt what we know in order to be effective in what we do.

I have taught thee in the way of wisdom; I have led thee in right paths. (Pro 4:11 KJV)

To walk in the way of wisdom means that one has become clear and focused on his basic purpose in life: to know, love and glorify God, and enjoy Him through eternity.

It also means that, though he desires a prosperous life on earth, he will not try to find it outside the will of God. So, he will live by God's priorities. He will take a little with righteousness rather than great gain with wrong (Pro 16:8), and he will choose peace and love with simple fare over feasting with strife (Pro 15:16-17).

Above all, he will choose faithfulness to God over possessions, family, and life itself (Luke 14:25-33). He will not try to save his life at the expense of disobedience to God (Luke 9:24). He will lose his life in this world in order to save it for eternity (Mark 8:34-38). His operational goal throughout life is to hear from the Lord at the final evaluation, "Well done, good and faithful servant—come and share your master's happiness" (Matt 25:21)!

As life moves along, he will pursue his goals within the boundaries of righteousness and wisdom (Pro 8:20). And, he will handle the various facets of life in line with God's will.

The way of wisdom appears to have at least eight facets of life that must be handled in line with God's will. Scripture gives a great deal of information on each.

These facets of life have a domino effect on one another. One impacts another, which impacts another, and so on. Problems or success in one affects problems or success in the following ones. The flow of effects seems be

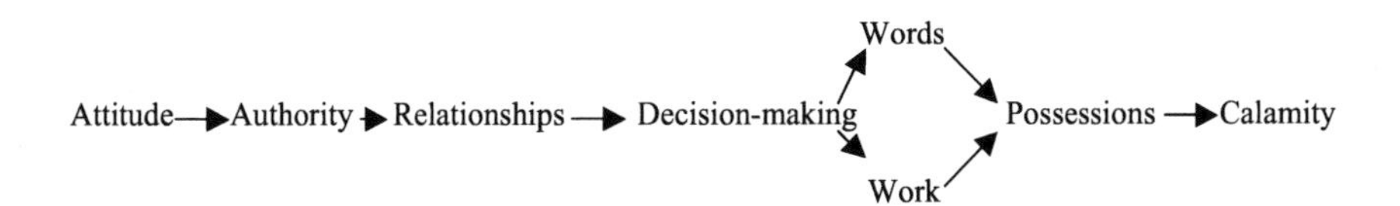

An *attitude* is a mental and emotional preset with which we meet life. There are several attitudes which are promised tremendous blessing in the Scriptures. If one has a wrong attitude, it draws discipline from the Lord and creates problems. It also affects all arenas that follow it. For example, one who lives in "fear of man" will end up trapped as a result of his decision-making process (Pro 29:25). Pride also is a cause for financial problems, as the Lord destroys the possessions of the proud (Pro 15:25).

Every human being must learn to deal with *authority* properly, both in exercising authority and in following it. How one exercises authority can build his authority or tear it down (Pro 20:28; 29:4). How one follows authority can bring him trouble (Pro 24:21) or it can bring him blessing (Pro 16:15; 14:35). One's manner of dealing with authority impacts his relationship with parents, with a mate in marriage, and with his children (Eph 6:4). It will also affect his decision-making and all arenas down line.

Relationships are the threads from which life is woven. The great commandments are about love in relationships: love to God and love to one's neighbor. Handling relationships rightly brings blessing to the relationship, but it also impacts all of life downstream. A person who is caustic and reactive to others will find people are not frank with them as they seek input on major *decisions*. If one has chosen to relate to the wrong kind of friends, he is likely to make wrong, costly *decisions* (Pro 13:20; 22:24). Unfriendliness makes it difficult to succeed in life (Pro 18:1). Rotten relationships within the family can preclude one inheriting *financially* (Pro 11:29). Failure to build relationships results in no help in *calamity* (Pro 17:17; 27:10). Back-stabbing in a relationship can cause repeated disasters down through the years (Pro 17:13).

One's approach to *decision-making* affects his ability to deal with people and to make money. The wrong approach to decision-making leads to job failures and financial failures. It also can mess one up in the sudden onset of calamity.

Work patterns (Pro 10:4) and word patterns (Pro 12:14; 18:20) both impact one's financial success.

How one handles all that has gone before, including money, impacts his ability to deal with calamity, the sudden eruption of trouble (for example, see Ecc 7:12).

In a future book, I hope to deal with the specifics of the way of wisdom in each arena of life. What follows at the end of this chapter is a chart showing what appears to be the key principle for handling a given arena of life according to the ways of God. The statement will be general, but is the "guiding light" for wisdom in that arena of life.

SUMMARY

Wisdom is a great blessing. It begins with the fear of the LORD. It builds by finding information that adequately shapes spiritual perspective to be in line with God's. It grows as we learn to evaluate life based on what we have come to understand about life. Wisdom enables us to better handle life as we develop the ability to make good decisions, learn what is appropriate, learn to plan and to detect covert plans in operation, learn to assess and respond to situations, develop the ability to start with ideas and turn them into realities, and grasp the deep principles behind success across all of life.

Wisdom has several facets, several components. Particularly in the realm of decision-making and choosing strategies, the abilities of wisdom appear to have differing orders of complexity to them. We have looked at one possible organization of them moving from simpler to more complex. In summary they are:

1. *Da'ath*—Perceptual Wisdom: knowledge that shapes spiritual (and thus, real) perspective, and changes how we perceive things, situations, and people. It involves contents, categories and connections; a knowledge of how things, people and life work.

2. *Biynah*—Analytical Wisdom: the ability to analyze people and situations, identifying underlying components, causes and motives.

3. *Leb*—Decisional Wisdom: the ability to make decisions with good sense.

4. *Ta'am*—Tasteful Wisdom; the ability to choose what is tasteful, appropriate.

5. *Mezimmah*—Procedural Wisdom: ability to devise or detect plans for good, or plots and schemes for ill, plotting, conniving.

6. *Sekel*—Situational Wisdom: ability to assess a situation and come up with a highly appropriate solution/ response to it.

7. *Twushiyah*—Fruitional Wisdom: the ability to bring into being; the ability to start with a plan and bring it to fruition.

8. *`Ormah*—Managerial Wisdom: The ability to excellently plan a complex undertaking and excellently execute the plans, carefully managing oneself, one's resources and contingencies.

9. *Tabuwn*—Architectural Wisdom: possession of the deep principles and insights upon which a person draws to create new approaches and solutions.

10. *Hokmah*—Global Wisdom: skill in the whole realm of life; high level skill in a specific arena (as, metalwork).

Wisdom—understanding and doing things God's way—is the way to eminent success in life. As one follows the way of wisdom, he is trying to learn from the Holy Spirit how to do what is pleasing to the Lord Jesus. It is to the one who pleases Him that God gives wisdom and knowledge and happiness (Ecc 2:26).

Below is a chart of the fundamental principles guiding wise responses in the key arenas of life.

GUIDELINES FOR THE ARENAS OF LIFE

Arena	Guideline	Key Scriptures
Attitudes (Mental presets)	Start with the fear of the LORD.	Pro 22:4; Pro 16:20; Pro 16:32
Authority	Use your position to serve.	Lead: Matt 20:26-27 Follow: Ro 13:1
Relationships	Act from sacrificial love.	Luke 6:31; Eph 5:1-2
Decision-making	Seek God's priorities in God's way.	Eph 5:15-18
Words	Speak only what is beneficial to hearers in the situation.	Eph 4:29
Work	Work whole-heartedly serving Christ.	Eph 6:7; Pro 14:23
Possessions, Money	Use your resources as God's steward doing His will.	1 Thes 4:11-12; Matt 6:19-20
Calamity	Go to God first in crisis.	2 Cor 1:11

Think About It

Which of the components of Wisdom is most appealing to you? Why?

In which arena of wisdom do you feel you have made the wisest choices? Why?

YOU'VE GOTTEN A PICTURE OF WISDOM
AND THE WAY IT GROWS AND HANDLES LIFE.
WANT TO SEE THE OPPOSITE—HOW FOOLS BEHAVE?
READ ON!

Chapter 9

WISDOM'S OPPOSITE

A Survey Of Foolishness

Proverbs presents two realms in life: wisdom and mockery (Pro 9:12). Those who are wise are rewarded by their wisdom as time goes on. Mockers, however, suffer. We have looked at the wise in some detail. In this chapter, we will briefly look at wisdom's opposite. Two other books by the author, *Fools and Follies and Self-Defeating Strategies*, will give a more extensive outline of this realm along with the scriptural connections. A Map of Folly is included at the end of the chapter. Referring to it may help you follow the discussion below. The map is an attempt to display visually how the terms relate conceptually.

WISDOM AND THE FEAR OF THE LORD

One who would enter the realm of wisdom must do so by the one port of entry: the fear of the LORD. The fear of the LORD is the beginning of knowledge from which wisdom is built (Pro 1:7), and also the breakthrough point into wisdom (Pro 9:10). One who has not entered into the fear of the LORD is outside the realm of Wisdom. (From the author's own studies, the fear of the LORD and the Lordship of Christ in one's life is the same point of entry into wisdom.)

THE BARRIERS TO WISDOM

Only God possesses wisdom in the absolute sense (Job 12:13). While the world can derive some insight from observing the patterns woven into the creation by the Creator, human intelligence alone cannot derive the full divine wisdom (Job 28:12-13, Ecc 7:23). To attempt to do so only results in frustration and grief.

The human heart keeps getting in the way of wisdom. Three things packaged into all human hearts militate against developing wisdom: *'ivveleth, howlelah* and *ra'*.

'Ivveleth (iv-veh'-leth)

Folly ('ivveleth) is bound up in the heart of a child, but the rod of discipline will drive it far from him. (Pro 22:15 NIV)

'Ivveleth is a Hebrew word for obstinate self-will, the stubborn determination to have what I want, when I want it; that is, I intend to have life on *my terms*. Bound up in the hearts of all children, *'ivveleth* can be "driven out" with corrective training by the parents, using corrective instruction and physical discipline, if necessary (Pro 22:15). Unless it is trained out, the child grows into an adult who will settle into a lifestyle like the *Keciyl* fool or the *'Eviyl* fool, or perhaps a *Cakal* fool—or some mix-and-match combination of these. These fools are discussed in the following pages.

If *'ivveleth* remains ineffectively challenged, the grown adult will find it impossible to change without the help of God (Pro 26:11; 27:22). And, the *'ivveleth* will keep undercutting the adult's success (Pro 19:3).

For the adult to acquire wisdom, he will have to first enter the fear of the LORD, the willingness to have life on God's terms, not his own (Pro 1:7; 9:10). He will have to be willing to do God's will before he is allowed discernment (John 7:17). Someone in the grip of *'ivveleth* is fully committed to his own will, self-will. Apart from a special work of God in the person's heart, he or she will tend to remain ignorant of what is truly important in life.

Howlelah (ho-lay-law')

... Truly the hearts of the sons of men are full of evil (ra'); madness (howlelah) is in their hearts while they live, and after that they go to the dead. (Ecc 9:3 NKJ)

Howlelah (ho-lay-law') is a term for our tendency to exalt ourselves, to treat ourselves as more important than others (pride), to demand more for ourselves than is due to us (arrogance), and to look down on others (haughtiness). We not only want what we want when we want it, we also feel we *deserve* it.

Howlelah never leaves the hearts of the children of Adam. It remains life-long (Ecc 9:3). One cannot get rid of it; he must simply learn how to deal with it and then deal with it daily. As *'ivveleth* undercuts the success of its devotee, the pride that runs through *howlelah* creates repeated problems for *howlelah's* fans. The pride sets the person up for failure and embarrassment (Pro 16:18; 11:2).

Pride resists humbling. As a matter of fact, it is one of the major characteristics of that individual who will never know wisdom, the mocker (Pro 21:24).

Without humility, a person will never find wisdom. Remember? Humility is a prerequisite to wisdom (Pro 11:2). Indeed, wisdom *hates* pride (Pro 8:13).

Pride always brings failure and embarrassment. Sometimes it brings a person low enough that the door opens to new possibilities in life. If, as a result of his troubles, the proud one develops a lowly spirit, he may, through the humility, acquire genuine honor that comes with developing wisdom (Pro 29:23).

Until an adequate "fall," however, pride keeps a person in ignorance, excluded from the wisdom from God.

Ra' (rah)

Ra' is a Hebrew word referring to natural or moral evil. Located in the hearts of people, it shows up as a willingness to harm others in order to get what we want. To get what we want, we are willing to *say* and *do* things that hurt others. Some of us don't harm others *that* much. Others among us are willing to do great damage to others to get what we want.

Our willingness to do harm lasts all our lives. Like our native arrogance, it will not go away, even at conversion. We must learn how to deal with it—and then *deal with it* repeatedly as long as we live.

Again, our willingness to harm others blocks the way to wisdom. Wisdom *hates* evil *(ra')* ways (Pro 8:13). It simply will not go near someone who is nurturing *ra'*. To find wisdom, we have to enter the fear of the LORD, live in a way pleasing to Him.

A major part of the will of God is that we sacrificially love others, and the kind of love God has in mind will do no harm to its neighbor (Rom 13:10). My understanding of the Scriptures is that there is a time to do harm, as when war is necessary or the wicked must be resisted (Ecc 3:8; Pro 24:11-12). However, other than at the extremes of human existence, we need to lay aside our willingness to harm. You might want to read the sections on war and self-defense in *Christian Ethics* by Norman Geisler.

The Drives Behind The Follies

These three drives in the human heart can be summarized in three sentences. I *want what I want when I want it ('ivveleth)! I deserve to have it (howlelah)! And, I don't necessarily want to hurt you, but if you get in my way, I will (ra')!*

Each of the five Old Testament fools wants to *have what he wants*, and feels he *deserves it*. And each is *willing to harm* others—in various ways and to varying degrees—to get what he wants. The three drives appear to be "mixed-and-matched" in various ways to come up with the different follies (ways of thinking and approaches to life) that drive the various fools. For example, one fool is self-willed and arrogant, but operates mainly out of his self-will. Another operates mainly out of his arrogance.

FOLLY / MOCKERY

In English, the opposite of Wisdom is "folly." Folly is a lack of good sense or normal prudence and foresight. A fool is one who uses poor judgment.

In English, we tend to feel the cause of his poor judgment is a *mental* deficiency. In the Bible, the fools' poor judgment comes from his *moral* deficiency. To be wise, in the Bible, involves being righteous; it is the righteous who have wisdom (Luke 1:17). The one who does wrong has ceased to act wisely (Ps 36:3), that is, he is acting foolishly. It is the moral deficiency of the person that accounts for his folly.

Unlike English, in Hebrew, there is no single term for "folly." Rather, there are nine different Hebrew word groups that indicate different kinds of poor judgment. Each of the terms for poor judgment is used in opposition to Hebrew terms for wisdom, but there is no *single* term for "folly" that covers the whole field.

Five of these Hebrew word groups indicate well-established thinking and behavior patterns. Individuals who indulge in these appear as different kinds of "fools" whose approach to poor judgment has its own particular style. The three problems of the heart, *'ivveleth, howlelah* and *ra'*, show up in each of the fools. The fools create their own style of poor judgment by the way they mix-and-match the three heart problems. We will look at the fools and their core styles (follies) in a moment.

While there is no single Hebrew word equivalent to the English "Folly," there is a Hebrew word that may qualify as the comprehensive term to designate the whole realm of "un-wisdom." However, that term is not translated "folly" but "mocking." Proverbs 9:12 sets the terms "wisdom" and "mocking" opposite one another. The choice appears to be between two ways to live, one looking for ways to do life God's way, and the other making light of the things important to God. Perhaps "Mocking" should be the name of the whole realm outside wisdom. Each of the different types of fools engages in mockery in his own way.

We will use the term, Folly/Mockery, to describe the realm opposite to wisdom and look at different Hebrew forms of it. If the wise person is concerned for the fear of the LORD, the various fools neglect Him. The "follies" are strategies used by various fools to live life and attempt to achieve success without giving heed to God. The fools are convinced that God, in different ways, will not be a real factor in life.

SIMPLICITY

Though not yet a full-fledged folly, simplicity (Heb: *pethiy* [peth-ee']) is inclined in the folly direction, and is capable of inadvertently foolish decisions.

The core meaning of the Hebrew term is "open, roomy." The simple person believes—and *wants* to continue to believe (loves his simplicity Pro 1:22)—that life is not all that complicated, and that success is not all that hard to attain. The simple fail to take seriously the possibility of harm through making wrong decisions. So the simple tends to easily believe ideas and people without checking them out (Pro 14:15). They do not look ahead as they make decisions (Pro 27:12). Therefore, they make excellent prey for human predators (see Pro 7).

Characteristic of children and adolescents, "simplicity" is a temporary state. The simple one is envious of what older and wiser people possess (Job 5:2). Though not yet a mocker, he has inclinations in that direction (Pro 1:32). Either he must choose to aggressively pursue wisdom, or over time he will drift into ("inherit") folly (Pro 14:18). Under the eroding influences of external pressure (from friends or tempting situations) or internal drives (envy and waywardness) he will cross the line into *'ivveleth*-folly, the stubborn determination to have what one wants in life regardless what God says.

FIVE FOOLS AND THEIR FOLLIES

The Old Testament presents five types of persons with differing styles of foolishness. We will call them the *five fools.* They are motivated by different ways of thinking and approaching life, which we will call the *follies* of the fools.

It appears to the author that, while all five fools indulge all three basic drives (*'ivveleth, howlelah* and *ra'*) they find in their hearts, three of the fools build dominantly out of 'ivveleth, the fourth builds his life around arrogance, and the fifth builds his life around the last drive, doing harm. Consider the following comparative listing:

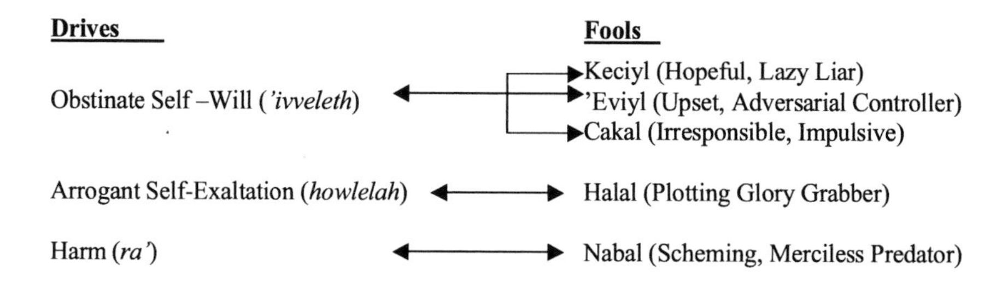

'Ivveleth (iv-veh'-leth) And Its Devotees

As we saw above, *'ivveleth* is the obstinate determination to have one's own way, to have life on one's own terms. According to Proverbs, it is packaged into all children and can be "driven out" by adequate instruction and correction (Pro 22:15). If it is not driven out, it will shape the life of the growing child, and will become a part of the foundation of their adult life. *'Ivveleth* is the foundation for two fools whose focus in life is the determination to get what they want, though they use two different strategies to achieve it. It may possibly also be the foundation underneath a third, the Cakal.

- The *Keciyl* (kes-eel') is a person with a lazy streak and a willingness to lie in order to make life go more smoothly for him. His name comes from a word meaning "hope." He is a confident person who has high hopes, for he is sure he will achieve his goals. However, he is repeatedly disappointed because he sets his hopes on something other than God. Rather than do life God's way, he is sure he can find an easier path to success. Diligence and righteousness require more than he intends to do. He keeps trying to find the easier way, now excited over this possibility, and then excited over another. But his dreams never materialize. He will simply not place his trust in God. *Kacal* (kaw-sal'), *kecel* (keh'-sel), *kiclah* (kis-law'), and *keciyluwth* (kes-eel-ooth'), are different terms for his "folly of false hopes." His up-and-down lifestyle may set the stage for manic-depression or bi-polar disorder.

- The stubborn, adversarial, easily upset *'Eviyl* (ev-eel') is more noxious than the *Keciyl*. The *'Eviyl* does *not* want to be appointed "ruler," but *does* feel he knows best what others ought to do. He attempts to impress his agenda on others and so to control them. His contrary, upset, contentious, and bitter life focuses on achieving his own stubborn self-will through hostility, belligerence, manipulation and sheer stubbornness. Once provoked, the *'Eviyl* can become an unforgiving, life-long enemy. The *'Eviyl* is associated with wasting illnesses. The *Eviyl*, with his firm determination to control reality, may set the stage for psychotic breaks.

While each fool, *Keciyl* and *'Eviyl*, has his own theme for his folly, both also share characteristics of *'ivveleth*, their common, underlying folly: haste, anger, etc. *'Ivveleth* can reach the proportions of "great *'ivveleth*," leading its perpetrator to stray in directions that lead to his death (Pro 5:23).

Cikluwth And The Cakal

Cikluwth (sik-looth') is a disastrous, unthinking folly, a folly born of the intent to fulfill a strong desire while refusing to think of one's responsibilities or the consequences of his actions. It comes from a word that means to take a disastrously foolish step, one that draws unforeseen but serious consequences.

While an ordinary person might make such a mistake once (see 1 Chr 21:8), *cikluwth's* devotee, the *Cakal* (saw-kawl') fool, makes a career of just such choices. He does not particularly plot, premeditate, or connive. Rather, he simply experiences a desire, and then acts to gratify himself.

To the author, the *Cakal* folly and lifestyle appears to be rooted in the "stubborn self will" of *'ivveleth*. His approach to life is more destructive than that of either the *Keciyl* or the *'Eviyl*. Some linguistic evidence argues that the *Cakal* is a *Keciyl* gone to the extreme. If so, then the *Cakal's* folly, built on that of the *Keciyl*, would indeed be grounded in *'ivveleth*.

The *Cakal* has experienced consequences of his foolish actions in the past, and should know the consequences of his choices. However, under the spell of a temptation, all else in the world seems to fade from his sight as he contemplates the object of his desire. He *does not want* to see the consequences. Willfully blinded by his own desire, he seizes his opportunity for gratification. Then, he suffers the horrendous consequences. When he has survived the storm, he will go into another cycle of irresponsible, impulsive behavior.

Unrestrained, blind desire rules his life. The *Cakal* is so controlled by thoughtless gratification that he is said to be expert in ruin without a clue how to do the good (Jer 4:22). He is spiritually blind and deaf (Jer 5:21). Those guided by *cikluwth* are the most stupid of the fools, and have a reputation for their incredibly stupid choices and inability to handle even the simplest matters (Ecc 10:3). Disastrous consequences multiply for the impulsive *Cakal* so that he lives a very deprived life (Jer 5:25).

The *Cakal* way of life appears to set the stage for an addictive lifestyle.

Beyond *cikluwth*, one moves on to follies that can be criminal.

Howlelah And The Halal

In Ecclesiastes *howlelah* (ho-lay-law') is translated "madness." *Howlelah* comes from the Hebrew word for "praise," *halal*. The same Hebrew word, *Halal* (haw-lal'), names the self-praising fool. The Halal is an impudent, self-exalting person (Ps 75:4-7). His folly is madness because it challenges the sovereignty of God as the Exalter, the one who determines who rises and who falls (Ps 75:6-7), and so, earns the direct opposition of God (1 Pet 5:5-6).

The *Halal* wants to rule over others and be the center of attention. Caught up in pride and arrogance, the *Halal* is a self-promoter. He will do even the criminal in order to gain the power and prestige he wants. So he uses threats, oppression, bribery and if necessary, violence, to secure his power (Ps 5:5-6; Ps 73:3-12). He is a perceptive leader with a good sense of timing. His frequent successes fuel his wickedness (Ps 73:4-5), secure his leadership of his henchmen (Ps 73:10), and stimulate his arrogant boasting and blasphemy (Ps 73:7-11).

A full blown *Halal* may become a crime boss like Al Capone. Less than full-blown, these people are the source of many splits in churches and community organizations. Howlelah may set the stage for the criminal personality.

According to Ecclesiastes 9:3, this folly is in the hearts of all humans until the day they die. One cannot get rid of it, but he can learn to control and rule over it.

Nebalah And The Nabal

Nebalah (neb-aw-law') is the villainous, predatory folly of the *Nabal* (naw-bawl'), the intentional scoundrel, the devotee of the low and cruel.

The *Nabal* is the only confirmed atheist among the fools, and makes decisions based on the non-existence of God. He believes that since there is no God, there are no ultimate moral or ethical boundaries for him (Ps 53:13). So, the *Nabal* does reprehensible things that violate the covenant of God, bringing the community into "uncleanness" before God, and in danger of divine retribution.

Nebalah contains such things as immorality, adultery, homosexual rape, gang rape and murder, high sacrilege, and false prophecy.

The *Nabal* fool may be a social outcast or may be part of the social upper crust—or, even in a religious vocation. But, he is devoted to doing the hurtful and harmful in order to get what he wants. He will readily return evil for good. Given a choice of accomplishing his goals in an honorable way or a harmful way, he prefers to render harm.

Willingness to harm others in order to get what we want *(ra')* is one of the problems in the human heart (Ecc 9:3). Over time the person developing into a Nabal becomes a specialist in harm.

The *Nabal* is a predator (sexual, religious, financial, etc.) and dangerous. He may hide his predatory nature under a guise of social respectability until he gets the opportunity to strike (Isa 32:5-6). The *Nabal* appears to share many characteristics with the psychopath/ sociopath.

PROGNOSIS FOR THE FOOLS

The fools blossom over time. Fully developed, they may experience different measures of short-term success, from the Cakal's momentary gratification followed by disaster to the temporary glory and splendor of the *Halal*. Ultimately, their own approach to life undermines their success, and God brings judgment to them.

Fools desperately need wisdom, but in their present state, they will never find it. Changes will have to take place in their hearts before wisdom dawns for them. Fortunately, with God all things are possible (Matt 19:25-26).

The three, basic negative drives in the human heart block the way to wisdom. Whoever would walk toward wisdom is going to have to learn a different set of motivations and different responses to life and people. He is entering an *upside down world.*

His normal responses to people and to situations are going to have to be significantly altered. One way of living must be replaced by another.

Below is a diagram summarizing some of the radical changes, the replacements for the old drives behind the follies with new drives behind a godly life. On page 160 is a "map" attempting to relate wisdom, mockery, fools, and follies.

Replacements For The Old Drives

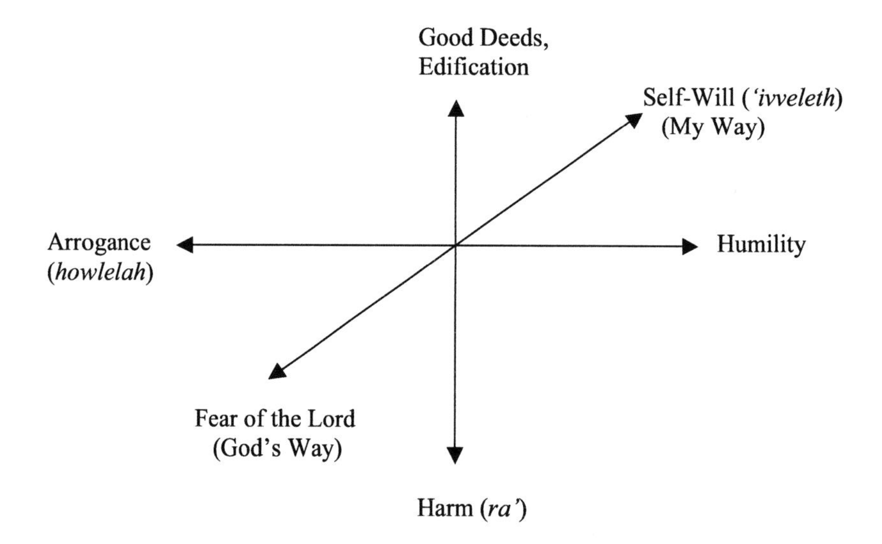

THINK ABOUT IT

Which Fool (or mixture of them) might come closest to your approach to life? Identify some of your specific inclinations that would fit this category of fool.

Which Fool seems most different from you? Why?

Just for fun, based on the sketchy information provided above, describe what life would be like for a close friend of a *Keciyl.* How about for the close friend of an *'Eviyl?* How about the close friend of a *Cakal?*

WANT AN IDEA OF HOW UPSIDE-DOWN THE WAYS OF GOD ARE TO THE OPERATING GUIDELINES OF OUR CULTURE? READ ON!

A MAP OF MOCKERY / FOLLY

INCREASING WISDOM ↑

WISDOM — THE FEAR OF THE LORD: THE DOORWAY TO WISDOM

MOCKING — REALM OF THE PETHIY /PATHAH, THE SIMPLE: THE "SOON-TO-BE" FOOL

PETHIY: SIMPLICITY Credulous Gullibility

INCREASING 'IVVELETH ↓

'IVVELETH: THE FOLLY OF PERVERSITY

REALM OF THE UNREALISTIC KECIYL	REALM OF THE CONTRARY 'EVIYL
The Follies Of False Hope: KASAL, KECEL, KICLAH KECIYLUWTH	The Folly of Adversarial Manipulative, Control

"GREAT" 'IVVELETH — REALM OF THE IMPULSIVE CAKAL

CIKLUWTH: The folly of blind unrestrained desire

REALM OF THE ARROGANT, SELF-EXALTING HALAL

HOWLELAH — HOWLELAH: Self-Exalting Folly

REALM OF THE PREDATORY NABAL

NEBALAH — NEBALAH: Folly Of Villainy

Chapter 10

THE UPSIDE DOWN KINGDOM

Key Principles For Living In The Real World

On the movie screen, an ocean wave of incredible height sweeps across the sea, bearing down on a huge luxury liner now dwarfed by the wave. Amid screaming alarms the wave overwhelms the ship and rolls it over. The ship floats upside down on the waves. Inside, chaos reigns for a time. Finally, people begin to find one another. Many have died. The remaining ones must find their way to the bottom of the ship—which now is atop the waves. If rescue comes, rescuers will cut through the exposed hull to remove survivors. In a world turned upside down, the journey begins. The survivors struggle to ascend upside-down stairways and navigate across floors that once were ceilings. *The Poseidon Adventure* is the story of an upside-down journey to safety.

The followers of Jesus Christ find themselves in a similar situation. When they yield their lives to Jesus Christ, they experience a gigantic rollover. The Kingdom of God operates upside down to the ways of this world. (Actually, the Kingdom is right side up; it's the world that is upside-down—but we won't worry about that right now.)

Jesus identified the difference in the ways of God when he commented to the religious leaders of his day that the things highly esteemed by the people of the world are an abomination to God (Luke 16:15). He had already called his followers to lose their lives in order to save them (Luke 9:23-24).

As the Gospel moved from Asia Minor into Europe, some opponents recognized its completely upside-down way of thinking and living. In Thessalonica, a mob charged that the people who had turned the world upside-down had come there also (Acts 17:6 KJV, RSV). John warned believers not to set their affections on the wrong things, for these had nothing to do with God, though the world thought them quite important (1 John 2:15-17).

When we set out to follow Christ, we are starting on an upside-down journey to rescue (salvation) and freedom. Many times, the *value structure* by which we operate is upside-down to the world's. The *manner* in which we operate is upside-down to the world's. The way we handle relationships is quite different from what the world would do. We are on an upside-down journey to freedom. The way we operate looks "down" to the world," but it is actually the only way "up," the only way to freedom and good things.

The journey toward Wisdom is upside down to the way the world tries to achieve success. The journey of walking with Jesus Christ, the Wisdom of God, is in the same upside-down direction. The God we fear has been made clearer to us in Jesus Christ, than in Old Testament times (John 14:9). The spirit of God's intentions in the Scriptures has been clarified (Matt 19:3-9; 5:21-22) as God has spoken to us, not merely through prophets this time, but through His Son (Heb 1:1-2). As we walk in the fear/respect of the Lord Jesus and trust Him with our lives, He lives within us in the Holy Spirit. Our communion with God is closer than that of people in the time of Solomon.

But, we still have to walk/live our lives in a way radically different from the culture around us. We are still in the world, but we are not of the world (John 14:17-18). While the rest of the world pursues its passions and pleasures (Titus 3:3-4), we live a different kind of life (Titus 2:11-14): self-controlled, upright and godly lives looking forward to fulfillment at the return of Jesus—and eager to do good to people, just like Jesus was. Rather than living for our passions, we live now for the will of God (1 Pet 4:1-2).

Occasionally some of our old friends don't understand our change in point of view. They feel that we have gotten messed up, that we are committed to a direction in life that can only take us down. They make fun of us. Amid the misunderstanding and laughter, we need to stay clear-headed and doing the right things (1 Pet 4:3-1).

Since Christ came to the earth, to pursue the way of wisdom is to walk with Jesus Christ doing the will of God. The characteristics of the wise (chapter six) look much like the fruit of the Spirit (Gal 5:22-23) and Peter's list of essential Christian qualities (2 Pet 1:5-8). And, they look a great deal like the qualifications for the elders/overseers of the New Testament church (1 Tim 3:1-7; Titus 1:5-9).

The Counterfeit Wisdom whispers to us through our culture that one does not have to be so extreme in following Christ, that there is some way to work out a compromise with the ways of this world so that one can be "good enough" to get into heaven and yet still "bad enough" to enjoy the good things of this world. It is a lie. Jesus would prefer us hot or cold—lukewarm only makes Him "sick to His stomach" (Rev 3:14-16). And, life only works in line with the way its Author designed it and with the way He runs the universe.

We do not want to be simple-minded in our approach to life. We do not want to be naïve, but we "know whom we have believed" (2 Tim 1:12). And, *He* is leading us to safety. Regardless what the rest of society thinks, we have to intelligently follow Him, even though it looks "down;" He knows the way to rescue and freedom! As we take up our cross and follow Him to what looks like certain death, we find life itself (Luke 9:23-24). In this upside-down world, the way of the cross (self-denial, to the point of death, if necessary, for Christ) is the way to *life*.

In order to help understand the upside-down journey, we will look at some themes from the teachings of Jesus and what they mean practically for living in the will of God. These "themes of the upside-down Kingdom" are challenging for they are very different from the way the culture around us operates. They are also different from our native self-will, pride, and willingness to hurt others. But, they are the only way to freedom. There is no alternative to living in line with these *if* you want a good life on this planet—and in the next world.

One could write on many more themes, but these will help identify the "upside-down" way to safety and freedom.

THE UPSIDE-DOWN TREASURES: GOD'S VERY DIFFERENT VALUES

If we want to walk with God, we are setting out on a quest that will demand we redo the worldly value system that we have learned—and which, actually still has great appeal to us. Our concept of "what is more important than what" is going to go through a drastic revision.

He said to them, "You are the ones who justify yourselves in the eyes of men, but God knows your hearts. What is highly valued among men is detestable in God's sight. (Luke 16:15 NIV)

The world's system is built around getting what we want, gratifying our appetites (sex, food, drink, power), gratifying our desire to have "cool" or beautiful things, and doing or possessing the things that give us status and feed our sense of superiority to others (the lust of the flesh, the lust of the eyes and the pride of life—see 1 John 2:14-17). We are capable of altruism, but *high* in the human value system are those things that enable us to get our way and gratify our wants: money, power, good looks, fame, pride, and being praised by others. These things are quite appealing to us, but they are much less important in God's scale of values. So, we must guard against being trapped by them lest we waste our lives.

God's value system is built around loving sacrifice for the good of others, even if they don't yet return love to the lover. He wants us to accept His love for us, and in return, love Him enough to do what pleases Him. What pleases Him is not only our love expressed to Him, but our imitation of Him as we love, care for, and help others (1 John 3:1; Matt 22:36-40; Eph 5:10; 1-2).

Out of His grace (undeserved favor) toward us, God took the *initiative to love* us (2 Thes 2:16) *before* we loved Him (1 John 4:19). So, we love God because He first loved us (1 John 4:19). This God-like initiative is the first component of the love that God wants us to display to others (1 John 4:10).

The second component of God's love to us was His *deep personal sacrifice* for our sakes, as His Son came to be the atoning sacrifice for our sins—and He did it even *before* we loved God (1 John 4:10; Rom 5:8).

This caring initiative to personally sacrifice for the good of others—even if they don't love us yet—is the kind of love God wants displayed to others (1 John 4:11). It is not merely an emotion or a theoretical concept. Rather, it shows up in practical acts of need-meeting (1 John 3:16-18). The refusal to meet the real, legitimate needs of others indicates that God's love doesn't dwell in us (1 John 3:17).

High in God's value system are those things that are like Him in heart: love, humility, serving, purity, justice, etc. In terms of God's values, this love-in-action is supreme. It outranks supernatural gifting, such as speaking in tongues or prophecy. It outranks the greatest of perceptive abilities, even the ability to fathom all mysteries and knowledge. It outranks incredible faith. It outranks vows of poverty. It even outranks martyrdom for the sake of Christ (1 Cor 13:1-3).

People who are trying to solve their problems or who are strategizing to get ahead in life must realize that God is going to use circumstances to wean them away from the world's value system and to teach them to value what God values. Some people insist on keeping one foot in the world and one in the Kingdom of God. Because God loves them, He will deal out discipline to them (Heb 12:5-11), a flow of events that will frustrate and redirect them—and will do it their life-long, if necessary.

WE LIVE BY FAITH, NOT BY SIGHT

We live by faith, not by sight. (2 Cor 5:7 NIV).

This principle means at least four things:

1. We must trust God and do what is right even if it costs us dearly. God's Word will call us to do what is right before God even at risk to ourselves. And, we have to start doing right *even though we cannot see* "how things will work out." We just trust God and do right. We live by faith, and faith in God means risk, especially risk to do right.

That means that we will repeatedly have to choose against living in anxiety over how things are going to work out (Matt:6:33-34; Phil 4:6-10). And, we must pray and *rely on God*, His character, and resources, to enable us to make it through difficult situations and to accomplish the good things He wants us to do in life (see 2 Cor 1:8-11).

2. We will *never not* *need* the help of God, especially His help through the Holy Spirit in our lives. Whatever good happens in our life, it will come as we continue to, moment by moment, trust God. The "walk" (way of living) is by faith. We never come to a point that we can slack off.

No matter how long or how deeply we have walked with Christ, we do not count on our own goodness to propel us forward spiritually. We simply are not that good! (See Rom 7:18-25.) But *God*, living in us through the Holy Spirit, *empowers* the development of good in our lives, things such as the fruit of the Spirit (Gal 5:22-23). While our own effort is significant in seeing our lives change, we need to continually *depend on Him* for the growth of good things in us, not on our insight, strength or endurance. It is by daily and momentarily walking in trust of and obedience to Him that we will overcome the "works of the flesh" in our lives (Gal 5:16; Rom 8:13).

We simply *won't* have days or hours when we can handle it on our own, when we don't need God.

3. God will not give us a map of our future, lest we trust in it instead of Him. Instead, He will be our guide into the future. We will simply have to trust God day by day for ultimate direction in our lives.

We will not know when difficulty may strike. But, we will know the one who can take us through whatever comes (Phil 4:13f). The difficult events of life are going to repeatedly drive us back to desperately trust God (2 Cor 1:8-11), and will prepare us to be able to strengthen others as they go through difficulty (2 Cor 1:3-7).

Once we feel we have direction set for our lives, it can still be changed by God (Pro 16:9). We follow, *not the plan, but the man*—the God-man, Jesus Christ, who is the Way (John 14:6). And, the Lord will tell us just enough at a time to help us be effective but also keep our faith set in Him to keep leading us.

4. We need to operate with a clear conscience before God. Living by faith means that we stay within the boundaries of what is pleasing to the Lord.

If we are not sure whether or not an activity is really right, before God, for us to participate in, then we *just don't do it.* If you can't do something knowing that you are in the boundaries of what is pleasing to God, just don't do it—just say no!

Later on, you may be able to study the issue and come to the conclusion it is just fine for you. But until then, just don't. Whatever you do that doesn't grow out of faith is sin (Ro 14:23).

LOVE GOD WITH EVERYTHING YOU HAVE

Jesus replied: "'Love the Lord your God with all your heart and with all your soul and with all your mind.' This is the first and greatest commandment. (Matt 22:37-38 NIV)

Jesus is basically saying, "Love God with everything you are and have." Or, to say it another way, God must have first place in your life. In the words of Proverbs, you must enter into the fear of the LORD.

One's **heart** represents the real thinking, feeling, and willing inner person. It is especially the true, inner person viewed from the angle of motives and decision-making. The heart could be called the "cockpit of the life;" it is in the heart that direction for one's life is set (Pro 4:23).

Your motives and goals must be wrapped around God. Decisions must be made with His concerns in the forefront. As Jesus said in another place: "Seek first His kingdom and His righteousness," and all the rest will be taken care of (Matt 6:33).

Your **soul** is the vital force that animates you. Your energy is to be given to God and to living life according to His priorities. Our relationship to God and His work in the world will require our force and energy, and we need to put our energy and strength and will into it.

You need to take some part of the action in the Kingdom of God, take some role in the fellowship of believers for the common good (Rom 12:7). For this you have been designed, and you have a part to play (Eph 4:16).

We also need to keep our spiritual fervor and watch that our zeal for God does not die down (Rom 12:11).

Our **mind** involves our thoughts, views and mentalities. God must have first place in our views, mentalities, and thoughts.

We need information about our Creator in order for the new life to grow in us (Col 3:10). Our minds are to be remodeled according to God's perspectives on life (Rom 12:2). We need to monitor our thoughts and not get into anxiety (Matt 6:34; Phil 4:6-7).

Because our ideas shape the way we live our lives, and because deceptive people are willing to inject false teaching into whomever will listen, over time, we need to check the teachings we receive to make sure they square with God's Word before we buy fully into them (Acts 17:11; Col 2:8; 1 Tim 6:20-21). Even more, we need to be selective about the thoughts we allow to remain in our minds. Different thoughts may run through, but we must screen every thought and allow to remain only those that are pleasing to the Lord (2 Cor 10:5).

To *love God with all our heart, soul and mind* is to put God first in the way we live our lives and make decisions. Jesus was adamant that one could not be His disciple unless Jesus were first over all that person's relationships, possessions, and his very life (Luke 14:25-33).

Many people *sort of* want to follow God as number one in their lives, but other things keep getting their attention—things that worry them, hassles with making enough money, and trying to get *some* pleasure out of life. People who keep getting their priorities messed up never bear the fruit God wants, and never find the good life that God desires for them. When we get preoccupied with worries, money or trying to have a good time, *the good things* that God could bring into our lives *never arrive* (Luke 8:14).

Life simply "cripples along" until we decide to put God first. Putting God first is the point at which wisdom and the resources of God begin to open up to us.

Please understand that we will not love God *perfectly*. We will finally be perfect only in heaven. Here on this planet, in even our best days, we could be deceived about the strength of our love for God. Some people get lost in introspection and guilt, wondering if they love God enough.

Actually, there is an answer to the question, "Do I ______ God enough?" (You can fill in the blank with "love," or "pray to," or "appreciate," or "thank," or "praise," or "give to," and so on.) The answer is "No!" We can always grow in every facet of Christian living. The real issue is not "enough," but "Am I doing what God wants right now?"

Rather than worrying if we love God enough, we simply need to take what we *are* and *have*, and present them to God. Then, we need to ask Him to take them and use them. Then, we need to do what He says.

To *hold back* from God *does not work.*

Many people who seek counseling are actually trying to come up with a way to *worry over their cares* less stressfully, *create riches (make money)* less stressfully, and be able to *indulge their pleasures* (have a better time, have more fun) less stressfully. That is, they want to reduce the stress of living for the things of the world (Luke 8:14).

Theirs is a self-defeating quest. They will merely keep riding the Mocker's Merry-Go-Round. The only way to get off the Merry-Go Round is to leave the realm of Mockery and start to fear the LORD. That is, they have to start putting God first in the matters of daily life and the use of resources. They must start to love God with all their heart, soul, and mind.

LOVE YOUR NEIGHBOR AS YOURSELF

Jesus replied: "'Love the Lord your God with all your heart and with all your soul and with all your mind.' This is the first and greatest commandment. And the <u>*second*</u> *is like it:* <u>*'Love your neighbor as yourself.'*</u> *All the Law and the Prophets hang on these two commandments." (Matt 22:37-40 NIV)*

Here, Jesus is *not* talking about "feeling good about your neighbor." Sometimes people interpret the verse this way and then conclude that we must first love (feel good about) ourselves before we can love others. Such an interpretation cuts the very heart out of what Jesus is saying. It takes our attention off our neighbor and puts it back on ourselves. We start trying to feel better about ourselves so we can ultimately feel better about others. Actually, if we do feel rotten about ourselves, we usually feel rotten about others. But Jesus is not addressing our feelings, He is addressing our *priorities.*

What Jesus is saying is this: "Put others' interests on par with your own" (see Phil 2:3-4). Even people who feel rotten about themselves still love themselves in this sense. They still put their own agenda ahead of the agendas of other people. Their disgust with themselves is actually one expression of their self-preoccupation. Focused on self-disgust, they do not notice others. They will jump line to get ahead of others, putting their own interests first. They cut in front of others in traffic, etc. They *will* press their own agenda ahead of others.

When we love our neighbors as ourselves, we are still taking care of our responsibilities. The difference is that we carry out our agenda in a way that is helpful to them as well (Phil 2:3-4), and we may even sacrifice our agenda for the sake of members of the family of God (John 13:34-35).

This is the royal law of love, the law that brings freedom (Jas 2:12). Love does no harm to a neighbor (Rom 13:10).

DO TO OTHERS WHAT YOU WOULD HAVE THEM DO TO YOU

So in everything, do to others what you would have them do to you, for this sums up the Law and the Prophets. (Matt 7:12 NIV)

Much contemporary wisdom urges us to be aggressive (demanding) and assertive (pushy) with others in order to make sure we get what we want.

Jesus sets down a different way of handling people. And, we will find favor and help from God as we do what He says, and trouble from God as we refuse to do what Jesus says.

Normally, we don't mind demanding that other people treat us the way we want to be treated. But, God demands that, as we deal with others, we approach them from the angle of how we would like *them* to treat *us*.

This basic law of being considerate stretches all across the Christian life, and includes parents, children, husbands, wives, friends, enemies, neighbors, and strangers. It actually is one way to define what Jesus meant when He said that we are to love our neighbor as ourselves, for Jesus makes the same statement about what we call "the golden rule" as He does about the two greatest commands to love God and neighbors: this sums up everything in the Old Testament (Law and Prophets) (see Matt 22:40).

This is a fundamental part of the will of God. Regardless how others treat us, we are to treat others in the kind, just, and merciful way we wish they would treat us. This does not mean we are to be stupid in the way we deal with manipulative or predatory people. But, it does mean that even predators on their way to just punishment, must be treated considerately by us.

We can be arrogant and demanding if we want, but the "Golden Rule" is the way life really works. Steven Covey, the business trainer, utilizes this principle in one of his seven habits of effective people: seek first to understand, then to be understood.

This is a key way to love our neighbors as ourselves.

DON'T WITHHOLD GOOD FROM THOSE WHO DESERVE IT

Do not withhold good from those who deserve it, when it is in your power to act. Do not say to your neighbor, "Come back later; I'll give it tomorrow"—when you now have it with you. (Pro 3:27-28 NIV)

We frequently have the power to do a good turn to others. The beneficial things we could do to others are a part of God's plan for our life (Eph 2:10). When we have the power to do good, and the opportunity to do it, we simply need to act—especially if the other person is deserving of the good we could do. For example, perhaps we owe them money and we have the cash available—then we need to pay it, and not say, "Come back tomorrow" (Pro 3:28). James even says that to *fail to do good* when we see the opportunity is sin (Jas 4:17).

We are to do good to all people, *especially* those who belong to God (Gal 6:10).

This includes several facets of life: paying debts when they are due, paying taxes when they are due, paying tariffs and wages owed, and giving others the respect due them, as a fellow human being made in the image of God or the additional honor due to people who hold office (Rom 13:6-8). It also includes paying double respect and salary (money is implied in the term translated "honor") to hard working pastors who preach and teach. (1 Tim 5:17). Respect is also to be shown to the aged (Lev 19:32).

This command to do good includes sex within marriage. It is wrong to withhold sex inside marriage. Our foolish culture tends to encourage us to use sex as a bargaining chip in marriage. But, sex is not a bargaining chip; it is a marital obligation and an opportunity to do good to one's mate. Husbands and wives are to meet the sexual needs of their mates (1 Cor 7:3-5). According to the Bible, the husband's body actually *belongs* to the wife and the wife's to the husband. The husband is to do good to his wife by meeting her sexual needs—she deserves it, since the husband's body belongs to her! Likewise, the wife is to do good to her husband by meeting his sexual needs. After all, he deserves it since her body belongs to him!

BETTER IS GIVING THAN RECEIVING

...the Lord Jesus Himself said: 'It is more blessed to give than to receive.'" (Acts 20:35 NIV)

People of the world are out to get what they can: stuff, gratification, money, admiration, etc.

Emotional health (that sense of living well, being "blessed") and other blessings depend on becoming a giver, however. Life *goes better*, and *is better*, for the one who is a consistent giver.

In a specific situation, *giving is the better course of action.* For example, Abraham let his nephew, Lot, choose the best pasturage for his flocks (and thus, the path to wealth and the easy life). Later, it turned out that the place chosen by Lot—the lush advantageous place that Abraham could have chosen—lay in the path of God's coming judgment and destruction! We do not know the future, we just know that God will take care of givers.

Many people have great trouble in their relationships, marriages, and careers because they are a *demanding* person and *not a giver.*

YOU GET IN PROPORTION TO WHAT YOU GIVE

Give, and it will be given to you. A good measure, pressed down, shaken together and running over, will be poured into your lap. For with the measure you use, it will be measured to you." (Luke 6:38 NIV)

Stingy people try to gather as much as possible and give as little as possible. Stingy people always give sparingly and make sure they have plenty for themselves. They don't want an experience of giving to wring them out or leave them exhausted. Some are stingy with money, others with praise, others with time, and others with personal energy or emotional expenditure.

Life is different from what we think: one man gives generously and gains all the more, while another tries to hang onto all he can, and loses even that (Pro 11:24). The way God operates heaven and earth is to *make sure stingy people lose* what they are trying to hoard. Thus, the stingy person has actually set out on a course of life that will lead to intense lack (Pro 28:22). And, those who are givers keep on being enriched and refreshed—financially, time-wise, praise-wise, and emotionally (Pro 11:25).

Jesus stated clearly the way God operates: God gives more back to us than we give, but *God uses the same size of package* that we use. We will get back more (pressed down, running over) than we gave, but if we used a teaspoon to measure out our gift, we get back a heaping teaspoon. If we used a wheel barrow to measure out our gift, we get back a heaping wheel barrow. If we used a dump truck to measure out our gift to another, we get back a heaping dump truck.

Note, however—we don't measure out with a teaspoon and get back a dump truck! God returns more to us, but it is the same kind of measure. The extra heaped on a dump truck is much more than the extra heaped on a teaspoon.

Many frustrated people are simply stingy. They want a lot in life, but they give only a bit. So God keeps running the universe His way and life returns very little to the stingy person. All that they want continues to elude them.

Married people who are trying to figure how to get more out of their mates are on a never-ending quest. One counselor has said many people approach marriage like a tick on a dog. The problem is that most marriages are two ticks and no dog!

The tick only takes, it never gives. So, given the way God runs the world, He matches one marital tick with another. And that other tick just *will not* turn into a dog !

The tick has to change its ways, even if the other tick does not! Once it becomes a giver (which may delight the other tick), God will begin to act in the changed person's favor. I am not saying that one marriage partner should become a doormat for the other to wipe their feet on. I am simply saying that a selfish, demanding approach to other people, especially in marriage, only moves God to guarantee that the demands will not be met.

Generous people are blessed people (Pro 11:25).

DIFFERENT STEWARDSHIPS FOR DIFFERENT INDIVIDUALS

For God, who was at work in the ministry of Peter as an apostle to the Jews, was also at work in my ministry as an apostle to the Gentiles. (Gal 2:8-9 NIV)

In a culture where everyone wants to be number one, it seems unfair that some—in particular, ourselves—should have less than others. In a culture that stresses "equality" (which we never seem to be able to adequately define or attain) rather than "justice" (which can fairly easily be defined and more easily attained), it seems that everyone should have the same—and all be *rich*, of course.

In the "economy of God" (i.e., theologians' words for "the way God has decided to carry things out"), people are actually given different assignments in life: some start life in great wealth, others in poverty (Pro 22:2); some are princes, others just ordinary citizens (Job 34:19). Some are of one nation, others of a different nation. God cares for all nations, and has helped even those who do not know Him (Amos 9:7). God does not favor one person over another, but treats them impartially (Job 34:19), and commands that we act impartially (Jas 2:1-10).

God's command to love others means that we are to treat *all*, not just the rich and powerful, with respect (Jas 2:8-9). While men and women play different roles in marriage and life, God respects the one as much as the other, and even more if they belong to Christ (Gal 3:28). A woman cannot disrespect her husband or a man his wife and expect God to be answering their prayers (Eph 5:33, 1 Pet 3:7). *Proper respect shown to one's mate is key to God repairing a marriage.*

Some of us are given great ability and responsibility in life (Matt 25:14-30). God requires much from those who have been given much, and less from those given less (Luke 12:48).

Some are given one type of spiritual gift and others another (1 Cor 12:7-11). There is a ranking among the gifts (1 Cor 12:27-31), and high ranking gifts are not "equally distributed" but are handed out as God sees fit (1 Cor 12:11). Some gifts have leadership associated with them and others do not. The "equality" God intends is not an equality of gifting or leadership, but an *equality of concern* for one another, regardless the gifting (1 Cor 12:25). Everyone's gifts are to be used in harmony (1 Cor 12:25) for the common good of the church (1 Cor 12:7). We are to use whatever gift God has assigned for the benefit of others (1 Pet 4:10-11).

Some people are assigned shorter lives on this planet, as were the Lord Jesus, Stephen, and James, the brother of John (Acts 12:22; 22:20; 9:10-11). Others are given long ones (Ps 139:16). The issue is not the number of days we have, but to live godly amid our days (Ecc 8:12-13).

Some people are initially given health, others come into life with physical problems, even though neither they nor their parents had rebelled against God (John 9:1-3). The difficulty comes so that the work of God may be displayed in their lives. The things that God chooses not to heal become the vehicles for God to display His greatness through the life of the afflicted person—if that person will seek to walk with Him and do His will (Rom 8:26-27; 2 Cor 12:7-10). Those who have health ought to be of help to those who do not.

What is important is that we take what we have been given—whether a spiritual gift, money, possessions, heath, even a public beating (Acts 5:40-42), imprisonment (Acts 16:23-25) or a martyr's death (John 21:19)—trust God to empower us (2 Cor 12:9), and use it to bless people and honor God (Matt 26:39, 42; Acts 20:24; Phil 1:21; 1 Pet 4:10-11). Self-pity only leads to *depression* (see Job 3:1-26); self-centeredness only leads to *subtraction* (Luke 12:16-20).

HARVEST HAS SOME LAWS

Let us not become weary in doing good, for at the proper time we will reap a harvest if we do not give up. (Gal 6:9 NIV)

We all want to see wonderful results at the end of our labor. We work hard and the results are there! Right?

Maybe not! It depends on what you are working on. If you work hard on something mechanical, like putting together a computer, or building a bookshelf, or making a soufflé, you can work hard for a short time and see results. But, if you are working on something organic, something that has life to it, results just don't come as fast as with a bookshelf. Crops (and animals) take *time* to grow, no matter *how* hard you work.

The Bible uses the imagery of sowing and reaping, an organic model, to describe our labor in the spiritual realm. There are several laws of the harvest you need to be aware of, lest you make a mistake or simply grow discouraged. Here are some:

1. There is no way to remove the risk. Take the risk.

I tell you the truth, unless a kernel of wheat falls to the ground and dies, it remains only a single seed. But if it dies, it produces many seeds. The man who loves his life will lose it, while the man who hates his life in this world will keep it for eternal life. (John 12:24-26 NIV)

When seed goes into the ground, several things could happen. Animals might dig it up and eat it. It could fail to germinate and only rot. It could produce a crop that gets wiped out by bad weather, pests or disease. Or, it could produce a crop that is a blessing.

What the planter knows is this: If he plants the seed, he is not going to eat it. If he does plant, he is losing his food. That loss may end up worth it, as the seed produces many more. Or, it could end up simply a loss.

To "go into the ground and die" means the seed will give up remaining unchanged. For a person, it means, at the Lord's bidding, saying no to all the things you would like to do, such as being well-known, well heeled, well-financed, well-connected, and well-rested. And, it means saying yes to so many things you would really not want: rejection, ostracism, caring for people who don't return it, spending money to help people come to know God, being tired because of helping others, etc. That's going into the ground and dying. There is a risk that it won't count for anything.

You just have to take the risk, endure the pain, and trust the Lord to be faithful. In time, there'll be a harvest of good things.

If you take the risk to plant, you can get so much more.

2. If you don't plant, you don't get.

A sluggard does not plow in season; so at harvest time he looks but finds nothing. (Pro 20:4 NIV)

Unless you actually invest money, time, effort, emotional energy and prayer in getting to know God and in helping others, you will get *nothing* over the long haul. You will simply grow old. Many people are "waiting for their ship to come in," but they have never sent one out!

3. If you plant, you get the *same kind* of stuff.

A man reaps <u>what</u> he sows. The one who sows to <u>please his sinful nature,</u> from that nature will reap destruction; the one who sows to <u>please the Spirit,</u> from the Spirit will reap <u>eternal life</u>. (Gal 6:7-8 NIV)

To sow to please your sinful nature means to spend your time, money, energy and effort doing the things that please you but displease the Lord. For example, many people spend a great deal of time and energy mentally rehearsing their hurts and anger over the past. They will only raise a crop of stress-related diseases and discipline from God. Many never really contribute a significant part of their money to the things of God They are too busy spending on their "worries, possessions or pleasures" (Luke 8:14). Where you put your money tells where your heart really is (Matt 6:19-21).

To sow to please the Spirit means to spend time, money, effort and emotions on doing the things that make God glad: helping others practically, helping them to know more about God, etc.

If we sow good things, good things come back to us! If we sow bad, wrong things, then bad, destructive things come back to us!

No one plants weeds intending to harvest wheat! Monitor what you spend your time and money on—it determines what kinds of things will be happening to you in the future as the stuff you planted starts coming up and bearing fruit!

4. You get *in proportion* to what you plant.

Remember this: Whoever sows sparingly will also reap sparingly, and whoever sows generously will also reap generously. (2 Cor 9:6 NIV)

If you plant fifteen or twenty corn seeds, you will get back *much more*—perhaps fifty or a hundred times more! There is a *great return* on what you plant, but planting fifteen or twenty seeds is *not* going to produce a *huge harvest*!

A huge harvest demands the planting of a great number of seeds—which is both a lot of work, and a lot of risk. What if the weather goes bad and the crop is not so strong? Perhaps one could plant a *few* seeds and hang on to the vast majority for another year! But then, that means only a tiny harvest this year!

The one who *really goes after it*, planting without sparing, is the person who will have great things happening in their future. The one who holds back simply won't have very many good things coming true as time goes on.

This also works in *planting the wrong things*. One frequently hears of someone who wants to "sow their wild oats" and then settle down. Sowing wild oats is a *cultural* metaphor for *doing wrong for a time*.

The *scriptural* metaphor is not "sowing wild oats," it is "sowing the wind." Wind is something that is non-substantial; it's only air. In a sense, it's worthless. The one who "sows the wind" does what is wrong and worthless before God for a time. The problem is this: If we sow the wind and do the empty worthless things, we are going to get back much more than we "planted."

They sow the wind and reap the whirlwind. (Hos 8:7 NIV)

When they sow the wind, they will reap a storm! (Hos 8:7 TEV)

The one who sows the wind gets back not *"wild oats,"* but a *massive storm.* What was sowed (the wrong stuff we did) we may have thought actually to be *refreshing*, like a cool wind on a hot summer day, or *impressive*, like a gust of wind in March. But what comes back is the *same kind of stuff but now in horrendous quantities with destructive force.* The one who sows the wind later finds coming back at him a tornado.

If we sow a lot of good seed (things done to learn about God, help others and help advance God's kingdom), a *huge* harvest of good stuff comes back to us.

If we sow *a little* good seed, *more* good will come back to us. The problem is that *more than a little just isn't much.* We need to "not spare."

And, in the *bad* seed realm, *breezes produce tornados.* What may appear refreshing in the moment turns into gale-force destruction later.

5. There's a *long time* and a *lot of hard work* between planting and harvest.

Do you not say, 'Four months more and then the harvest'? (John 4:35 NIV)

One has to wait. The harvest can only grow so fast. It takes so many days until the plants can mature—it simply will not happen faster, no matter how hard you work, wish or try to get God to alter His laws for plant growth. Patience is needed.

See how the farmer waits for the land to yield its valuable crop and how patient he is for the autumn and spring rains. (Jas 5:7 NIV)

One also has to work! Actually, hard work needs to be done in the fall before the spring planting, plowing up the field, getting the soil loosened, and plant matter plowed under to help fertilize the field. Then, there is the hard work of planting. Then repeatedly, daily, the soil must be loosened, weeds removed, and watering done when necessary—all just to keep the plants healthy. The work will not stop as long as the crop is in the field. It will continue until the harvest is ready.

Actually, when the harvest is ready, God sees that the first reward goes to the hard workers.

The hardworking farmer should be the first to receive a share of the crops. 2 Tim 2:6

How long does a spiritual harvest take to grow? In my own life, I have been able to see some results after three or four years. But these are not "harvest," they are merely like the young plants pushing their leaves above the soil. In our lives (my wife and I), harvest has taken about fifteen years. What we planted fifteen years ago, we harvest today. What we planted five years ago, we will likely harvest in ten more.

The spiritual farm we are working in seems to be more like an orchard: It takes several years for the newly planted trees to finally bear. Then, they bear repeatedly.

6. There are different roles to play as God prepares the harvest.

I planted the seed, Apollos watered it, but God made it grow. So neither he who plants nor he who waters is anything, but only God, who makes things grow. The man who plants and the man who waters have one purpose, and each will be rewarded according to his own labor. (1 Cor 3:6-9 NIV)

The type of work changes during different phases of the harvest. One is not always doing the same thing. There is time for planting-type work, then for gardening-type work, then for harvesting-type work. As God grows a harvest that we have planted, the nature of our work will change. Sometimes God also changes personnel, using more than one to create the same harvest. So Paul planted, and Apollos watered. And, God made it grow! And, God will see that each one profits from the harvest according to their own work.

If others get involved in helping you grow a harvest, do not become envious or jealous. God will still reward you. Just make sure you play your role well and work hard, so that when reward is handed out, there will be a lot for you.

7. The harvest requires one last demanding, exhausting push.

He who gathers crops in summer is a wise son, but he who sleeps during harvest is a disgraceful son. (Pro 10:5 NIV)

After a long summer of hard work, the crops ripen. Within a very short time, all the crops have to be harvested and stored in barns or they will rot in the field. In a brief time, the results of all the months of hard work and investment could be destroyed.

Harvest-time is not party time; it is "work harder and longer than ever" time. This is why it is shameful to sleep during harvest. Harvest is not a time to sleep.

Many times, after a long time of working hard at doing the right things, a crop of good things ripens for us. Then, we become busier than we ever thought we could be. It is possible to resent the extra labor, feeling we have already worked so hard and long. However, it is simply the nature of the harvest. This is simply what it takes. *If we will do what it takes*, we will enjoy the good things that we have planted. We will enjoy the fruit of our efforts if we do not lose heart.

The party comes *after* the Harvest.

SUMMARY

The challenge laid out by Jesus, "Follow me!" (Luke 9:23) is, in essence, the same as the challenge laid out by wisdom to walk in the fear of the Lord and turn away from evil. The King and His Kingdom *just handle life so differently* from this world's ways. Amid our own desires and the world's doubts, we sometimes wonder if we labor in vain. Keep on, however. Time will ultimately prove who is right (Luke 7:35). You will reap a harvest *if* you do not lose heart (Gal 6:9-10).

Think About It

Which of the above "principles of the Kingdom" have been easier for you?

Which seems to you to be the most difficult to implement? Why?

WANT TO UNLOCK THE TREASURES OF WISDOM?
WANT TO KNOW WHAT YOU HAVE TO DO?
IT'S IN THE NEXT CHAPTER!

Chapter 11

GAINING WISDOM

True wisdom is a possession of God (Ecc 8:22-26). Out of His common grace, He grants a basic measure of wisdom to human kind so that princes, nobles, kings, and all who exercise judgment on the earth can use it in their decision-making (Pro 8:15-16). However, He gives it in greater and deeper measure to those who please Him (Ecc 2:26), and to those who ask it of Him (Jas 1:5; Pro 2:6).

WISDOM AND THE HOLY SPIRIT

When the Holy Spirit entered the people of God on Pentecost (Acts 2:1-4), the very source of wisdom was now resident within the individuals of the church and in the church as a group. He is the Spirit of Wisdom, who gave Joshua and Daniel wisdom (Deu 34:9; Dan 5:11, 14), and who rested upon the Messiah, Jesus (Isa 11:2). He is the spirit of wisdom and revelation who allows us to know God better (Eph 1:17).
The Holy Spirit gives wisdom to His people, the church, in three ways:

- To some He gives a *gift*. To some He gives the gift of the "*word of knowledge*," an ability to perceive and communicate spiritual perspective on situations. To others, He gives the gift of "*the word of wisdom*," the exceptional ability to grasp and communicate the course of action that is pleasing to God (1 Cor 12:8). These gifts are to be used for the common good of the whole group of believers (1 Cor 12:7).
- To all who ask without doubting, He grants *situational wisdom* to deal with their immediate circumstances in a manner pleasing to the Lord (Jas 1:5). This situational wisdom reminds one of the *sekel* wisdom of the Old Testament (see p. 93-94).
- To those who do as Jesus said and put the word of God into practice (Matt 7:24), the Spirit grants an *abiding and growing discernment and wisdom* as they mature spiritually (Heb 5:14). The wisdom of the more

mature allows them to understand deeper matters of the faith (1 Cor 2:6). Their maturity is demonstrated by their willingness to adopt the apostolic (scriptural) viewpoint on matters (Phil 3:15), rather than the usual human viewpoint. Their wisdom identifies its presence in their good deeds (things that please God and bless others) done in the humility that comes from wisdom (Jas 3:13).

SPIRITUAL GROWTH IN THE NEW TESTAMENT (NT)

Spiritual growth in the NT requires that one yield to Jesus Christ as Lord and Savior, trusting Him with all that one is and has (John 1:12; Luke 14:25-33). Having received the Lord, one must live by/walk in the Holy Spirit—that is, live in line with the Holy Spirit's desires, relying on His resources (Gal 5:16, 25; Rom 8:11-14). Life does not lastingly change without walking in the Holy Spirit. To walk in the Spirit, one must:

- **Exercise faith.** One trusts God enough to do what the Holy Spirit wants, to do the things that are pleasing to God in situation after situation (such as, Eph 5:1-2,10). We exercise faith when we:
  - **Actually step out to obey God.** We trust God to keep His promises and to supply *all we need:* strength, increased faith, endurance, courage, help against the Enemy, understanding, wisdom, food, money, possessions, tools, love, joy, peace, patience, kindness, goodness, gentleness, faithfulness and self-control. Then, we take the step of obedience.
  - **Endure through difficult times.** Difficulties come to test our willingness to trust God (Jas 1:2-4; 1 Pet 1 6-7). We endure through them.
  - **Pray to the Lord.** We focus on Him, praise and thank Him, confess our sins, ask for what we need, and pray for others (2 Cor 3:18; 1 John 1:9; Matt 6:5-13).
- **Utilize the Spirit's resources.** The Holy Spirit has provided resources for us in the Word of God and the church. It is up to us to:
  - ***Implement* the Scriptures.** One must personally understand and learn how to put Scripture into practice in daily situations (Matt 28:19-20; 1 Pet 2:2; Col 2:6-8; 1 Tim 3:16-17, Heb 5:11-14), rather than operate out of one's old motives and perspectives just like the rest of the world (1 Cor 3:1-3). Time spent memorizing and understanding the Scriptures is one way we get spiritually strengthened.

- ***Participate* in the fellowship of believers.** We are to aggressively learn from the example and teaching of its pastor-teachers. We are to personally give and receive encouragement and correction ("speaking the truth in love"), and ministering through the gifts the Holy Spirit has given. We especially need to take some role in the ministry, so that not only do *we* grow beyond spiritual childhood, but, also the *whole church* grows up into what Christ wants (Eph 4:11-16; Heb 3:12-13; 10:24-25; 13:7). Our growth prospers as others in the church, especially leaders, pray for our spiritual development (Col. 4:12; Eph 1:16-19).

ACQUIRING WISDOM

Proverbs 2 contains a description of the process of *developing abiding wisdom.* It is a parallel to the process of spiritual growth in the New Testament. In the passage, the Christ-follower who wants to develop wisdom can see a clear layout of what is needed.

Our survey of acquiring wisdom will begin with the humility and fear of the LORD (faith) that underlie wisdom, and then look at the process through which wisdom increases by engagement with the Word of God, with people who know God, and engagement with daily life.

Note that one step is not completed before the next is begun. Rather, one step tends to fade into the next. For example, one does not "complete" storing up God's word; one continues to expand his store as life endures. But, as he is storing up God's word, the next steps are engaged. So, also, it is with prayer.

THE FIRST STEP: HUMBLE FEAR OF THE LORD

When pride comes, then comes disgrace, but with humility comes wisdom. (Pro 11:2 NIV)

The fear of the LORD is the beginning of wisdom, and knowledge of the Holy One is understanding. (Pro 9:10 NIV)

The one who wants to find wisdom must first humble himself or herself before God and live out that humility in daily life. See Appendix Two, Actualized Humility.

One facet of the needed humility is submitting oneself to Jesus Christ as Lord and Savior. That is to say, one must have decided to walk in respect of and obedience to the Lord Jesus and not be equivocal (willy-nilly) about it. Persons who have made a formal commitment to the fear of the LORD, but inwardly do not actually intend to obey Christ in the matters of practical living (dating, relationships, money, marriage, etc.), are "double-minded." Their prayers for wisdom will receive no answer from God (Jas 1:5-8). One must intend to do the will of God before the discernment arrives (John 7:17).

The fear of the LORD is the breakthrough point into wisdom. No matter what one professes verbally, if on the inside, in his heart, he has not entered the fear of the LORD, wisdom *cannot* begin, no matter how hard he prays. Unless one has entered the fear of the LORD, true wisdom is simply unattainable. As the punch line of an old joke says, "You can't get there from here."

If one does not submit to Jesus Christ in the fear of and trust in the Lord, the best one can attain is not full, true Wisdom, but her seductive counterfeit, the appearance of wisdom (Col 2:23; 1 Tim 6:20-21). The "appearance of wisdom," is a mixture of some valid insight and much skewed perspective that may perhaps lead to a few successes but will definitely lead to a great deal of frustration and disappointment (see Pro 9:1-6, 13-18).

If one has decided to humbly walk in the fear of the LORD, Proverbs 2 gives an extended layout of the path to wisdom. Presented as a father's instructions to his son, it is the Heavenly Father's instructions to His sons and daughters regarding how to go about finding genuine wisdom. Sidetracks are possible. This world offers a variety of ideas that are falsely called knowledge (1 Tim 6:20-21), empty philosophies that snare inquiring but unsuspecting souls (Col 2:8), and a stupidity that advertises itself to the naïve as the path to sophistication, but is actually the doorway to destruction (Pro 9:13-16). There is, however, a path to genuine wisdom.

Pro 2:1-12 (NIV)

1 My son, if you accept my words and store up my commands within you,
2 turning your ear to wisdom and applying your heart to understanding,
3 and if you call out for insight and cry aloud for understanding,
4 and if you look for it as for silver and search for it as for hidden treasure,

5 then you will understand the fear of the LORD and find the knowledge of God.
6 For the LORD gives wisdom, and from His mouth come knowledge and understanding.
7 He holds victory in store for the upright, He is a shield to those whose walk is blameless,
8 for He guards the course of the just and protects the way of His faithful ones.
9 Then you will understand what is right and just and fair— every good path.
10 For wisdom will enter your heart, and knowledge will be pleasant to your soul.
11 Discretion will protect you, and understanding will guard you.
12 Wisdom will save you from the ways of wicked men, from men whose words are perverse...

SECOND STEP: HUMBLE ACCEPTANCE OF SCRIPTURE

My son, if you accept my words...(Pro 2:1 NIV)

As we saw in the first step, if you want to find true wisdom about how to succeed in marriage, career, family, society, church and more, *humble yourself before God.* Humility before God means "walking in the fear of the LORD," that is, submitting yourself and your life to the Lord Jesus Christ. This means that at a very practical level, you must *humbly accept God's Word as your starting point for understanding and dealing with life.*

In Proverbs 2:1, the Hebrew word translated "accept" by the NIV actually means *to take.* One must do more than merely see God's Word offered, one must take God's Word. It is not enough to hear God's word, you must act related to it (Jas 1:22-23). To gain Wisdom, you must aggressively lay hold of the Scriptures. You must take it in to your heart and life. It will play a major purpose in your life, helping you to understand and obey God. He has revealed it for you to obey (Deu 29:29).

One takes God's Word into his heart for the purpose of obedience without arguing with it. One bows his heart to God and says, "Your word is right. I accept it. By Your help, I will learn to understand it. Help me to learn to obey it."

Not all the Scriptures are immediately clear as to their meaning (2 Pet 3:15-18). It is okay to question what Scriptures mean—*if* the question is raised in order to obey intelligently. Many times people raise questions like a smokescreen to cover their rebellion. To debate the meaning of Scripture in order to *dodge* having to obey it is both arrogant and foolish. If this has been your pattern, quit debating with them and trying to justify your disobedience; just receive the Scriptures with meekness. The "disputer (debater) of this age" will never attain wisdom (1 Cor 1:20 NKJ).

The *Scriptures* are able to make you "wise for salvation" (2 Tim 2:15). Indeed, Proverbs was written specifically to help one gain wisdom (Pro 1:1-6). Though philosophy has some contribution to make to an understanding of God and life, you cannot start with philosophy. Though science can elucidate an understanding of God, you cannot start with science. Though you may have previously come up with some of your own ideas about God, you cannot start with your own ideas. You must start with the Word of God, the Scriptures, the Bible.

God's Word has been revealed to us that we may know Him and obey Him (Deu 29:29). The quest for wisdom starts at the acceptance of God's Word, receiving it for the sake of understanding, and living in line with it (Pro 2:1). Until you decide to receive God's Word for obedience, you will never find wisdom.

In fact, you will remain trapped by your own ideas and unable to find the freedom you want in life. Freedom comes as one gets to know the truth. But the truth that sets one free comes only to those who "abide" or "continue in" God's Word (John 8:31-32). To continue in God's Word is like moving along a freeway. One continues to progress along the freeway and stays within the boundaries of it. Continuing to learn God's Word and conducting life within the boundaries of it are the keys to coming to know the truth that sets one free.

If you are unsure about the validity of the Bible, do some research on its veracity. For a start, you might want to read Josh McDowell's *Evidence That Demands A Verdict.*

If you are unsure of the meaning of certain passages, and are, therefore, unsure how to obey them, put the unclear passages aside for a time. Focus on the passages that are clear. As your understanding grows, you may be able to deal with the difficult passages. The key is to deal with what you *do* know, not what you *don't* know.

The journey to wisdom begins with humbly taking, accepting God's Word. As God's Word begins to enter a person's life, spiritual light dawns on the issues of life, and spiritual understanding begins to grow (see Ps 19:7-8).

The unfolding of your words gives light; it gives understanding to the simple. (Ps 119:130 NIV)

THIRD STEP: STORING UP THE COMMANDS

My son, if you accept my words and store up my commands within you, (Pro 2:1 NIV)

The one who accepts God's Word must begin to *acquire* it. He needs to "hide my commandments with thee" (KJV). The Hebrew word translated "hide" means to "hide by covering over," and implies to horde or reserve something, thus the NIV translation "store up."

The person who wants wisdom must "receive" God's Word for the purpose of reshaping his views and his lifestyle, not for debate.

Then, he needs to begin to accumulate an understanding of the Scriptures, especially by hiding them within him. The verse does not *literally* command memorizing Scriptures, but Scripture memory certainly lies within the realm of hiding God's Word within one. Proverbs 22:18 expresses a similar idea. Speaking of a father's words, it encourages one to "keep them in your heart" and "have all of them ready on your lips."

In particular, the wisdom seeker needs to store up God's *commands.* The Bible contains a variety of material: stories about people who walked with God, letters, songs about God and life, prophecies about the future, and proverbs about how to conduct life. Interspersed in the different parts of the Bible are God's commands on how to live life. We have had our own ideas about how to live life. God's commands are *quite often different* from our ideas and opinions about how to handle life.

Some of God's commands set boundaries for us, limits that we are not to pass over—such as forbidding adultery or the lustful look (Matt 5:27-28), or "do not lie to one another" (Eph 4:25). Others of God's commands set direction or define duties for us, such as "love your enemies" (Matt 5:43-45).

The wisdom journey requires us to store up God's specific commands.

Were we to start our wisdom journey by memorizing *general statements* about reality, we would face few situations where we would have to engage our "store" of God's Word. For example, consider the statement, "Hear, O Israel: The LORD our God, the LORD is one" (Deu 6:4 NIV). The statement is true, and theologically is quite important. However, in the contemporary western world, few of us are passing recognizable altars to other Gods as Paul did in the ancient city of Athens (Acts 7:16, 22-23). So, we do not immediately see multiple situations in daily life where we would have to engage that particular stored part of God's Word.

However, by memorizing pointed specific statements (God's commands) that deal with our behavior in daily life, we begin to be forced to deal with daily issues from the perspective of God's concerns and value system. It happens as we "bump into" a situation and suddenly recall—because we have committed God's commands to memory—what God wants us to do in this kind of situation, either a boundary to maintain or an action to take. Perhaps we are on the verge of deceiving someone with a "white lie," and Ephesians 5:25 comes back to us. Or, we encounter someone who has hurt us and are about to speak cruelly to them, and the command to love your enemies comes to mind.

Memorizing God's commands can lead to change in the ways we respond to life (Ps 119:9, 11). And, because we encounter situation after situation that requires us to revise our responses to life, we set the stage for beginning to see daily life from God's perspective—which turns out to be *knowledge*, the foundational component of wisdom. It is by the practice of this "piece-by-piece," situation-by-situation application of God's Word that we train our "faculties" so that we develop our "spiritual radar" system, our capacity to discern, *distinguish* good from evil (Heb 5:11-14 RSV). Distinguishing, by the way, is related to the second component of wisdom: *understanding* (Heb: *biyn*—to analyze).

Excellent passages to examine for God's commands are Romans 12:1-13:10; Ephesians 4:22-6:10; Colossians 3:1-4:2, 1 Thessalonians 4:9-5:2; 2 Thessalonians 3:7-15.

I learned to memorize by using a small blank card the size of a business card. First, I would write upon it the *topic* that the verse dealt with (as, "money" or "speech"). Then, I would write the verse *reference* on the next line (as, Pro 11:25 or Pro 10:19). On the third line and following I would write the *verse*, and below the verse, write the *reference again*. I would carry the cards with me, and in slow moments during the day, I would pull out the card and work on the verse, memorizing topic, reference, verse, and reference again. When I thought I had it down, I would ask a friend to check me on the verse and hand the card to him. As he read the card, I would recite what was on it, trying to get it "word perfect." (Remember? "Have *all* of them on your lips.")

Over time, I was able to commit many verses to memory. The Lord used those verses in many different situations to direct me toward His will, and also, to help me interpret situations from His viewpoint. Without the memory, the direction and interpretation would have been unavailable. And, a major vehicle for developing *understanding* (the second level of wisdom, *biyn*, analysis) would not have been in place.

FOURTH STEP: TUNE TO THE "WISDOM CHANNEL"

...turning your ear to wisdom and applying your heart to understanding, (Pro 2:2 NIV)

The next verse in the directions for acquiring Wisdom speaks of "turning your ear to wisdom and applying your heart to understanding."

Both parts of the verse deal with *making adjustments to our mindset and the things we allow to go on inside our minds.* In essence, we need to prepare to discover and process Wisdom and its components. Someone who wants to get a certain channel on satellite TV, must make sure the antenna is set in the optimum direction. Then, he must set the TV itself to process the incoming signals so that one channel stays on the screen. In a similar fashion, we must tune in to the "wisdom channel" and stay there.

First, Adjust Your "Attention-Preset"

"Turning your ear" in the Hebrew is actually "pricking up your ear." A deer in the woods keeps its ears alert, turning them in different directions to pick up faint sounds, trying to discern the approach of a predator.

The person who wants to acquire wisdom needs to similarly go on alert, scanning for *wisdom.* He must set his mind on "ready alert" and keep it there. He is to keep his mental faculties ready to grasp insight that God may allow him to discern. His search for wisdom will have to become more intense than mere passive listening. We will discuss that below. However, like a person with satellite TV must make sure the antenna is pointed in the right direction, the wisdom hunter must set his "attention" to scan for the right things, lest he/she miss wisdom as it passes. Below, we will also discuss learning wisdom from the situations around us.

The verse is saying that we must adjust our "attention preset" to scan for and identify wisdom. Wisdom has to do with the full range of *knowledge* (perspective shaping information that enables us to see life more accurately from God's point of view), *understanding,* and the ways to make *good decisions* at different levels of complexity.

Some people go through the day with their mind set on previous hurts, ruminating over past injustices, gradually forging a bitter outlook on life. Others go through the day *wanting (*lusting for*)* something they don't have or wish they had, such as sex with a certain person, a relationship, a certain kind of car, or a certain house. Some go through life with anger ready to spring into action. They are scanning for perceived insult or attack so their anger can be unleashed.

Many go through the day with their mind set on *nothing*. Whatever happens around them gets their attention and shapes their internal thought-flow for the next many minutes until something else engages their random mind. Perhaps their thoughts flow from the words and emotions of songs on the radio on the way to work, then turn to anger over a traffic problem, shift to gladness at seeing co-workers, adjust to the emotions carried by the backdrop music at the office/business, become anxious during an interaction with a customer or co-worker, etc. They use their minds to get to work, get a job done and get back home, but they are, in reality, scanning for nothing—and they get what they scan for.

This verse is saying that you must daily, intentionally, get your mind out of neutral and set it to scan the words and events of the day for wisdom. You need to develop a *preset attention* directed toward wisdom. You need to set your antenna to detect wisdom. Get your mind in gear! Quit daydreaming and blanking out. You need to stay ready to detect wisdom. Prick up your ears for wisdom! If you do not scan for it, it will get past you. It is especially your "ears" that need to scan for Wisdom. *Eyes* are helpful in learning by observation or in reading. The *ears* are useful in conversation and in learning from people as we interact with them. Many conversations are simply about the business of the day and allow us to get done what we need. Some conversations are about sheer foolishness. But, sometimes Wisdom shows up amid interaction with others, especially when we interact with wise people. To "prick up the ears" means especially to scan the interactions with people during the day, looking for the brief appearance of Wisdom.

As you get up in the morning, ask God to speak to you during the day and to help you identify Wisdom as it comes across your path. Then, scan the conversations and events of the day for the Wisdom God will bring to you.

Second, Adjust Your "Internal Processor"

A satellite TV dish feeds the incoming signal from a satellite to a set of equipment that will process the signal and turn it into an image on a screen. We call the equipment a "TV." The processing equipment has to be adjusted to process a certain signal in order to get a certain station. The owner uses a remote to punch in a channel number. The equipment starts processing the signal from that channel, and owner gets to "watch" the show on that particular channel.

Our minds tend to be processing things, "working on stuff," throughout the day. Thoughts enter our heads through our eyes and ears, and our minds tend to latch on to them and process them: toying with them, stewing over them, lusting over them, running mental scenarios of just how we'd like to... We rarely pay attention to the thoughts that land in our minds or to the processing we do with them.

The Scriptures call us to be *selective* about what we let remain in our minds, encouraging us to make sure that what is bouncing around in our heads is actually serving Christ. As Paul, we are to take captive every thought to make it obedient to Christ (2 Cor 10:5). If the thought is not a captive to Christ, it should be brought into servitude to Him—or chased out! It is nearly impossible to stop negative thoughts from entering our minds. You may have heard people say that you can't stop thoughts from coming into your mind any more than you can stop birds from flying over your head. That is fairly true, though one has to admit that, if you feed your mind on trash (porn, revenge, etc.), you tend to have a lot of trashy thoughts flying about. However, while one may not be able to keep the birds from flying over his head, he for sure can keep them from making a nest in his hair!

Proverbs encourages us to be highly selective about what gets into our hearts. What we let into our hearts will actually *set the course of our life and shape our personal history* (Pro 4:23). Things seep from our minds (mental processing) into our hearts (decisional core).

The heart is the inner thinking, feeling, and willing person seen especially from the angle of motive and decision-making. One thinks in his heart—what he thinks about is crucial; it shapes his life direction. One feels in his heart—the feelings he rehearses there shape his life direction.

In his heart, unseen by others, one decides what will have priority in his life. Though unseen by others in the present, his secret decision will one day be realized by others, for it will shape his personal future.

What one thinks about, reminisces over, gets emotional over, and secretly decides will determine who he will be, what he will do and what will come to him as the future unfolds.

It is important that we set our minds and hearts (our thoughts, our tendency to stew over things, the feelings we rehearse and allow to well up within us, and the priorities we secretly begin to prefer) toward understanding. The Hebrew says we are to "incline" our hearts, that is, to make them *bend in the direction* of "understanding." "Understanding" translates the Hebrew "*tabuwn*" (taw-boon'). *Tabuwn* can be translated understanding or intelligence. It is especially the higher level understanding that is the subject of discussion among the wise (as in Pro 18:2). It appears to be more the principles behind the practical matters of wisdom. The person of tabuwn has a keen grasp of how to deal with practical situations, but he has more than just an intuitive ability. He also knows the principles that guide the practice. We are to look for and grapple with the principles behind how the various facets of life work.

Around us the people of the world are simply processing and following the desires of their bodies and minds, ultimately in tow behind the Enemy as he sets the agenda for this world (Eph 2:1-3). Enslaved to various passions and pleasures, their minds are easily preoccupied with malice, envy, and hatred (Titus 3:3). They mentally focus on, stew over, and talk about getting what they want and doing foolish things outside the will of God (Pro 15:14 *'ivveleth*).

Proverbs 2:2 is saying that the wisdom-hunter needs to change his internal processing equipment from its "cultural default" setting of desires, passions, pleasures, malice, envy and hatred to a new setting. He must intentionally set his mind and heart, his inner thinking, feeling, and choosing person to process the principles behind how life works.

What one allows to preoccupy his mind should in some way be related to wisdom, not just to his desires or passions. What he stews over should not be his anger or resentment at the events of the day, hurts from the past or lusts for the future. Rather, he should "stew over" the application of Biblical principles to the situations he is facing. Or, he might mentally search for Biblical insight to apply to his situation. The LORD tells Joshua, the leader who came after Moses,

Do not let this Book of the Law depart from your mouth; meditate on it day and night, so that you may be careful to do everything written in it. Then you will be prosperous and successful. (Josh 1:8 NIV)

"Meditate" translates a Hebrew word meaning "to murmur over." The picture is of Joshua keeping God's Word in mind and talking under his breath to himself about how to put it into practice as he faces situations of the day, or of sitting in his tent at night, reading the Scripture and thinking over its application to life. Joshua should be "stewing over" how to apply God's Word to the situations he faces. If he obeys God's Word, he will be prosperous and "successful." "Successful" translates the verb form of "*sekel,*" the practical wisdom that knows how to read situations and construct a response that is highly successful. Joshua's practical wisdom, and the success that comes from it, will depend on obeying God's Word. His obedience is going to require him to keep the Word in mind and "*stew over*" its application.

Rather than let his inner being dwell on and process whatever stray thought enters his awareness, one needs to be highly selective about what he lets hang around in his brain. He needs to intentionally input helpful information into his mind, not trash. Thus, he is going to become much more selective in what music he listens to, what TV and movies he sees, the magazines and books he reads, and the video games he plays. Why listen to, watch or read stuff that is going to set your internal processor (mind and heart) on the wrong channel?

And, the person who wants to find Wisdom will have to choose to mentally and emotionally process the situations he comes across during the day in the light of the principles of God's Words, *not* simply in line with his own natural reactions.

If he will adjust his "momentary mental focus," that is, his attention, to scan for all forms of wisdom and his "thought-habits" (processing) to grasp the principles that apply to the situations he faces in life, he will be ready to receive and process wisdom. He is tuned to the "wisdom channel" and needs to stay there. Proverbs 22:17 expresses the same idea: *"pay attention...listen...apply your heart to what I teach."*

To change the illustration, the wisdom hunter who has adjusted his mental focus to scan for wisdom and his internal processor to process the flow of life from the perspective of God's Word is like a treasure hunter who has his metal detector tuned to the right settings and is now *ready for the search.*

FIFTH STEP: PRAY EARNESTLY

...and if you call out for insight and cry aloud for understanding, (Pro 2:3 NIV)

The wisdom hunter has to "call out" and "cry aloud." These words might be taken as calling out the names of the things sought, but actually indicate a calling out loudly, in earnest, to God to supply the things sought. To the one who calls out, God gives (see verse 6).

James is clear about this. If anyone lacks wisdom, he should not be embarrassed about it. He should simply ask God for it. And, God will give it freely without rebuking the petitioner. However, the one asking for wisdom must not be equivocal, willy-nilly in his commitment to Christ. If he is, he will get nothing, for God will not answer such a prayer from a "double-minded" person. The fear of the Lord is the beginning of wisdom; without it, there is no wisdom.

Some misconstrue James' statement and say that the acquisition of wisdom does not need to be a Christian's concern, since God will supply wisdom on a moment's notice in any situation. However, while God is a gracious Father, He wants His children growing in their ability to grasp the difference between good and evil through the practical application of His Word (Heb 5:11-14). The one who would be wise for salvation must draw his teaching, reproof, correction, and training in righteousness from the Scriptures (2 Tim 3:14-17). There is a category of person who is "full of wisdom" (Acts 6:3). James is not saying there is no need to grow in our understanding of God's ways, but that in real life, we are all going to hit situations where we need more wisdom than we have. We can cry out for it, and God will answer those whose hearts are his.

The verse in Proverbs 2 instructs us to call out for "insight." The Hebrew is *biynah*, the understanding that allows one to effectively analyze both people and the situations of life. It also stands for the insight gained from such analysis.

We are to call aloud for "understanding." Here, the Hebrew word is "tabuwn," indicating the *principles* which guide wisdom in its decision-making at complex levels.

The person who can accurately "see" situations and grasps the principles by which to respond to them is a blessed person.

Prayer is the next step to attaining such blessing. Many times, we are frustrated in our efforts simply because we have gotten busy attempting the right things, but have not prayed to the Father asking for them. God may withhold success until we humbly learn our need for His hand to act amid and beyond our efforts.

SIXTH STEP: SEARCH DILIGENTLY

...and if you look for it as for silver and search for it as for hidden treasure, (Pro 2:4 NIV)

I once watched a PBS documentary about one person's search in the Caribbean Sea for the wreck of a Spanish treasure ship. Convinced by historical documents of the existence and general location of the wreck, the person searched for nearly twenty years, day after day, season after season, for the wreckage. After more than a decade and a half of searching and nearly at the end of investment money, the person found the wreck—and over a billion dollars in gold! The investors were paid off, and the searcher became incredibly wealthy.

We are to search for wisdom like someone looks for hidden treasures. Hidden treasure is not immediately obvious, nor is it found on the first try. It may not even be found on the hundredth try. But, if one is certain that it exists, it will one day be found by the person who looks in the right place. The search for wisdom is similar. One does not simply look once and then give up. The Hebrew for "look for" means to search out by any means possible, and especially through worship and prayer. Wisdom really does exist! Wisdom really will bless the finder (Pro 8:15-21)! So, one persists in the search and searches diligently, that is, energetically, thoroughly, and persistently. Wisdom rewards such diligent persistence (Pro 8:17, 34-35). The impatient one who will not persist until wisdom appears will never know her (Pro 8:34).

The wisdom-hunter must search diligently for wisdom—then the breakthrough into wisdom pays off. The fear of the Lord arrives with the knowledge of God and the discernment, discretion, success and protection that come with them (Pro 2:5-12).

Make It Your Top Priority

Wisdom, knowing how to do things God's way, must become one's top priority. Indeed, though Wisdom belongs to God, she is *different from God in one respect*: God loves those who do not yet love Him (Rom 5:8, 1 John 4:9-10, 19). *Wisdom*, however, *loves only those who love her* (Pro 8:17). To love Wisdom means to place it above other things in your scale of values.

The Wisdom-quest must have first place in your *finances*. Wisdom—knowing how to do life God's way—is the supreme thing to seek in life (Pro

4:7). Therefore, one must set his mind to acquire it—*even though it costs all that he has.* Indeed, Jesus sets this as the cost of discipleship (Luke 14:25-33). To truly learn of the Lord requires the disciple to choose Jesus as first over one's family, possessions, and even one's own life. Wisdom must be chosen over money or investments: silver, gold or rubies (which were the diamonds of the ancient Middle East) (Pro 8:10-11). A person who spends money on possessions but will not spend money for key books, seminars or retreats simply will not find Wisdom. He misunderstands the purpose of money. So, he continues to be a fool (Pro 17:16).

Wisdom must have the top priority in your *time use.* Wisdom will be found by those who seek her (Pro 8:17). But she may not arrive immediately; the one who really desires audience with her must wait patiently at her door until she comes out (Pro 8:34). If you do not have time for her, she has no time for you.

If you are a normal person, you will have to spend many hours at a job. You will need to take care of your property (wash clothes, mow a lawn, get the car serviced, and so on). You ought to be spending part of your time in ministry to people. Amid all these things and beyond them, you need to be seeking Wisdom, God's way of handling people and the situations of life.

Watch that you spend your money and time pursuing real Wisdom and not her seductive counterfeit. Getting a high school education is prudent. Getting a college degree is prudent—it helps in the job market. However, such education does not normally contain true Knowledge, the perspective changing information that allows one to see life from God's point of view. You must go *further* than geography, science and math to find the stuff of Wisdom. Watch out for what *appears to be wisdom* but is *not.*

SEARCH IN THE RIGHT PLACES

My son and I once went to dig for diamonds. We did not simply go down the street to an empty lot and begin digging. Small children, with their naiveté and imagination, might do that. But, we were not small children, and we really wanted to find diamonds. So, I researched where diamonds could be found in the continental United States. Crater of Diamonds State Park in Arkansas turned out to be our best option. So, we drove to the park for our great search.

We made the trip because one doesn't find valuable things like diamonds just *anywhere.* Quartz crystals, which the naïve might mistake for diamonds, can be found just about anywhere. But, real diamonds only occur in certain places.

Neither does one find that most desirable thing, wisdom, just anywhere. Sure, just about anywhere one can find ideas that others want to pass on to you as genuine wisdom. And, the naïve are often deceived. However, the wisdom-hunter tracking down genuine wisdom must look, not just anywhere, but in certain places.

1. KEEP CHRIST AT THE CENTER

Crater of Diamonds State Park was only so large. When one drifted outside the crater area, diamonds were just not to be found. Staying within the crater areas was crucial to finding diamonds.

So it is with the search for wisdom. Jesus Christ is the one in whom are hidden all the treasures of wisdom and knowledge (Col 2:2-3). One must keep both his life and his quest for wisdom oriented around Christ. Outside the "Jesus Area," genuine wisdom will not be found.

Jesus Christ is not merely "true," He *is the truth* (John 14:6). Truth is ultimately a Person, Jesus Christ, who reflects the God-head, the Trinity. To say that Jesus is the truth means *there is a certain God who truly exists and who has made reality in a certain way and operates it in the manner that He pleases (Ps 115:3, Eph 1:11). "Truth" is that which conforms to the person God is, the way He has made the universe, and the way He operates it—physically and spiritually.*

The statement that the world is approximately 25,000 miles around at the equator is "true," because it conforms to the way God has made the world. The statement that all gods worshipped by mankind are basically the same is false, for only a certain God, the God of the Bible, exists.

What About Science?

Science does not currently accept the Biblical standard of truth. It tries to produce an increasingly accurate "picture" of the universe based on observation and reason alone. Because God made the universe with patterns to it, science can come up with some pretty good pictures of physical realities. However, it is always improving the accuracy of its views, refining its models of reality. *A Christian has no problem with such a hard-nosed approach to observation and reason.* Science may actually find out a great deal about how God really made things and is governing them.

When science grows arrogant, and demands that one adopt an atheistic view of the universe in order to have a valid picture of things, science has ceased to be *science* and becomes propaganda, a smoke screen for an ideology, not an intelligent investigation of the universe. At this point, people who are searching for genuine wisdom want to point out the intellectual hypocrisy of science and begin to doubt its conclusions.

Science tends to arrogantly demand an atheistic approach when it is discussing the *origins of the universe and of life*, neither of which was ever *observed* by a human. Darwin's ideas about evolution appeared to give science an opportunity to explain the origin and development of life and human kind completely apart from any ideas about a god or a creation. Happy with such new freedom, atheists who were involved in science began propounding the ultimate legitimacy of Darwinian thought. Time and research have not treated Darwin well. Darwinian ideas are under increasingly effective siege. Many books are currently on the market showing the problems with evolution, such as *Darwin's Demise* by Drs. White and Comninellis. If science continues to operate by observation and rigorous reason, rather than a kind of atheistic evolutionary "orthodoxy," the picture of "origins" is going to change significantly over the next fifty years.

Science also tends to demand an atheistic approach to understanding human beings as it tries to construct its models of how human beings operate individually (psychology) and in groups (sociology, anthropology). People searching for Wisdom begin to part company with psychological or sociological ideology at this point. If human beings are spiritual as well as physical entities, then an adequate understanding of a human person must include the spiritual as well as physical matters. And, to attempt by an atheistic psychologist to ascribe *all* the struggles a human has to merely physical (and thus, non-spiritual) causes is just as perceptive as a tribal shaman trying to ascribe all the physical problems a person has to only demonic/spiritual causes. In each case, there are "real causes" that exist outside the practitioner's perspective.

Psychological or sociological approaches that demand an atheistic interpretation and explanation of human situations simply are not adequate—they may contain some insight, but they are not fully *true*. God exists, and human beings are both physical and spiritual entities. To solve significant human problems, the spiritual nature of human beings must be included in the analysis and the solution. The wisdom about how to live a blessed, prosperous life begins with Jesus Christ in whom are hidden all the treasures of wisdom and knowledge, no matter what propaganda psychology and sociology falsely promote in the name of "science."

Please note that *I am not saying* that only Bible-believing people can come up with true ideas about nature or about human beings. I discussed this earlier: God's common grace allows for many to discover God's world, regardless their religious persuasion. However, *I am saying* that science is often used as a disguise for what is actually a *philosophy*, a belief about life that is not rooted in science but in another source. In the realm of chemistry, one's philosophy has less to do with one's conclusions about the interpretation of experimental data. In the "soft sciences" dealing with people (psychology, sociology, etc.), however, one's philosophy tends to highly color one's interpretations of his data. This is so true that some call psychology "the bastard child of philosophy."

Secular psychological ideology tends to shape our popular culture's ideas of how to live a happy life. Therefore, a person seeking Wisdom finds himself in frequent conflict with popular ideas. He simply must get used to the discomfort.

In Christ, not in the culture nor in its guru, atheistic psychology, are hidden all the treasures of how to live life in a manner pleasing to God, how to solve personal and relational problems, and how to be as happy as one can on this broken planet.

The Appearance Of Wisdom

One must keep Christ in center focus as he tries to determine what is true-and-real and what is only the appearance of wisdom.

Many things appear to be wise, but are not:

- **Secular Ideologies.** These are ideas about how to live that are built upon human wisdom and not Christ. They are usually more "philosophical" in their roots. The ideas are packaged into pop psychology and promoted through TV shows, movies, magazines, music and college classrooms. Scripture says these ideas are *falsely* called "knowledge" (1 Tim 6:20-21) because they give a *wrong spiritual perspective* on life. Those who build life out of these wander from the faith to their hurt (Col 2:8; 1 Tim 6:20-21).

The person who wants to follow Christ needs to live a life that is both kind and exemplary. However, he must accept that the *real wisdom* that he seeks is not the same as that which is popular in the world around him. He has a different starting place (Christ) for his standards of what is wise (1 Cor 3:16-18). He must be prepared to be thought "foolish" by his peers as he pursues genuine wisdom.

• **"Liberal" Christianity.** There has persisted in the church through the centuries, a movement that tries to "adjust" Christian teaching to fit the popular ideas, morals and lifestyles of the times. There are pastors of "Christian" churches who accept as valid the values, morals and lifestyles of the current culture, though such practices are clearly out of bounds according to the Scriptures. They use "fine sounding arguments" to persuade the spiritually naïve and ignorant toward popular ideas of the current culture (see Rom 16:18). The books of Second Peter and Jude deal extensively with these people.

In recent decades, this stream of thought has called for "secular Christianity" in the 1950's and 60's, for a "new morality" (re-packaging of the old immorality) in the 1970's, for a "multi-culturalism" (the rejection of any absolute truth) in the late 1980's and 90's, and now for a "new pluralism" (actually a radical individualism that prefers to ignore the social consequences of individual sexual choices or of occult practices). This stream of non-Biblical Christianity is responsible for the current movement to legitimize homosexual marriage in the church and to ordain homosexuals as pastors.

• **Asceticism.** Some are attracted to movements that involve strict religious rules and observances, and severity to the body (as in many Eastern practices and some "Christian" mysticism). These things have an "appearance of wisdom." However, asceticism has no ability to actually help one deal with the deep root of his struggles (Col 3:23).

• **Supernatural Excitement.** Leaders rise up to describe their visions of angels and the demonic and go into great detail about what they have seen (see Col 2:16-23).

Actually, the angelic and demonic are both real, and visions of them can occur.

However, when those who supposedly have the visions begin to *focus* on the visions, they cease to focus on Christ. The movement becomes about the vision, not about the Lord. Sometimes the visions relate to the end times.

These "mystical" type stirrings arise within the Bible-believing part of the church and generate excitement. They often get combined with some form of asceticism (Mosaic food laws, holy day rituals, excessive fasting, body cleansing rituals, etc.). They lose touch with the Head (Christ) and are just another form of a spiritual trap.

The person who wants to find Wisdom and really know Christ must move beyond these "appearances of wisdom" when he comes across them. And, he must walk in the fear of the Lord. Keeping Jesus central and walking in obedience to Him unlocks the treasures God has for us.

The LORD is exalted, for He dwells on high; He will fill Zion with justice and righteousness. He will be the sure foundation for your times, a rich store of salvation and wisdom and knowledge; the fear of the LORD is the key to this treasure. (Isa 33:5-6 NIV)

2. STUDY THE SCRIPTURES

The law of the LORD is perfect, reviving the soul. The statutes of the LORD are trustworthy, making wise the simple. (Ps 19:7 NIV)

Your word is a lamp to my feet and a light for my path. (Ps 119:105 NIV)

...from infancy you have known the Holy Scriptures, which are able to make you wise for salvation through faith in Christ Jesus. (2 Tim 3:15 NIV)

The Scriptures are the Word of God. They give light and understanding to a person and can make one wise (Ps 19:7). They can provide the components of Wisdom (Ps 119:97-104). The Scriptures can make one wise for salvation (2 Tim 3:14-16). Indeed, they are the comprehensive equipment of the godly person (2 Tim 3:17). One needs to study them in order to become an effective worker for God, one who has no reason to be ashamed (2 Tim 2:15). The Proverbs especially are written to help one develop wisdom (Pro 1:3-5). The one who learns the teachings of Jesus and puts them into practice is demonstrating wisdom (Matt 7:24). Obedience to the teachings of Christ allows one to see the truth that is liberating (John 8:31-32). The person who delights in God's Word and meditates in it day and night in order to understand how to obey it—he is the one who keeps on being refreshed, even in dry times, and keeps on bearing good things in his life (Ps 1:1-3). He is the one who succeeds (Josh 1:8).

If you want to develop wisdom, you must get to know God's word and how it applies to life.

Here are some suggestions:

- Listen to messages by Christian speakers who deal accurately with the Bible. Use their tapes or CDs in your car as you drive around town. Hearing God's word can stimulate your faith (Rom 10:17).

- Get an easy-to-read version of the Bible (Living Bible, Today's English Version or New International Version), and read through the core books of the Bible: John, Acts, Romans. Then, branch out and read until you have read the whole Bible.
- Get a commentary on Ephesians and study that small book in the Scriptures. The paperback commentary by Curtis Vaughn is excellent. Next, go to First Peter and then to James. Investing a bit of time (twenty minutes to an hour) each week in consistent study of the Bible will benefit you tremendously over time.
- Pick out a couple of verses from Proverbs that deal with one of your problems and memorize them. Later, select another area of struggle and find a couple of verses to memorize in that area.
- In "empty moments" (waiting for traffic to unsnarl, waiting in the dentist's office, etc.) pick one of the verses and meditate on it. Mull over its meaning.

I learned to use the *who, what, where, how, why,* and *when* questions of the news reporter. *Who* is this verse directed toward? *What* do these words mean? *What* does the verse say to do? *Where,* in what situations, does the verse apply? What does the verse imply regarding *how* to go about what it encourages one to do? *Why* should a person do this? *When* should a person do this?

One can also simply meditate on each word in the verse for its contribution to the overall thought of the verse.

Forcing your mind to engage a verse in these ways will grant you insights into wisdom.

3. LEARN FROM WISE PEOPLE

Wise people are a tremendous source of wisdom—for those who will learn from them. Instruction from a wise person is insightful and motivating. Their speech makes one want to learn (Pro 16:21, 23). And, it motivates one to action, to change.

In ancient times, a farmer used an ox goad to guide his ox. The goad was a long nail on the end of a nine-foot stick. It not only *directed* the ox but also *motivated* it, by unpleasant gouging, to go that direction. The words of the wise can also guide and prompt us (sometimes uncomfortably) in the right direction (Ecc 12:10-11).

Earlier we looked at the profile of a wise person. Search for people who match the profile and aggressively learn from them. If you are going to learn from them you must:

• **Associate with them.** To learn from the wise, one must "walk with them."

He who walks with the wise grows wise, but a companion of fools suffers harm. (Pro 13:20 NIV)

One can associate with the wise through their writings or tapes/CDs. Books bring you to the minds of teachers who are separated from you by distance or time. If you want to profit from them, you must *read and analyze* them. To save yourself time, ask a wise friend to recommend some *key* books for you to read—and read them. Even better, you might get recommendations for a couple of books in a key *area you are dealing with* in your life right now.

The best way to learn from the wise is by walking with living people, that is, getting in on their schedule. Most wise people are busy. You will have to get on their timetable, not try to get them on yours.

If you know a wise person, offer to help them around their house or with a chore. Discuss while you work with them. Take them out to lunch or dinner. Get into a Bible study led by them.

Be an aggressive and appreciative learner (remember this characteristic of the wise?). As you learn from the wise, give them gifts in appreciation for what you are learning (see Gal 6:6).

• **Listen to their teachings** (Pro 22:17). One of the barriers to learning is wanting to do all the talking and impress the wise with your own wisdom. Listen. Don't do all the talking.

A fool takes no pleasure in understanding, only in expressing his opinion. (Pro 18:2)

Another barrier to learning is resisting the instruction by debating—even debating silently in your own mind—or fault-finding rather than learning. Ask legitimate questions, but if the instruction challenges your life, don't disguise your "value struggle" under the mask of "debate."

Just accept, take the word of God. Listen intelligently to their corrective instruction—it will make you wise (Pro 19:20).

• **Apply your heart** to what they teach (Pro 22:17). Expect to have to use your brain and not to be spoon-fed. We live in a mentally weak time and are used to pre-digested insight fed in sound-bytes over the media. Interestingly, much of Jesus' teaching was not immediately clear to people. He left mental work for them to do in order to understand His point (for example, see Luke 8:8-10).

Certainly, ask questions to clarify meanings and to understand what is being said. But, also, put your mind to work at understanding the application to yourself.

- **Memorize what you are learning**—"have them all ready on your lips" (Pro 22:18).

- **Take their advice.** The wise are excellent sources of advice, guidance on what courses of action to take, or how to go about a matter. They know proper timing and procedures (Ecc 8:5). Listen intelligently to their advice and heed it, and you will become wise (Pro 19:20). Fools will not take advice. They scorn it, so Proverbs encourages people with good sense not to advise fools (Pro 23:9).

- **Heed their correction.** The wise will speak kindly and graciously, but they will speak the truth in love (Eph 5:15) and correct someone if necessary. Actually, the willingness to be corrected is part of the price of admission to the fellowship of the wise, for correction simply takes place in that realm. Indeed, that is what keeps mockers from consulting the wise.

He who listens to a life-giving rebuke will be at home among the wise. (Pro 15:31)

A mocker resents correction: he will not consult the wise. (15:12)

Heeding correction is one of the major means to acquiring wisdom. Below, we will take a look at learning from "*muwcar*" (moo-sawr'), a Hebrew concept translated as instruction, discipline and/or correction.

4. LEARN FROM LIFE

- **Visit The House Of Mourning**

The heart of the wise is in the house of mourning, but the heart of fools is in the house of mirth. (Ecc 7:4 NKJ)

Parties are about laughing, celebrating and enjoying the moment now. It is not amid the parties that we assess what we are doing with our lives and decide to make needed changes.

Rather, it is "in the house of mourning" that we consider what is really worthwhile (Ecc 7:4). At the funerals of our friends and relatives, we are "in the house of mourning." Visiting in the home of a grieving widow or husband or parent, we are "in the house of mourning." Time spent in the house of mourning causes us to ask the big questions about what is really important in our lives, about *what we are doing that really matters*, about what we need to stop doing, and what we need to start doing.

We have an inclination to seek only the parties and run from funerals and grieving persons. To look into the face of a dead person confronts us with our own mortality. To encounter a grieving person and be at a loss for words to comfort is uncomfortable for us.

But, beneath our loss of words is also a desperate fear. The visit of death to any house is a reminder that one day death will come for us. We desperately fear that insight. As a matter of fact, human beings live out their lives in bondage to the fear of death. Because we are unsure there is an after-life, we live for our passions and pleasures in this one. Cornered by our fear of death, and desperately clinging to our passions and pleasures, we are actually enslaved, not only to them, but also to Satan (Titus 3:3; Eph 2:2; Heb 2:14-15). In the words of an old beer commercial: "*You only go around once in life, so you gotta grab all the gusto you can get!*" Or, as the Apostle Paul wrote, if there really is no resurrection of the dead, "*Let us eat and drink, for tomorrow we die*" (1 Cor 15:32 RSV).

Jesus came to destroy the work of the Devil and to liberate the slaves (1 John 3:8; Heb 2:14-15). Jesus' resurrection gave assurance that there is a life after death for us with Him. His death and resurrection removed "the sting of death" and reassures us to keep on doing what is right (1 Cor 15:52-58). But the "scorpion" of death still looks formidable—it takes faith to see that the sting is gone. And, even with faith, it is uncomfortable to look at the scorpion. We want to avert our eyes!

Like the wise, we need to visit the "house of mourning." It is right to show respect at the passing of someone made in the image of God. It is also pleasing to God that we comfort those who mourn. And, it is quite healthy for us to confront death and to reacquaint ourselves with our own coming demise.

In the fresh awareness of our own mortality, we reassess our lives and decide to do the truly important things, to do more with our energy, money, time and influence than merely accumulate "stuff" (see Ps 39:4-6). For this reason, the heart of the wise is in the house of mourning. The fool seeks only a continuing party. When the death of a friend or relative intrudes into the life of the wise, they visit and comfort the bereaved. And they reflect on what is important to do in the life they have remaining.

- **Number Your Days**

The length of our days is seventy years— or eighty, if we have the strength; yet their span is but trouble and sorrow, for they quickly pass, and we fly away... Teach us to number our days aright, that we may gain a heart of wisdom. (Ps 90:10, 12 NIV)

In scriptural perspective, *today* is the day of salvation (2 Cor 6:3). Today is the day that we are alive and experiencing the opportunities that God is sending—and the day we need to wisely make the most of them (Eph 515-17). Today is the day we need to be aware that we can "go to sleep at the wheel." We need to make sure that we are not deceived by sin *today* (Heb 3:12-13). Actually, we will only be alive "today." Tomorrow will be "today" when it gets here.

Though we know better, we tend to live in a kind of "make-believe" mentality feeling we will live on and on. Because we tend to think we have many days left on the planet, we get lax about "making the most of the opportunity." Days come and days go and we never think about what is really important *right now*. Therefore we waste days, months and years doing trivial things that matter little.

To make the most of the opportunities, we need frequent reminders that our time is passing so we need to do the important.

Besides visiting the house of mourning, there is another way to keep mindful of the shortness of our life and the importance of doing *today* what really counts: "number our days." Years ago, at the encouragement of a wise man, I "numbered my days," counting up the number of days left until I would turn age seventy, the usual length of a human life. One might continue to live and grow older, but the Scripture encourages us to think of age seventy as a "target." As my wise friend said, anything past seventy is grace from God and to be enjoyed in obedience to the Lord. Up until seventy, one should be thinking about priorities and strategies for doing what is important. My friend kept a calendar on his desk with the "number" of the current day he was living. His calendar was numbered to count the days downward toward his seventieth birthday, which was day one. When I first numbered my days, I had about 16,000 left until age seventy. I now have a bit over 4000 left. I have not had a downward-counting calendar, but watching the time tick down has helped me keep a sense of doing the will of God *now*.

One could become morbid about the disappearing time—and that would be foolish. Morbidity only results in depression and loss of time to do the important. One needs to remember the time left from a wise perspective, not a foolish one. Numbering my days has provided me incentive to make wise choices. It is a route to getting a value-system (heart) shaped around wisdom.

How many days are left until you turn seventy?

- **Listen To The Fear Of The Lord**

The fear of the LORD teaches a man wisdom, and humility comes before honor. (Pro 15:33 NIV)

The fear of the LORD is not only the point of breakthrough into wisdom, it is also *one of the instructors* who teach wisdom. The verse could also be translated, "The fear of the LORD is the corrective-instruction of wisdom..."

As life moves on, the follower of Christ has to bring his general commitment to the Lordship of Christ to bear on the many, specific, individual situations of life. Over and over again, he/she will face a choice of how to respond to people, which priorities to enact, how to deal with his/her attitudes, authority, relationships, decision-making process, work, speech, possessions or trouble that has erupted.

A follower of Christ needs to survey the options, and choose the one that is pleasing to the Lord, no matter how difficult it is. When he enacts what is pleasing to the Lord, he will have acted in the fear of the Lord.

Over time, the difficult choice to fear the Lord will work out for blessing. Then, the Christ-follower can see how the chosen path was not only the path of the fear of the LORD, but also very definitely the path to success, the way of wisdom. The believer now has acquired wisdom out of experience guided by the fear of the LORD. In this way, the fear of the LORD teaches wisdom to those willing to live by it.

- **Assess Life Around You**

Several times the writers of Proverbs and Ecclesiastes refer to lessons (wisdom) learned from observing and studying life. The human realm is one arena for fruitful observation, watching how humans relate, observing their choices and consequences, etc. The other realm is nature, looking at the way animals live and work. The Creator of the Universe made animals according to patterns and illustrates through them, not only his fabulous intellect and power, but also some truths about life.

There are three stages to coming up with such "lessons learned." They are illustrated in the lessons from the wasted vineyard in Proverbs 24:30-34:

I went by the field of the lazy man, and by the vineyard of the man devoid of understanding;
And there it was, all overgrown with thorns; its surface was covered with nettles; its stone wall was broken down.
When I saw it, I considered it well; I looked on it and received instruction:
A little sleep, a little slumber, a little folding of the hands to rest;
So shall your poverty come like a prowler, and your need like an armed man.

First, one *observes*. As one is going about life (*I went by*), he views and listens to what is occurring, taking it in (*I saw it*).

Second, one *considers* (*I considered*). What one observed, one now thinks over. The Hebrew literally says, "I placed the heart." The heart, the internal person, is put to work on this situation and "chews over" this set of observed circumstances, especially to see what it says about making choices, since decision-making is the business of the heart.

Third, one "*receives corrective instruction*" (*muwcar*). Insight comes to mind, a kind of insight that not only provides ideas, but also sets direction for a person. It is the valuable instruction, *muwcar*, the corrective instruction that enables one to redirect his life and set it in a profitable direction.

1) Decipher The Analogies Of Nature

One of the fundamental assumptions of Wisdom is that the Creator God made the world according to patterns that reflect Him (see p. 75ff). As one observes the majesty and complexity of nature, he gets insight into the mind and power of God (Rom 1:18-20).

However, God has also made nature in such a way that it provides analogies to our human experiences. Nature presents many situations that illustrate spiritual truths to the person willing to observe and consider God's creations. For example, the lilies of the field in their beauty and temporariness tell us something of the willingness of God to care for and clothe his more majestic creation, human kind (Matt 6:28-30). The birds, without complex brains, still know the times of their migrations, and set out to return to their homes at the appropriate times—in contrast to God's people, intelligent humans who yet cannot discern when it is time to return to God (Jer 8:7). And, sluggards would do well to go to the ants and observe their voluntary diligence in gathering while goods are available in order to prepare for lean times ahead. Such insight could lead the sluggard to wisdom (Pro 6:6-8).

Sometimes, nature's animals exhibit qualities for humans to imitate, such as the providence of the ants, the voluntary cooperation of the locusts, the prudent sanctuary of the coney or the exceptional achievement of the ordinary spider or lizard (Pro 30:24-29). The book *Character Sketches* contains numerous examples of admirable qualities exhibited by animals. The folk tales of many cultures relate animal traits to the human situation, such as "The Ant And The Grasshopper."

Other times, nature provides parallels to human tendencies and makes a bit more obvious something about the human situation. Examples of such clarifying insight would be what is really going on with a parading king (Pro 30:29-31), or how unfathomable it is that a woman would let a man take advantage of her (Pro 30:18-19), or the consuming need felt in barrenness (Pro 30:15-16).

Life around us provides illustrations of spiritual things, if we have the eyes to see and the willingness to consider. I was once on a trip by auto across northern Texas. To pass the time, I was trying to find in the passing scenery examples of spiritual principles. I was driving through ranch country. On ranch after ranch, windmills pumping water whirled in the steady Texas breeze. As I sped along the freeway, my eye caught one windmill that was not turning. The rancher had "locked it down" so that the blades refused to be moved by the wind. Instead of facing the wind and drawing useful power from it, the locked blades merely acted like a weathervane, buffeted by the wind, but drawing nothing from it. The windmill was a contrast to all the other windmills. I decided to consider it and see if there was a lesson there.

I saw, and now, *I considered.*

For a few weeks, I had been reading about the work of the Holy Spirit in the lives of believers. I thought about how the Holy Spirit had come like a mighty wind at Pentecost. Suddenly, the thought came to me: When I am refusing to cooperate with the Holy Spirit as He is prompting or leading me to do something (like, admit I am wrong), I am just like the locked windmill. The power of God is still flowing, but I, stubbornly refusing to do what God says, am "locked down" just like the windmill and will draw nothing from the Holy Spirit's available power.

I decided I didn't want to live in such a condition. I wanted the free flow of the power of God in my life. The image of the locked windmill has come back to my mind many times as I struggle to yield to the Lord's leadership. It has prompted me to "let go and let God."

My experience with the locked windmill parallels that of the learner in Proverbs 24. As I drove along and viewed the locked windmill in the stiff breeze, I "went by" and "I saw it;" I *observed.* Then, I *considered.* And then, I *received corrective instruction*, insight that helped me make some choices about how I wanted to live.

The wisdom that I gained from the experience does not have the same authority and weight as a statement made by Scripture, but it is still a practical guide in making wise choices. Actually though, the wisdom I gained from the experience *is* rooted in such scriptural statements as: *"Do not quench the Spirit" (1 Thes 5:19 NKJ), "do not grieve the Holy Spirit" (Eph 4:30), and "you always resist the Holy Spirit" (Acts 7:51).*

In order to keep from erroneous conclusions as you draw out a lesson from nature or life, it is a good idea to identify the Scripture or the scriptural principle illustrated by the experience you had.

2) Backtrack From Results To Causes

One way to learn from life is to observe *results* and trace them back to their *causes.* Life has a cause-and-effect flow to it. Individuals make choices, and the choices produce consequences. Many times, we see the results of choices, either a mess or a success. We tend to observe the mess or the success and then go on about our way. If the mess or success is significant, one needs to learn to ask questions about how the situation came to be—and its implications for one's life in the future.

So, the man in Proverbs 24 goes by a property that is capable of producing considerable income, a vineyard. Instead of being in prime, income-producing condition, the property is in shambles and will produce little of value. The contrast catches his attention. Looking at the ruined vineyard, he asks how it came to be in this condition. What would motivate someone to let such devastation occur? He remembers the character of the man who owns the property: lazy. Suddenly, the reason for such ruin is clear: the cause is a little laziness in situation after situation over time. The day comes when the opportunity for income is gone, and poverty replaces it. Laziness causes the breakdown of valuable things and the loss of their potential for income. The cause-effect relationship is clear: laziness → ruin → poverty.

The same is true for the wounds of the drunkard (Pro 23:29-35). What causes a person to awaken sick, bruised all over, and not exactly sure how it all occurred: drunkenness.

When the simple (naïve) person sees a mocker get due punishment, the naïve one begins to gain wisdom. Insight about a cause-effect connection dawns on the simple one: mockery → punishment (Pro 19:25; 21:11). In his heart, the simple makes a choice to "not go there." He develops the wisdom to avoid mockery. That wisdom comes by observing consequences and drawing conclusions about causes.

Tracing situations back to their causes allows one to draw important lessons about the flow of life.

Writing "Lessons Learned." Years ago, a wise person challenged me to record the lessons about life that I learned from observation and experience. I purchased a small three-ring binder and began to record lessons somewhat along the following outline:

1. **Name of the Lesson—**Pick the name you like best.
2. **Relevant Scripture—**List Scriptures that related to the lesson.
3. **Principle—**Write a concise statement of the principle or lesson learned. State it the way it means the most to you. Don't worry about style.
4. **Background—**Write a summary of the situation or events from which the lesson was learned.

I kept the lessons and reviewed them occasionally. Having "paid the price" to learn the lesson, I did not want to forget it and have to learn it all over again.

"Lessons Learned" tend to have a certain limitation to them. They are not able to give us *new information* from God, but they do provide new perspective on, striking examples of, or deeper insight into things we already know.

- **Learn From Correction**

Correction comes to us in many different ways. It may come from the Scriptures, from another person, or from the frustrations or disappointments of life. It is important to learn to recognize and heed *correction.* It turns out to be a major vehicle through which God intends to teach us wisdom. We will look at that in the next chapter.

Think About It

Wisdom *can* be gained. For the person who humbles himself and walks in the fear of the Lord, there are steps that lead to abiding wisdom.

Which of the wisdom-search steps have you already taken?

Which of the steps is the easiest for you? The most difficult? Why?

Are there any remaining steps you need to take?

WISDOM CAN COME TO US THROUGH MANY DIFFERENT CHANNELS. BUT, IT COMES THROUGH ONE CHANNEL SO FREQUENTLY THAT YOU COULD CALL IT "WISDOM'S PIPELINE."
WANT TO KNOW WHAT IT IS?
READ ON!

Chapter 12

WISDOM'S PIPELINE

All cultures have some form of "training program" for their children. It could be tutelage under Dad and Mom. It may involve time spent with tribal elders. It may involve classes under teachers. In Europe and America, we have made the center piece in our child training the instructional process in the public school classroom.

WISDOM'S DIFFERENT APPROACH

In our American educational system we stress the acquisition of *ideas* and *facts* as the key part of education. So, we teach and learn facts, such as *the world is approximately 25,000 miles around*, or the facts of mathematical relationships.

We usually are concerned to make sure no one's feelings get hurt in the educational process. Indeed, we are so socially concerned with hurt feelings that we have tried to create "politically correct" terms to make certain persons feel better. We use them to somehow make all or us feel more equal and more "right." Sometimes the terms become nearly ridiculous as we try to make the hard things of life appear minor or interesting in order to make those in the hard situation feel better about themselves.

Wisdom has a quite different idea of "education."

First, *wisdom's goal* in training is the *development of skill in dealing with people and life in a successful manner.* The acquisition of information about the facts of the world or science or math is not unimportant, but is not adequate to develop a wise person. Wisdom's quest for knowledge goes beyond that of science. It seeks to know the God who is really there, how He has made and runs the world, how to connect with and cooperate with Him, and how life flows under His rulership.

The categories of education are the topics of public school: science, math, language, geography, social studies, etc. The categories of Wisdom are the person of God, the ways of God, the kinds of people, the consequences of actions, how to read people, and how to deal with life. One needs to learn how to choose the right attitudes, how to deal with authority, how to relate to people, how to make good decisions, how to speak wisely, how to work rightly, how to handle possessions, and how to deal with trouble—all in a way that is pleasing to God.

To develop such *skill,* we need more than mere *ideas* about what we ought to do. We need a better *pattern for dealing with life* than we are currently using, and we need skill in working the new pattern. We are going to have to exchange our current approach (to enemies, to dating, to work, etc.) for a better one. And, we are going to need coaching (correction, instruction, and encouragement) in our new way of doing things until we are skilled at it.

Wisdom's goal is to help us change both ourselves and our approach to life to something better and more successful, more in line with how God does things. Wisdom is not trying to change our *information*, it is trying to change *us*!

The native arrogance in our hearts (Ecc 9:3 "madness") reacts negatively to such a goal. *Change me? Who do you think you are? I'm fine just like I am. And my approach to life—it's my own! I created it myself, and I like it! Who are you to say that your approach is the right one and that mine is wrong? My momma didn't raise no fools! I know what I am doing, and I would appreciate it if you would go bother someone else!*

Not only is wisdom's goal offensive to the arrogance of our hearts, Wisdom's *method* is even *more* offensive. Wisdom's first approach to us is with *correction* of what we are doing.

In public education, we go to great lengths to make people feel good about themselves and to try to find something positive about even *wrong* answers.

Wisdom does not intend to make us feel *bad* about ourselves. The Lord, to whom wisdom belongs, is kind and has compassion on us. He understands that we struggle (Ps 103:13-14). Indeed, he gives us His Sprit that we may know peace and joy in Him (Rom 15:13; 1 Thes 1:6). So, wisdom will deal with us graciously, but her goal is not to build our "self-esteem," but our perspective and skill.

Wisdom is genuinely concerned that we *succeed*, so she is willing to correct us, and to "speak the truth in love," using a NT phrase. She is also *testing us*. She knows that one has to humble himself in order to learn the difficult lessons of wisdom and make actual changes in life, so her corrective approach is also *a test* to see if we qualify as a learner.

Therefore, Wisdom's first address to us is likely to be a rebuke, a correction—something that pricks our arrogance. So, Wisdom is personified in Proverbs 1, chiding the simple (the too-long naïve) and fools for rejecting, *not her concepts*, but her *rebuke* (v. 22-25). To the one who accepts her rebuke, she *then* pours out her heart/spirit and thoughts/words (v. 23). Rather than a "kinder, gentler," principles-first-optional corrections-later approach, wisdom turns the process around and comes toward us with correction first. If correction is heeded, she then pours out her principles and reasons.

But, if one refuses her rebuke, she never tells him more—except that disaster is already on its way to him. The refusers will never know her concepts and principles. When their disaster arrives, though they cry out to wisdom, she will not answer them. As they have mocked her in more placid times, she will laugh at them amid the overwhelming storm of troubles and calamity that come upon them (v. 26-28). They will eat the fruit of their ways; they will get everything coming to them!

First comes the willingness to heed correction, then comes the insights of wisdom. This approach is in line with the principle that one cannot know wisdom until he enters into the fear of the LORD (Pro 9:10). First comes the fear of the LORD, the profound respect for the LORD that desires to obey Him. Then wisdom begins. Wisdom's rebuke enables us better to walk in the fear of the Lord; it is an invitation to break through into wisdom, not simply a criticism of inadequate performance.

Jesus says much the same thing when he declares that the ones who will have adequate discernment about His teachings are those who are willing to do God's will, for willingness to obey is a prerequisite to discernment (John 7:17).

Thus, our first invitation to a dialog with wisdom likely will not be an invitation to contemplate ideas or discuss concepts. Rather, it will be a situation that tests our willingness to obey God, some advice, a correction, or a rebuke (Pro 1:23, 25, 29-30). If we receive the correction, the treasures of wisdom are unlocked. If we ignore or reject the correction (advice or rebuke), the mind of wisdom does not open to us. The treasure remains hidden away, unavailable to us.

This is difficult for Americans, for again, our attitude toward correction tends to be, *"Who are you to correct me?"*

A STRANGE STATEMENT

It is difficult for the citizens of our society to imagine why *anyone* would make a certain strange statement found in the book of Psalms:

Let a righteous man strike me— it is a kindness; let him rebuke me— it is oil on my head. My head will not refuse it. Yet my prayer is ever against the deeds of evildoers... (Ps 141:5 NIV)

Contemporary Americans have a hard time receiving even gentle rebuke. We take offense at even *hints* of correction. But the psalmist says he is quite willing to receive two *severe* types of correction from a righteous man:

- A blow is severe reproof or punishment for a serious offense. The Hebrew indicates willingness to take a *severe* blow: "Let him *hammer* me."
- A rebuke, being set straight, the emotional equivalent of the physical blow.

The Psalmist promises to regard the blow as a merciful, faithful, almost beautiful kindness (implied by the Hebrew word). He will regard the second as a refreshing courtesy and honor (the anointing with oil).

What could motivate a person to make such a strange statement?

Could he just enjoy pain? There are guilty people who develop an emotional need for punishment and pain. Some sexualize it into masochism. But, the psalm makes it clear that the writer does not like the pain of his circumstances.

Maybe he is just a whiner with no guts. Perhaps he just cowers before strong personalities! The rest of the psalm, however, indicates that the psalmist is a courageous, committed person bearing up under very dangerous times.

The writer makes his strange statement because he has an accurate perspective (*knowledge*) regarding himself. His chosen perspective on the blows that he would receive means that he sees the blows as being just (deserved). He knows that he could *intentionally* do wrong, or *unintentionally* do wrong. In either case, he would deserve correction. He apparently understands that human beings, himself included, have an inclination to selfish agendas The writer also has two motives that drive his amazing statement:

- First, he is committed to the fear of the LORD. He *would prefer punishment among the righteous* to pleasure taken with the wicked (Ps 141:4-5), and he wants to make that clear.

· Second, he knows the correction would *be to his good.* A righteous/just (the Hebrew could be translated either way) person would not do what was wrong. Therefore, he would give a blow or rebuke only if it were really appropriate, if something really out of line had occurred. That is, the righteous would only strike or correct if the psalmist had really erred. By the corrections, the erring writer would be set more clearly on the right path. And that, to him, would be a blessing.

In other words, the psalmist *really believes*

Like an earring of gold or an ornament of fine gold is a wise man's rebuke to a listening ear. (Pro 25:12 NIV) or in the Living Bible: *It is a badge of honor to accept valid criticism.*

Wounds from a friend can be trusted, but an enemy multiplies kisses. (Pro 27:6 NIV)

...the corrections of discipline are the way to life, (Pro 6:23 NIV)

The rod and rebuke give wisdom...(Pro 29:15 NKJ)

The Scriptures say that an attitude toward correction like that of the psalmist reveals a person of discernment, prudence and wisdom:

... rebuke a discerning man, and he will gain knowledge. (Pro 19:25 NIV)

... whoever heeds correction shows prudence. (Pro 15:5 NIV)

...rebuke a wise man and he will love you. (Pro 9:8 NIV)

The discerning, the prudent, and the wise understand that *wisdom, especially, comes through correction.* It is this understanding that lies behind two striking statements about the crucial nature of correction:

... the corrections (Heb: towkechah) of discipline (Heb: muwcar) are the way to life... (Pro 6:23 NIV)

Hold on to instruction (muwcar), do not let it go; guard it well, for it is your life. (Pro 4:13 NIV)

To the ordinary human heart, correction by another person is insulting and receives a resentful or abusive reaction from the corrected one (Pro 9:7-8). But, the persons who have made the breakthrough into wisdom realize that *correction is the clothing that wisdom will wear as she approaches them.*

Correction is so crucial that it is the *way to life*. Whoever wants to find safety, refreshment, enjoyment, and meaning must travel a certain road to get there: Correction Highway.

Even more, the form of correction called "*muwcar*" (moo-sawr') turns out to be *life itself.* When it arrives, one hangs onto the correction. He does not let it accidentally escape through poor memory. It is so valuable that he protects it. He does not let it be kidnapped by distraction. He will not let it go until it he has assimilated it into his life. If it gets away from him, he has missed safety, refreshment, enjoyment, and meaning—life itself has gotten away from him!

How different is the societal attitude that sees correction as life-removing, not life-giving. The culture-wide perception of all correction as degrading and humiliating means that people simply *miss life itself.* They keep on with inadequate strategies for handling life with an arrogant determination to have others respect their right to do life their *own* way. As a result, they are ineffective in dealing with life, and their problems are arrogantly perpetuated.

THE NATURE OF CORRECTION

The primary Hebrew words representing "correction" are *towkechah* and *muwcar.*

Towkechah (to-kay-khaw'), or in another form, *towkachath* (to-kakh'-ath), means chastisement and is translated rebuke or reproof. Both words are from a Hebrew word meaning "to be right" or "to put right." *Towkechah* is particularly the act of correction or the specific correction delivered.

Towkechah is the way Wisdom makes her approach to us (Pro 1:23, 24, 30). God, Himself, hands out *towkechah* (Pro 3:11). Heeding correction indicates a person is prudent (Pro 15:5). It fits one for the company of the wise (Pro 15:31), because correction is common there. Heeding correction enables a person to gain understanding (Pro 15:32), and leads to honor (Pro 13:18). The one who refuses correction is a person who will lead others astray (Pro 10:17). Along with physical discipline, correction (*towkechah*) is a key tool for developing wisdom in a child (Pro 29:15).

To despise correction will cause a person to end up at the edge of disgrace and ruin (Pro 5:12). Resisting repeated reproof will ultimately lead to devastating, permanent disability (Pro 29:1). Hating *towkechah* indicates a person is as stupid as a cow (the Hebrew word indicates food-on-the-hoof) (Pro 12:1) and will lead to his death (Pro 15:10).

The second Hebrew word *muwcar* (moo-sawr'), meaning chastisement, is used figuratively of reproof or instruction. It comes from a word meaning "to chastise," either quite literally with physical blows or figuratively with words. However, *muwcar* is not simply a rebuke or a piece of advice, though it could contain these. It is *instruction with a corrective edge* to it, somewhat like the instruction a coach gives. A coach shows an athlete how to do a skill or speaks about the mental focus or attitude the athlete needs in order to perform well. Then, the coach corrects and encourages the athlete until his performance is up to standards.

Muwcar shows up as instruction that intends to change us and help us achieve far beyond what we are currently able. The coach's initial presentation of the skill, focus or attitude is *muwcar*, for it presents things that are different from (and corrective of) what the athlete is currently doing. The coach's motivational correction is also *muwcar*; it is the same set of understandings now in the form of correction. If the coach perceives a need, he may deal out a form of punishment for failure to perform ("Give me twenty laps around the gym!"). That, too, is *muwcar*. It is the same set of goals for performance now dealt with from the angle of discipline in order to advance the learner. So, *muwcar* can be translated "instruction" (Pro 19:20 NIV), "correction/rebuke" (Pro 23:13 NKJ), or "discipline" (Pro 13:24 NIV).

MUWCAR AND TOWKECHAH

In several scriptures *towkechah* and *muwcar* are practically synonyms indicating a correction (for example, Pro 15:32). In concept, however, *muwcar* appears to be a larger category, including not merely wise rebuke, but also wise instruction and disciplined training. In one verse, the two terms are related to one another:

...the reproofs (towkechah) of instruction (muwcar) are the way of life, (Pro 6:23 NKJ)

Here, *muwcar* (corrective instruction) appears as a source from which *towkechah* (rebuke, correction) can be drawn. The reproofs that have *muwcar* as their source—these are the *way of life*.

Reproofs can have their origin in many sources: differences of opinion, differences of taste, another's personal ire or irritability, etc. One might dismiss or ignore reproofs that are rooted in a mere difference of taste or in irritability.

However, the reproofs that come from *muwcar*, from the realm of wise corrective instruction—these are to be heeded! They are the very *way to life* itself! Therefore, the one who dismisses the *towkechah* of *muwcar* is missing the way to life—he will find its opposite! The one who heeds Wisdom's *muwcar* will become wise (Pro 8:33). He finds Wisdom, and therefore, finds life (Pro 8:35). Those who will not heed Wisdom's *muwcar* fail to find her. They harm themselves; in effect, they love death (Pro 8:35-36). Therefore, one needs to get a firm grip on corrective instruction (*muwcar*), and not let it get away from one, but maintain it and assimilate it. It is one's *very life* (Pro 4:13)!

THE PIPELINE

All of us come into the world equipped with stubborn selfishness, arrogant self-justification, and a willingness to hurt others in order to get what we want. Our attempts to get what we want in life flow out of our personally preferred mix of these three elements. The strategies we develop out of our mix tend to run contrary to the way God rules the universe. He rewards sacrifice, humility, diligence and doing good to others. He disciplines selfishness, arrogance, sloth, and hurting others. Our native strategies incline toward the latter.

The result is that most of us learn to handle life adequately enough to get through, but not excellently, and not with resounding, enduring success. What successes we do achieve tend to be short-lived because of the selfish, arrogant, hurtful way we have gone about creating them.

There *is* a way to achieve *enduring success* in a universe run by the sovereign, moral, creator God—even in a world where people can be adversarial, antagonistic, and even dangerous. To learn the way to success, however, requires a *major shift* in our ways of thinking and behaving. It requires a great deal of correction. But correction is *so* offensive to stubbornly selfish, arrogant people: *Who do you think you are to correct me?*

In reality, there is a whole fund of corrective instruction we desperately need. *Muwcar* is the name of that fund of ideas, perspectives and skills—and the corrections. That is why *muwcar* can be practically a synonym for wisdom.

Muwcar occupies almost the same status as wisdom and understanding. For example, the Proverbs are written to enable one to attain wisdom (the skill to handle life well), and *muwcar* (the knowledge of more correct, better ways) (Pro 1:2). They allow one to receive the corrective instruction (*muwcar*) that wisdom, justice, judgment and equity each would give to one (Pro 1:3). One needs to apply his heart to *muwcar*, to think over how to apply it to his life (Pro 22:12), as he would apply his heart to understanding (Pro 2:2). One needs to pursue truth to the extent of paying money for it. Once he gets it, he should never let it go—and the same applies to wisdom, *muwcar* and understanding (biynah) (Pro 23:23). When the observer of the lazy man's vineyard considered the situation, he received a kind of wisdom: *Muwcar* (Pro 24:32).

Wisdom is to be chosen over wealth. Wisdom calls us to prefer her *muwcar* to wealth (Pro 8:10), and to heed it in order to become wise (Pro 8:33). The one who heeds *muwcar* will lead others to life, not into error (Pro 10:17). The one who loves *muwcar* is actually the one who really loves knowledge (Pro 12:1), the foundation of wisdom, since *muwcar* is one of the major means of acquiring knowledge.

By the way, one application of this verse is that a person can be tested to see if they are on the track to wisdom. One can offer them a valid correction and see if they love correction or resent it! The person who really loves knowledge will love the *muwcar*.

Muwcar is both the fund of corrective instruction we need and the vehicle (instruction, correction, discipline) for acquiring it.

Muwcar is somewhat like the term "Xerox." Originally, "Xerox" was the name of a company that invented copy machines. Other companies quickly tried to get into the market. In time, Xerox was just the name of only one company delivering photocopiers. But, over time, "xerox" came to represent the very act of photocopying. Formally, it was the name of only one means of delivery of photocopies. Ultimately, the "means of delivery," Xerox, became the term that stood for the whole realm: "I need to xerox this stuff, and then I'll get it to you."

So it is with *muwcar*. It names the stuff we need, corrective instruction. And, it names the major means of delivering the corrective instruction—correction. The corrective approach is not the *only* means that Wisdom uses to convey itself to us, but is *the major means. Muwcar* is Wisdom's pipeline. It is both the stuff we need, and the channel for getting it to us. If we do not hook up to the pipeline, the good stuff of Wisdom courses on past us, and we never benefit from it.

A person who ceases listening to *muwcar* will stray from knowledge (Pro 19:27), that is, from an adequate perspective on life. He is like an athlete who misses the coaching sessions. Not only will he fail to improve, his performance will gradually decline.

One who ignores *muwcar* will end up in poverty and shame (Pro 13:18). Therefore, the one who ignores *muwcar* actually despises himself (Pro 15:32). The person who persists in evil will die for lack of *muwcar* (Pro 5:23).

MUWCAR AND PARENTING

Muwcar plays a key role in the development of healthy children.

Folly (*'ivveleth*, the folly of stubborn determination to have one's own way) is bound up in the heart of children, but the rod of *muwcar* (corrective instruction) will drive folly from a child's heart (Pro 22:15). If the child grows to adulthood with the stubborn, selfish, folly intact, it becomes the determinative factor in his life, either part of the fabric of his person (Pro 27:22) or an addictive pattern of behavior that cannot be abandoned (Pro 26:11).

A child not adequately trained (instructed and corrected) but left to himself will fail to develop wisdom, and will grow up to disgrace his mother (Pro 29:15), who may, be the source of the reluctance to discipline the child. Rather than appreciate her reluctance to discipline him, a foolish adult will actually despise his mother (Pro 15:20). Instead of caring for her in her old age, he will be likely to drive her out to fend for herself (Pro 19:26). If her child grows into a foolish adult, a mother finds unending depression (Pro 10:1) and grief (Pro 17:25).

When a child grows into a foolish adult, he brings his father anxious turmoil (Pro 17:25). Joy is gone for the father of a fool; he lives in depression (Pro 17:21). A foolish son will ruin his father's estate (Pro 19:13). He may even rob his father and mother, bringing not only financial trouble to them, but also disgrace in the eyes of the community (Pro 28:24, 19:26). If he comes to the point of mocking his father or scorning obedience to his mother, he is headed for an early and ignoble death (Pro 30:17).

In contrast, a child raised to be wise is not only personally successful, but brings continuing delight to his father and his mother (Pro 10:1; 15:20; 23:15-16; 24-25; 27:11). He gets going on the right path in life and stays with it (Pro 22:6). He will honor his father and mother, setting the stage for a long and prosperous life for the child (Ex 20:12; Eph 6:2-3).

Therefore, one should not withhold discipline (*muwcar*) from a child. To punish a child with a rod, physical punishment, will not kill the child; it is an effective training tool to keep him from rebellious patterns that lead to death (Pro 23:13-14). (This verse implies that *muwcar* includes physical punishment.) The one who refuses to punish his son actually hates the child—he is condemning the child to a hard and frustrating life. The one who really loves his child will be careful to *muwcar* him (Pro 13:24).

Both fathers and mothers will teach a child the statutes and precepts of the Lord. Fathers, however, will also hand out *muwcar*, corrective instruction based on the principles of life (Heb: towrah [to-raw']) (Pro 4:1). Mothers may focus more on the statues and precepts themselves (towrah), and communicate in a more kindly manner (Pro 1:8; 4:1; 15:5; 31:26). A mother needs to watch that her concern for kindly instruction does not prevent appropriate discipline for her child. Otherwise, she will later come to heartache (Pro 29:15; 15:20).

A father needs to make sure that his inclination to *muwcar* does not anger, exasperate, and ultimately dishearten his children (Eph 6:4, Col 3:21). Rather, he is to "bring them up" (the Greek implies to *nourish up to maturity)* in the "training and instruction of the Lord." "Nourishing up" implies a warm and encouraging environment.

"Training" translates the Greek "paideia" (pahee-di'-ah), meaning the training of a child, including instruction. The term has an instructional focus, but also embraces the forming of the child over time through correction and discipline. It is analogous to the Old Testament (OT) *muwcar.*

"Instruction" translates the Greek "nouthesia" (noo-thes-ee'-ah), a noun related to the verb "noutheteo" (noo-thet-eh'-o), meaning "to put in mind." Nouthesia means a calling attention to, implying a mild rebuke or warning. It seems analogous to the OT *towkechah.*

The child is to grow in a warm and encouraging environment by means of aggressive instruction with a training edge to it, and by calling his attention to words, deeds, or attitudes that need to be corrected. The whole instruction and correction are to be about the things and ways of the Lord and be done in a manner consistent with God's character.

The LORD is Himself a good Father. He gives out *muwcar* (Pro 3:11; see also Deu 11:2; Job 5:17; Isa 26:16; Jer 2:30). We will look at the Lord's *muwcar* in the next chapter.

Heeding a father's corrective instruction (*muwcar*) indicates that a son is wise (Pro 13:1); the one who spurns his father's *muwcar* (instruction, correction, discipline) is a fool (Pro 15:5). Indeed, even an older adult should consider his father's input on matters (Pro 23:22).

AVOIDING REPROACH

Reproof or "rebuke" is one of the major ways we learn wisdom. To heed a rebuke is prudent (Pro 15:5), and leads to honor (Pro 13:8), to a greater understanding (Pro 15:32) and to wisdom (Pro 29:15). To ignore reproof is stupid (Pro 12:1) and sets the stage for personal disaster (Pro 1:23-31, Pro 29:1). For one to despise reproof is deadly (Pro 15:10).

One gets a "rebuke" so that he will not get a "reproach." A rebuke is a correction that, if heeded, keeps one on track to honor and to good things (Pro 13:18). A reproach is severe reproof that attaches lasting shame to a person (as in Jer 24:8-9; 42:18). If one will heed reproof from the right sources, he can avoid coming to lasting shame. Certain things lead inexorably to shame: pride (Pro 11:2), mockery (Pro 3:35), wickedness (Pro 13:5; 18:3), adultery (Pro 6:32-33), robbery of parents (Pro 19:26), betraying confidences (Pro 25:9-10), answering before one fully hears (Pro 18:13), ignoring correction (Pro 13:18), and hasty litigation (Pro 25:7-8). If one ignores correction, he continues down the path toward the disgrace awaiting him.

LEARNING FROM REPROOF

Reproof comes to us from different sources:

From the Scripture. While we are reading the Bible or listening to messages by Christian teachers, we get our viewpoints, values, decisions and life patterns corrected. Indeed, one of the great helps that Scripture gives us is correction (2 Tim 3:16). As we study and memorize it, the Holy Spirit will use it to correct and guide us.

From circumstances. Sometimes God uses circumstances to correct us. We will look at this in the next chapter.

From parents. A wise child listens to and heeds his father's rebuke and his corrective instruction (*muwcar*) on how to succeed. Fools and mockers won't listen to either form of correction (Pro 13:1; 15:5).

From friends.

Perfume and incense bring joy to the heart, and the pleasantness of one's friend springs from his earnest counsel. (Pro 27:9 NIV)

Wounds from a friend can be trusted, but an enemy multiplies kisses. (Pro 27:6 NIV)

Genuine friends want to see us succeed in life and will tell us the truth when we need it. Their earnest counsel points us in better directions. Even if we are hurt by them, we can trust them, for they are out for our best.

Enemies who want us to fail will notice our ineptitude and applaud us in order to get us to continue in ways that will bring us disappointment.

We need to trust and receive correction from friends.

From our superiors.

If a ruler's anger rises against you, do not leave your post; calmness can lay great errors to rest. (Ecc 10:4 NIV)

The superior could be a supervisor at work, a teacher at school, or a leader in an organization we have joined. When we have angered our superior by our performance, the easiest things is to go off in a huff, angry that someone is angry with us. Rather, we need to calmly figure out what we need to do to make things right.

From fellow Christ-followers. The importance of correction as a channel to wisdom lies behind the NT's encouragement to admonish, to correct, and to speak the truth in love (Col 1:28; 3:16; Heb 3:12-13; Titus 2:15; Eph 4:15). Loving correction has no desire to harm another. It is actually seeking the other person's good, and is willing to risk a negative reaction in order to help.

For example, Paul describes his rebuke of Peter in Galatians 2:11-14.

Peter, a major leader in the early church, had been raised in the Jewish traditions. He visited the primarily Gentile church in Antioch. He was having great fellowship with the Gentile believers until some other Jewish Christians arrived from Jerusalem and held back from the Gentiles in line with Jewish customs. Peter did not want to offend the Jewish visitors, especially since they were from his home church. So he joined their separation from the Gentile believers. Even Barnabas, the great-hearted Jew so concerned for the salvation of the Gentiles, was swept up in the error.

Paul, raised in the Jewish traditions but a major leader among the Gentile churches, realized that the Gospel was at stake. Paul had to do something. He chose the only route through the mess, open rebuke to Peter in front of the church. Paul's rebuke was not an arrogant or vengeful move. It was "*muwcar*" aimed at spiritual health for Peter, Barnabas, the visiting Jews, and the Gentile believers. Peter recognized his error and repented.

Given the deception of our human hearts, correction is simply *necessary* in the church. The only way the fellowship of believers can really progress in Christ, is to "speak the truth in love" (Eph 4:15).

From the wise. If we consult wise people for advice, we need to be ready to receive correction, for they will correct us if they feel it is needed (Pro 15:2). That fact keeps mockers away from the wise. Should we want to associate with the wise in order to gain wisdom (Pro 13:20), we need to be familiar with receiving correction, for correction is a way of life among the wise (Pro 15:31).

A rebuke from a wise person is actually an extension of trust from them and a compliment. They are trusting us not to resent them, as a mocker would. And, if they thought we were a mocker, they would not have corrected us (Pro 9:8). Their willingness to reprove us means that they think we have already begun the journey to wisdom.

Actually, a rebuke from a wise person is preferable to songs sung in one's honor by a bunch of fools (Ecc 7:5). The raucous singing of the fools is only so much noise (Ecc 7:6). But the rebuke of the wise comes to benefit us; it can add attractiveness and distinction to the life of the person who will heed it (Pro 25:12), and open the door to honor in the eyes of others (Pro 13:18).

So, wise people highly value correction given to them. A rebuke deeply impresses a discerning person who will gain knowledge from it (Pro 17:10; 19:25). The prudent heed correction (Pro 15:5). And a wise man will love the one who rebukes him (Pro 9:8).

From Wisdom. Wisdom is actually the one trying to get to us through the rebukes given to us by others. If we would listen to *their rebukes*, we would be listening to *her rebuke*. Then she would pour out her mind to us.

But, if we ignore *their* rebukes, we flout *her* rebuke. Then she will refuse to help us when trouble overwhelms us. Instead, she will laugh at us as we are filled to the brim with the fruit of our ways, with the trouble that comes from the arrogant, sinful, stupid path we chose when we ignored her correction through others (Pro 1:23-33).

From God. God is behind it all, wanting to get through to us the changes we need. He is capable of dealing with us directly, but often works through others to shape our lives and to bring us correction.

In our early days, He uses our parents. Parents yielded to Him are better tools for shaping, but God uses even parents who do not know Him to train and discipline us.

In our adult years, God uses the authorities over us. He somehow is able to direct the hearts of even kings and supervisors who do not know Him (Pro 21:1). He works through the state to keep order among its citizens (Rom 13:1-5). Indeed, to take a rebellious stance against legitimate authority is to oppose God and draw judgment on oneself (Rom 13:2). God will also speak to us through friends and people in our church.

When we are corrected by others, our deep concern needs to be: Is God trying to say something to me through this?

God can also correct us and teach us through the circumstances of our lives. Actually, God has a whole training program for our lives that utilizes corrective instruction, individual corrections and even punishment if necessary. We will look at God's corrective training program in the next chapter.

SUGGESTIONS FOR RECEIVING REPROOF

When someone offers you a correction, you will feel a need to defend yourself. You will be inclined to make statements that show your irritation or try to immediately explain why the correction is not really applicable to you. However, immediate self-defense usually shuts down the person trying to offer the correction—actually that is probably why we react defensively in the first place—to shut them down!

Instead of rushing to your own defense, calm down and *explore* what the other person is saying. Remember, we tend to be innocent in our own eyes. So explore. Ask, "How did I do that? When do I do it? Where do I do it?" Ask clarifying questions until you really understand what the other person is saying.

Then, *thank* the other person for caring enough about you to take the risk of correcting you—they have given you a "badge of honor," and you deeply appreciate them doing so (Pro 25:12).

If you immediately see the way in which you were wrong, admit your wrong and ask forgiveness of the appropriate parties. Say, "I sinned against you when I did such-and-such, will you forgive me?" Or, if your error was not a matter of sin, but poor taste or poor judgment, go to those it affects and admit your poor taste or judgment. Apologize—say, "What I did was in poor judgment (or poor taste). I am sorry for the discomfort or ill-ease I caused you. Will you please forgive me?"

Just to keep yourself sharp, if you have *sinned,* do not excuse it by calling it "poor judgment" or "poor taste;" just call it *sin.*

Indeed, don't make excuses. Just *admit* your sin or error and ask forgiveness. When we get into extended explanations about why we did such-and-such, we may be seeking "understanding," not forgiveness. That is, we may be asking the other person to not be offended by what we did because what we did was not really that bad, and we are not really that bad a person. Seeking "understanding" is merely a way to massage the relationship with the offended person so that we do not have to humble ourselves and admit we were wrong. Just humble yourself, admit you were wrong, and ask forgiveness.

If you are unsure that the rebuke given to you is actually valid, explore, thank the person. Then, tell them you will take it to the Lord, pray over it, and ask Him to confirm it to you. Then, actually do that. If the Lord does not confirm it to you, do not worry about it. If He does, however, deal with it promptly when He shows it to you.

One day my wife and I were on several errands. I became upset at something she did and, rather than discuss it with her, I began to give short, abrupt answers to questions she would ask. We stopped at a supermarket, and my wife went inside to pick up a few items. I remained in the car with our three-year-old daughter, who had been sitting in the back seat. As we sat in the car, my daughter unbuckled her seat belt, stood up and leaned on the back of the front seat.

"Daddy, you were harsh with mommy," she said seriously. I wasn't ready to admit it to myself.

"I don't think so, darling," I said uncomfortably, "but if you think I was, I will pray, ask the Lord, and see if He confirms it."

We bowed our heads and closed our eyes. "Father," I prayed, "Jessica says I have been harsh with Deborah, and I am not sure. If I have, would you confirm it to me? I ask in the name of Jesus. Amen."

Immediately I realized my daughter was right.

"Darling," I said to her, "God just showed me you were right. I was harsh with mommy, and I will ask her forgiveness when she comes back to the car."

And I did.

THE REBUKE WE DON'T HEED—*USUALLY*

We are not required to heed every rebuke that comes our way.

Some people merely have a negative critical attitude toward others and freely criticize and rebuke them. Two types of fools are especially likely to rebuke others (see *Fools & Follies* and *Self-Defeating Strategies* by the author):

- 'Eviyls (ev-eels'), who are stubborn, reactive, easily upset and determined to have their own agenda enacted. Due to their pushy, manipulative, controlling ways, they tend to be surrounded by ill-will.
- Nabals (naw-bawls'), the predatory fools who tend to treat people very harshly and have a habit of reproaching decent people (Ps 39:8 KJV; see also 1 Sam 25:1-12).

The rebukes we *need to heed* are those that come from *muwcar*, not from fools (Pro 6:23). When a righteous person rebukes us, then we need to pay attention quickly (Ps 141:5).

However, since the LORD used a lowly donkey to speak to an erring prophet, Balaam (Num 22:29-35), it is possible He could use a human "jackass" to speak to us. So, we need to consider, not merely the source, but the content of the rebuke. It is this possibility that motivated David not to kill a man who cursed him (2 Sam 16:5-13).

Therefore, we do not necessarily and immediately heed the rebuke of merely negative or foolish people, but we do consider our actions to see if we have been in error.

SUMMARY

We actually need considerable correction if we are to succeed in life. Some of us need more than others. Correction is one of the major ways wisdom will come to us—it is wisdom's pipeline. We need to learn how to receive it graciously and, if it is valid, to act on it.

Think About It.

What has been your response to correction in the past?
Whose correction has God most used in your life?
How has God used superiors, friends and circumstances to correct you?

WOW! DO WE GET CORRECTION IN LIFE!
PARENTS, TEACHERS, OLDER BROTHERS AND SISTERS,
POLICEMEN, THE IRS—IT COULD COME FROM ANYWHERE!
INTERESTINGLY, THE CORRECTION MAY NOT BE
AS RANDOM AS IT APPEARS.
IT COULD BE PART OF A TRAINING PROGRAM GOD
IS CONDUCTING FOR EACH OF HIS CHILDREN.
WANT TO KNOW MORE?
READ ON!

Chapter 13

GOD'S TRAINING PROGRAM

As any good father, our Father, the Lord, is interested that His children grow up to be well-developed, prosperous adults who know Him, enjoy Him, and whose lives really count as their days pass on earth. He has given us His Spirit, His Word, and His people to strengthen us and to help train us. He also uses the circumstances of life, both to correct and deepen us. In this chapter, we will take a look at God's use of the flow of life to develop us.

HAPPINESS AND HOLINESS

As any good father, the Lord delights when His children are blessed.

As God created the ancient nation of Israel and gave them His law, His desire was that they would enjoy the land He would be giving them and prosper in it (Deu 29:9; 30:9). People in ancient Israel who obeyed God received from Him wisdom, knowledge and happiness (Ecc 2:26). Yet, over time, the nation turned away from God. Through the prophets God pled with them to turn back to God and live (Eze 33:11). Even while Israel was being disciplined by God through the destruction and deportation of the nation, God spoke to them of the *"...plans I have for you ...plans to prosper you and not to harm you, plans to give you hope and a future" (Jer 29:11).*

The Lord Jesus assured us that He came for the purpose of giving us *life to the full* (John 10:10). So, those who believe in him are filled with inexpressible and glorious joy, especially as they come through the testing times (1 Pet 1:8). We sense the love of God, for His Holy Spirit within us sheds it abroad in our hearts (Rom 5:5). There is a joy that rises up from within as we fill ourselves with God's word and relate to one another based on it (Eph 5:18-20). Fellowship with other Christ-followers helps shape us into Christ's likeness and also encourages us (Eph 4:15-16; Heb 10:24). God responds to our faith and we see answers to our prayers—to our joy, both in having the answer and in knowing our God is real (2 Cor 1:11).

God delights to see His children happy. However, the only way we can live happily in the long run is to *walk with God* throughout the days of our life on earth. In the words of the old hymn, "Trust and obey, for there's other way to be happy in Jesus, but to trust and obey." To say it a different way, the path to a happy life is to become like Christ—the pathway to happiness is holiness. Those who become distinctively like Christ are the ones who really enjoy life. Others may have joy for the moment, but walking deeper with Christ brings increasing joy. The further we progress in His kingdom, the more we experience righteousness, peace and joy (Rom 14:17).

As we earlier noted, human beings have three things in their hearts that militate against walking with God and turn us toward the lusts of our own flesh and eyes (Num 15:39; 1 John 2:15-17):

· *'Ivveleth*, the stubborn determination to have our own way: *"I want what I want when I want it!"*

· *Howlelah, the feeling that we are superior to others and deserve more and better: "I deserve it!"*

· *Ra', the willingness to do wrong and harm others to get what we want: "If I have to hurt you to get it, I will!"*

God gives us His Holy Spirit to deal with these things. However, we also must learn to cooperate with the Spirit and choose rightly in life (see for example Eph 4:25-32). We have to "grow up" spiritually (see Heb 5:11-6:1).

God, the Father, who loves His children, wants to raise His kids to maturity, to see them grow into people who really enjoy life. So, He *will deal with* these three things in their hearts that incline them towards foolishness and not toward God. He has given us many resources to help us grow: His Word to guide us, leaders and teachers to instruct us, fellow Christ-followers to encourage and help us, and Himself, in the Holy Spirit, to motivate, give insight, comfort and strengthen us.

God also uses the flow of life to train us and develop Christ-likeness in us. In the flow of life, both good and difficult things come our way. Especially as difficulties arrive we are motivated to learn what the Scripture says and use the resources of God to deal with the difficulties (see Ps 119:71). As we deal rightly with them, we grow.

We will look at several verses in different parts of the Bible that talk about God's training program.

AN OVERVIEW

My son, do not despise the LORD's discipline (muwcar) and do not resent His rebuke (towkechah), because the LORD disciplines (yakach) those He loves, as a father the son He delights in. (Pro 3:11-12 NIV)

The LORD is in process of training His children.

Every child He delights in He disciplines. The Hebrew for "delights in" indicates that this is the child with whom the father is already pleased. The father's correction is not motivated by His displeasure with the child. He is not trying to turn the child from being *unpleasing* to *pleasing*. Instead, His work of discipline is done because the child *already pleases* Him.

"Disciplines" translates the Hebrew yakach (yaw-kakh'), meaning to be right or to put right (correct). This is the verb that *towkechah* is built on. The child who pleases a father is corrected by him. Why? Because the father knows that his child must be trained in order to enjoy life as an adult. If the father did not care for the child, he would not bother (Pro 13:24).

Corrected Out Of Love

So also, the LORD corrects His children, not because we are unlovely and He wants to change us into someone He can love, but because He *already* loves us. He is already pleased with us and loves us.

The punishment that made us pleasing to God actually fell on Christ for our sakes (Isa 53:5). Now, even though our hearts are stained by sin, those who trust God are treated by Him as though they are righteous, completely clean (Rom 4:5-6). Those who have received Christ have their sins forgiven and are "clothed in" His righteousness (2 Cor 5:21; Phil 3:9). We are declared as righteous as Christ. The Father is pleased with us. He is not disciplining us so that we can become loveable. He already loves us deeply as we are (Rom 5:8).

Instead of being out to punish us for our *sins*, the Lord is on a "*muwcar*" training track with His children. He will "*muwcar*" us. That is, He will give us corrective instruction, correct our performance (attitude, heart, deeds and words) in line with it, punish us if necessary to get our attention, and get us to focus on what is right. The "rebuke-event" (*towkechah*) will be one of His major tools.

Actually, from long ago the LORD has been disciplining His people to get them to observe commands, walk in His ways, and respect Him.

Know then in your heart that as a man disciplines (yacar) his son, so the LORD your God disciplines (yacar) you. Observe the commands of the LORD your God, walking in His ways and revering Him. (Deu 8:5-6 NIV)

"Yacar" (yaw-sar'), translated discipline, means to chastise with blows or words and is used figuratively of rebuke. *Yacar* is the verb that "*muwcar*," corrective instruction, is built upon. The LORD disciplined His people, ancient Israel. The Proverbs passage we looked at above (3:11-12) said that such discipline applied not only to the nation but to individuals.

The book of Hebrews indicates this process God used in the Old Testament is still going on with Christ-followers:

And have you forgotten the exhortation which addresses you as sons?— "My son, do not regard lightly the discipline of the Lord, nor lose courage when you are punished by Him. For the Lord disciplines him whom He loves, and chastises every son whom He receives."

The writer of Hebrews considers the statement about God's discipline an "encouragement." The Greek term indicates it is an exhortation that brings solace, comfort. We are under the Lord's discipline—and, it is a good thing.

Serious Training

"Discipline" translates the Greek word, "*paideia*" (pahee-di'-ah), the same term used for the human father's training efforts in raising his child in Ephesians 6:4. "*Paideia*" is a tutorage that covers the whole training and education of children, cultivating mind and morals. It uses commands, warnings, reproof, and punishment. For children, it would also include care and training of the body.

Applied to adults, *paideia* focuses on the cultivation of the soul, and aims at increasing one's virtue, especially through the correcting of mistakes and reining in of passions. It can be used in the sense of chastisement. It is especially used of the difficulties God brings on people for their betterment (see *Thayer's Greek Lexicon*).

Paideia represents God's training program for us, His corrective instruction. It is similar to the OT *muwcar*. As part of His training program, God will "rebuke" us. The Greek word translated "rebuke" indicates that God will *reprimand* us *severely*, hold us *accountable* (not let us squirm out of things), and *punish* us if needed. Even further, God will punish His children quite painfully, if necessary. The Greek word translated "punish" is literally *flog* and can be used in a literal or figurative sense. Our culture is shocked at the idea of painful punishment, but God, who created human beings and knows them intimately, understands how to get their attention and redirect them.

Taking It Seriously

Faced with God's corrective training program, or amid one of its challenges, we need to avoid two major errors:
1. Blowing it off. We could disdain the stuff we have to deal with and feel that we are worthy of much better treatment. We could treat it as if we care very little for it. Such "making light" is mockery and draws severe consequences (Pro 3:35).
2. Caving in. The Greek indicates we could "go slack." We could lose heart and collapse into self-pity and hopelessness. Caving in only results in the heat being turned up.

Caving in can especially occur when we suddenly discover that God is very serious about our training and is not going to let us off the hook when we have messed up. Instead, He is going to severely reprimand, hold us accountable, and punish us.

If we collapse into a hopeless heap, giving up on trying to do what God wants, the Father still will not relent. He knows exactly what we can and can't take. And He knows exactly what we need. The Father will view our "fainting" as a sign we need to be further toughened. He will not quit the training, but will "turn up the heat." God essentially said to Jeremiah, who was complaining about his difficulties, "You haven't seen anything yet!"

"If you have raced with men on foot and they have worn you out, how can you compete with horses? If you stumble in safe country, how will you manage in the thickets by the Jordan? (Jer 12:5 NIV)

Instead of making light, we need to take seriously God's training assignment, no matter how humbling it is. Instead of caving in, and perhaps earning a flogging, we need to step up to the challenge God has given us and bear responsibility like a genuine adult.

Again, the reason for the training program is that we are God's kids, and He is pleased with us. The Greek indicates He is so pleased with us that He brings us close to Him. He is like a father, who when he sees his children, kneels and his hands go out for his kids to run to him. God delights in us and wants us close to Him. And, God loves us and knows we desperately need to be trained out of our "upside-down" viewpoints and ways of handling life if we are going to enjoy this life and the next. He is committed to us and will not quit.

Endurance Training

It is for discipline (padeia) that you have to endure (hupomeno). God is treating you as sons; for what son is there whom his father does not discipline? If you are left without discipline, in which all have participated, then you are illegitimate children and not sons.

God's training program (*padeia*) requires that we have to endure under difficulties. The purpose in the endurance is the training impact.

"Endure" translates a Greek verb "*hupomeno*" (hoop-om-en'-o) meaning "to stay under," implying to bear up under difficulty and not abandon our post, to bear misfortune, trials, and ill-treatment bravely and calmly while hanging on to our faith. Difficult times and situations come upon us, and we have to bravely and calmly stay under them, hanging on to our faith and resisting the temptation to cave in or to run away screaming.

We are not unique in having to endure (bear up under) difficult things. This verb, *hupomeno*, describes what Jesus did with the cross: "He endured (calmly and bravely bore up under) the cross, despising the shame" (Heb 12:3). He also endured (stayed under) incredible opposition from sinners—and we need to focus on His example so that we do not lose heart when we have to "bear up under" (Heb 12:3). Indeed, the greatest of Christian virtues, love, endures (calmly and bravely bears up under) *all* things (1 Cor 13:7). Paul, the first century church starter, endured (calmly and bravely bore up under) all things for the sake of God's people (2 Tim 2:10).

So, Christ-followers are to be patient (calmly and bravely bear up under) in affliction (pressure against us) (Rom 12:12). As a matter of fact, one "endurance test" goes on throughout our lives: we have to "calmly and bravely bear up under" temptation. When we finish that endurance (that is, when we go home to be with Jesus) we will get the crown of life (Jas 1:12). Throughout the journey of life, if we endure (calmly and bravely bear up under) with Christ, we will reign with Him (2 Tim 2:12). This side of heaven, those who endure (calmly and bravely bear up under) difficulty will find the compassion and mercy of the Lord at the ends of the testing times—just as Job was incredibly blessed at the end of his endurance (Jas 5:11; Job 42:10-17).

While our having to "bear up under" difficult things is not easy, it is not extraordinary. In having to learn to endure (calmly and bravely bear up under), we are just following the same "training track" as the Apostle Paul, and before him, the Lord Jesus—and the same track as the Christ-followers of the New Testament (NT).

This cheerful, hopeful, steadfastness turns out to be the key to Christian maturity. "*Hupomone*" (hoop-om-on-ay') is a Greek noun related to *hupomeno*, the verb translated "endure." *Hupomone*, "staying under power," is translated "patience" or "perseverance." In the NT, it is the characteristic of a person who has not deviated from his chosen purpose, his trust in Christ, and commitment to a holy walk even though he has gone through the greatest trials and sufferings.

James encourages us to rejoice when problems come. Why rejoice? James says that when we have to go through trials that challenge our faith, we develop "perseverance" (*hupomone*). Extended *hupomone* generates full Christian maturity. In time, it produces a full and rich Christian character (Jas 1:2-4).

Paul agrees. He writes that we rejoice under various "pressures." The Greek word can mean oppression, affliction, difficulties, distress, or tight situations. The pressures produce in us perseverance (*hupomone*), and over time, *hupomone* produces "tested and tried character," that is, godly character that has set deeply into us.

Further, that kind of character produces hope, a confident, expectant outlook on life, knowing the certainty of the goodness of God and of our ultimate salvation (Rom 5:3-5). Our society yearns to be able to create such a positive, joyful outlook. It comes, not to those who go through inspirational seminars, but to those in God's endurance training program.

Because of "*paideia*," God's corrective training program, we have to endure different kinds of pressures calmly, bravely, bearing up under them. The pressures may be financial, relational, family-related, job-related, ministry-related, health-related, or related to other issues. Over time, the "endurance training" has effect. The character of Christ sets deeply in us and shapes in us a joyful, confident outlook on life.

Family-Only Training

Our experience of God's corrective training program is actually intended to give us confidence that we really belong to God. Only those who have the Holy Spirit inside them experience the conflict of the Spirit against their old way of living (Gal 5:17). Those without the Holy Spirit, those who are not Christ-followers, may occasionally have twinges of conscience. But they do not have the horrendous internal warfare between the desire for the things of God and the desire for the old life. They simply have the old life. Though the internal spiritual struggle is tough for Christ-followers, in a way it is encouraging. It marks us as a child of God.

In a similar manner, only the children of God go through God's training program. It is difficult to have to bear up under the hard things again and again. As the writer of Psalm 73 did, we sometimes we begin to look around and realize that the wicked don't have to go through all the stuff that we do. They seem to do so well!

...I envied the arrogant when I saw the prosperity of the wicked. They have no struggles; their bodies are healthy and strong. They are free from the burdens common to man; they are not plagued by human ills ..This is what the wicked are like—always carefree, they increase in wealth. (Ps 73:3-5, 12 NIV)

When we look at our own lives in comparison to the ease the wicked have, we appear to have been cheated. Like the psalmist, we try so hard to keep our hearts pure and to do what Christ wants in word and deed. And what do we get for it? We just get more troubles and more correction every morning! In our self-pity we begin to feel like noble martyrs. It certainly seems like God is unfair:

Surely in vain have I kept my heart pure; in vain have I washed my hands in innocence. All day long I have been plagued; I have been punished (towkechah) every morning. (Ps 73:13-14 NIV)

The psalmist finally gets perspective on things (you can read how in the rest of the psalm), and decides that he really is better off with God.

God's training program is sometimes extremely hard for us—and, those who are not Christ-followers seem to have it so easy! But let time go on, and see who really prospers in life. Once I heard it said, "If you think the wages are poor in the kingdom of God, look on the other side of the fence. They have Hell to pay over there!"

The struggle may be difficult at times, but in one way, the struggle is encouraging. It marks us as children of the Father. Like any father with sense, He disciplines only His *own* children. That we undergo the endurance training means that we belong to Him. If our life has been one of ease without discipline and correction, we need to check our spiritual birth certificate and *see if God really is our father*! God *always* trains His kids.

Not Unusual

Besides this, we have had earthly fathers to discipline us and we respected them. Shall we not much more be subject to the Father of spirits and live? For they disciplined us for a short time at their pleasure, but He disciplines us for our good, that we may share His holiness.

Actually, grasping what is going on with God's training program is not that difficult. We have previously experienced something similar. Earthly fathers train their children *as* they see fit and *when* they see fit. If you were raised by a dad, you know that the parent sets the training content and the training timetable; the child doesn't. Likewise, our heavenly Father has us in a training program, one that He sets; we don't get to choose it.

God's goal in the training may be different from our earthly father's however. Sometimes parents tend to discipline us in order to make their own lives less difficult and at their pleasure. God disciplines us, not for His convenience but for *our* good, that we may share in His holiness. He intends that our lives become *distinctly different* from the world's and distinctly like His. He wants to see a tested and tried, holy life set deep into us. As that kind of life grows deep in us, we have the possibility of really succeeding and enjoying life in a world run by a Holy God and in an eternity ruled by Him.

God wants to develop in us wisdom's understanding. He wants us to know directly what holiness is by participating in it. That will let us succeed in life, for the knowledge of the holy *is* understanding (Pro 9:10 KJV). As our lives grow toward holiness, our joy in life will increase and our grasp and understanding of life is vastly expanded.

Training Results

For the moment all discipline seems painful rather than pleasant; later it yields the peaceful fruit of righteousness to those who have been trained by it. Therefore lift your drooping hands and strengthen your weak knees, (Heb 12:5-12 RSV)

There is no way to get around it. God's training program seems painful, not pleasant, while it is in progress. Later on, however, as we have learned to think, value and perform in the ways God desires, there is a tremendous result. We acquire peace and righteousness. Our lives take on the character of Jesus Christ, becoming more and more righteous like Him in practical ways. And the result is peace—peace in our hearts, peace with God, and peace with people.

When a man's ways are pleasing to the LORD, He makes even his enemies live at peace with him. (Pro 16:7 NIV)

How wonderful when one's heart moves toward the right things, and one is surrounded and invaded by peace!

So, knowing the good end results over time, we need to get with the program! Like an athlete getting into the athletic stance, we need to change our posture from tired, droopy resignation on the edge of "wimping out" to a posture ready to go with God—arms, hands and knees poised and ready for the next tasks in the training.

We need to change our attitude about what is going on. The training is not done to hurt us; it is done to bless us! And, when we face difficulties, we face, not the random happenstances of the universe, but a set of circumstances that will enable us to develop our endurance. They are part of an intelligent training program developed by our father who is pleased with us. And, it is specially designed to fit us.

Over time the training program will wean us off the old, upside-down way of looking at life, and the selfish, arrogant, hurtful approach we developed to get what we wanted. With a new set of attitudes and a new way of relating to God, people, and life, we are going to find an increasingly positive outlook on life. And, we will be set to enjoy and utilize our time on this planet in a way that will bless ourselves and others for eternity! So, get with the program!

The last book of the Bible speaks of the same training process: those whom God loves, He rebukes (severely reprimands) and disciplines (puts through His corrective training program). Therefore, God urges us to "be earnest" and "repent." The Greek words indicate we need to get motivated and revise our opinions and viewpoints to match God's (Rev 3:19).

THE DISCIPLINE PROCESS

God rebukes and disciplines men for their sins (Ps 39:11). God's discipline creates *distress* (Isa 26:16) as God refuses to let us succeed or brings trouble upon us.

In a sense, we are always needing discipline. Our obedience to God is *relative*, not absolute. If we are "obedient," it is in comparison with our past disobedience or the disobedience of others. Our level of obedience to the Father is not the same as that of our older brother, Jesus Christ. His obedience was perfect (Heb 4:15). Ours is not quite so.

In this life we will not obey the Lord perfectly. The best among us will be less selfish than others, but until the day we die, we will still deal with pride, arrogance and self-justification of our actions that hurt others (Ecc 9:3).

Job realized this as he tried to sort out why suffering had come upon him. Job comments that human beings are born impure and do not produce purity alone (Job 14:3-4, Living Bible); they produce mixed deeds. In Job's case, he knew that he was not "sinless," but he was confident he had "kept short accounts" with God—that there had been no outstanding sin for which he had not confessed and sacrificed. So, Job couldn't figure out why he was suffering. We will look at his suffering later.

Even though we who follow Christ have been given the Holy Spirit, we still do wrong. By walking in the Spirit the deeds of the flesh are withered, and the new life in Christ asserts itself (Gal 5:16-23). Yet, our walk in the Spirit is imperfect. So, the Apostle Paul says of himself that, though he is aware of nothing against himself, he may not be without fault (1 Cor 4:4).

Crossing The Line

In a sense, God *could* stay on our backs all the time. But, He does not treat us with constant, unrelenting correction. When we go too far in disobedience, however, there comes a point at which the hand of God begins to move in discipline, a point beyond which we are definitely going to experience correction and punishment.

One such point is when we begin to flirt with other religions and participate in their worship; we can arouse God's jealousy and bring His anger on ourselves (1 Cor 10:21-22). The history of Israel provides cogent instruction on the actions that draw serious correction from God (1 Cor 10:6,11): idolatry, revelry, sexual immorality, and testing the Lord (1 Cor 10:1-11).

When we have "crossed the line," God will not let us get away with our disobedience. The discipline of the Lord *will* arrive. He will not let us go entirely unpunished (Jer 30:10-11). God disciplines us so that we will not be condemned along with the rest of the world (1 Cor 11:32).

We can, however, count on the Lord's discipline to be *just.* God corrects justly—that is, He corrects in a *manner* that is just, and corrects to the *extent* that is just. Were He to justly release His anger, we would be decimated. So, in the Scriptures, there is a prayer for God to not discipline in anger. When we have really pushed the limits with God, it is a good idea to pray for God's mercy in the discipline that comes (Jer 10:24, NIV).

Correct me, LORD, but only with justice— not in your anger, lest you reduce me to nothing. (Jer 10:24 NIV)

Straying, Affliction, Learning, Obedience

The discipline process is fairly straightforward. Three verses in Psalm 119 capture the essence of it:

Before I was afflicted I went astray, but now I obey your word. (v. 67 NIV)

It was good for me to be afflicted so that I might learn your decrees. (v. 71, NIV)

I know, O LORD, that your laws are righteous, and in faithfulness you have afflicted me. (v. 75 NIV)

We go astray, walking away from God's path, seeking out what our eyes and passions want. Then God, because He is faithful to us, *afflicts* us. This term in Ps 119:67 implies pushing us down; He "depresses" us. He brings the things to pass that "lower" us. What God does, what He brings to pass, hurts us. In the imagery of Scripture, God injures and wounds us (Job 5:18). When the pain gets bad enough, we repent; we turn to God and obey His Word (Ps 119:67). For an example of the wrenching emotional state that a person can reach until they begin repentance, see Ps 32, 38, 39, and

51. Then God binds up the wounds and heals them (Job 5:18). Note that the image of the doctored wound and healing implies the *passage of time.* When God must *severely* correct, it may take some time for the pain to go away, even after we turn back to God.

As God disciplines us, He is teaching us from His law (Pro 14:12). What we may have heard about in sermons or seen as we read the Bible, we now know is indeed true in real life, because we have *experienced* it. In the terms we used in an earlier chapter, we realize that *what God says* is not merely TRUE, it is REAL!

After the discipline is over, we realize that the trouble that came to us was actually good for us, because it resulted in us learning God's Word (Ps 119:71). God's correction brings an ability to see life more clearly, a change in our ways, and greater success in doing things God's way (wisdom). So, blessing comes to us through God's discipline (Ps 94:12). So, we should not "despise" it (the Hebrew term in Job 5:17 implies not only despise but also refuse).

Interestingly, even amid the LORD's punishment of us, God still *yearns* for us, delights in us, and has compassion for us (Jer 31:18-20).

WHAT DOES GOD USE TO CORRECT US?

Rather than speaking directly to us, God brings events to pass to correct us. The following is not a comprehensive list of God's means of correction, but it will help you get a grasp of major channels God does use. For a more extensive look at God correcting us through circumstances, you may want to read *Reading God's Lips: Understanding God's Silent Messages* by the author.

- **The Disappearance Of What Is Dear To Us**

When thou dost chasten man with rebukes for sin, thou dost consume like a moth what is dear to him... (Ps 39:11 RSV)

One way that God rebukes us is to consume what is dear to us. Like moths consume garments, God consumes the dear thing (Ps 39:11; see v. 7-13). The NIV has "consume their wealth" and the KJV "consume their beauty," but the Hebrew word means literally "to delight in." When we get into sin and persist, we draw the rebuke and discipline of God. To correct us, He "eats up" the thing that we delight in: money, a particular possession, reputation, fame, career, position, privilege—even family. For a sobering account of the latter, read Sheldon van Auken's *A Severe Mercy*.

- **Deprivation**

Sometimes God removes the dear thing we enjoy (see above). At other times wonderful things never even get to us. Our wrongdoing results in being deprived of good things (Jer 5:34-35).

"You expected much, but see, it turned out to be little. What you brought home, I blew away. Why?" declares the LORD Almighty. "Because of my house, which remains a ruin, while each of you is busy with his own house. Therefore, because of you the heavens have withheld their dew and the earth its crops. I called for a drought on the fields and the mountains, on the grain, the new wine, the oil and whatever the ground produces, on men and cattle, and on the labor of your hands." (Hag 1:10-11 NIV)

In the normal course of affairs, God grants to everyone "seed time and harvest" (Gen 8:22). He grows the crops of the earth to feed us, and lets us earn money with which we can buy food (Ps 104:14-15, 23; Acts 14:17).

When we start putting God's priorities last and ours first—financially or otherwise—things change. God will cause a drought of rain, crops and cattle (wealth), childbearing, and on the effectiveness of our work at our jobs.

Refusal to give financially as God says to, will result in destruction of one's efforts to make money, as "the devourer" destroys part and a curse of unfruitfulness destroys the rest (Mal 3:11).

Repentance means an end to the devourer and to unfruitfulness. When my wife and I realize we are in a sequence of "devouring" (the car tears up, the fridge dies, another appliance has to be repaired, and a child has to make a second trip to the doctor—all eating up money), we have learned to quickly check our giving records to make sure we are keeping God's financial priorities.

- **The Rod Of Men: Severe Pain And Difficulty Caused By Others**

I will be his father, and he will be my son. When he does wrong, I will punish (yakach) him with the rod of men, with floggings inflicted by men. (2 Sam 7:14 NIV)

God promised King David that Solomon, David's heir, would be treated as a son by the LORD. When Solomon did wrong, God would use the "rod of men" to punish Solomon. As a human father might use a switch upon a rebellious son, God would use painful things (literally "blows"), damage done by people to correct (Heb: yakach—put straight, the verb basis for *towkechah*) Solomon.

God brought this to pass as Solomon let his wives turn his heart from God. God raised up against Solomon three adversaries who were a constant source of hassle to him as they chipped away at his kingdom: Hadad the Edomite, Rezon, and Jeroboam (1 King 11:14, 23-26). The LORD did similarly with Jotham, king of Judah (2 Kings 15:37).

- **Severe, Life-Threatening Attacks**

All the nations surrounded me, but in the name of the LORD I cut them off...I was pushed back and about to fall, but the LORD helped me...I will not die but live, and will proclaim what the LORD has done. The LORD has chastened (yacar) me severely (yacar), but He has not given me over to death. (Ps 118:10, 13, 17-18 NIV)

God may chasten by allowing an attack from others bent on our destruction. But, He does not let them kill us. Ultimately, we overcome them. But the experience is severe enough that the writer of the psalm describes it by using "yacar" twice. "Yacar" means to chasten with words or blows. It is the verb basis for *muwcar*, the valuable corrective instruction. The writer says, in effect, that the experience was "double yacar" or a "yacar of yacars." It was an intense correction in God's training program.

- **Loss Of Sanity**

At the end of that time, I, Nebuchadnezzar, raised my eyes toward heaven, and my sanity was restored. Then I praised the Most High...(Dan 4:34 NIV)

Nebuchadnezzar, the most powerful king of the earth in his time, had been warned to turn away from his sins or God would remove his sanity. He did not. One day, he gloated over his accomplishments, giving himself entire credit for all that he had done. God intervened and removed his sanity from him for an extended time. He acted like an animal, ate grass like a cow, and lived outside until God restored his sanity (Dan 4:29-34).

- **Sickness**

Some became fools through their rebellious ways and suffered affliction because of their iniquities. They loathed all food and drew near the gates of death. Then they cried to the LORD in their trouble, and He saved them from their distress. He sent forth His word and healed them; He rescued them from the grave. (Ps 107:17-20 NIV)

Sometimes the affliction that comes to us is sickness. In the verses above, it is a deadly sickness. Some sins tend to bring sickness with them, as envy, which "rots the bones" (Pro 14:30). When Miriam began to undermine Moses' leadership, the LORD sent leprosy on her (Num 12:10-15). Failure to take the Lord's Supper seriously resulted in people being sick and some even dying (1 Cor 11:30).

- **Consequences**

Our actions have consequences to them. There is no escaping the fact. Many people think they can make certain choices and then negotiate whether or not they will receive the consequences of the actions. But, the consequences are not negotiable. They come anyway.

The laws of harvest operate. Wheat sowed produces a *wheat* harvest—not oats and not weeds. Weeds sowed produce weeds, not wheat. Little (few seed) sowed produces little harvest; much sowed produces great harvest. Wind (empty, worthless, sinful acts) sowed produces similar but overwhelming, consuming, destructive things (whirlwinds, tornados) (Hos 8:7).

The invisible choices we make in our hearts lead to actions (words and deeds) in the visible world (Pro 4:23; Matt 15:19-20). Good choices lead to good words and deeds. Foolish choices in heart lead to foolish words and foolish deeds. And, foolish words and deeds lead to *consequences* (Pro 18:6-7, Jer 5:25).

For example, adultery risks disease, extortion, revenge, public dishonor, and death—frequently consequences for those caught in its trap (Pro 5:8-14; 7:21-22). Immorality among believers causes God to discipline severely (1 Thes 4:2-8). Laziness leads to terrible jobs and poverty (Pro 10:4; 12:24). Being a general pain to one's family over the years leads to the loss of inheritance (Pro 11:29). Developing a hot temper leads one into all kinds of trouble (Pro 29:22; 22:24-25; 14:17). A person who stubbornly resists correction will ultimately come to a circumstance that "breaks" him beyond repair, one that leaves him in some way permanently disabled or dead (Pro 29:1).

Those who genuinely repent and seek God's forgiveness will find it—but they may still deal with consequences. So, David repented of his betrayal of a loyal friend through adultery with the friend's wife, and then the murder of the loyal man. God forgave David, but the sin caused the death of one child and brought a curse of bloodshed on David's descendants (Pro 17:13; 2 Sam 9:12-23). The curse resulted in the killing of some of David's immediate sons (2 Sam 13:28-29; 18:14-15; 1 Kings 2:23-25). The curse went on through succeeding generations, ultimately being borne by the Christ, Himself the descendant of David.

God will be kind to the repentant, as He was to David, granting another son to him by his ill-gotten wife, and blessing that son incredibly (2 Sam 12:24-25; 2 Chr 9:22-23)—but the curse still remained. For those who love God and are willing to serve His purposes, God will even bring blessing out of the consequences (Rom 8:28), though one would still wish the consequences to have never been. God did this, even out of the curse on David's family, when Jesus Christ, the Son of David, was unjustly killed, and out of His death and resurrection came the salvation of mankind. Yet, as wonderful as the salvation is, before the blessing arrived, great grief came through the curse David caused.

When people violate the will of God, sometimes consequences come in to their lives that must be dealt with for years, even if they repent. Children born out of wedlock must be raised to adulthood. While Christ can help with the pain, grief over aborted children remains a life-time. Deaths caused by a drunken driver do not go away because the driver subsequently finds Christ. A felon in prison does not immediately get out of prison because he became a Christian.

Lies undermine trust in relationships—and trust, once gone, will not return quickly. If the liar subsequently finds Christ, it is still likely to take years of "faithfulness" to the one betrayed in order to see trust return (Pro 16:6).

Manipulation results in abiding hatred for the manipulator (Pro 14:17). If the manipulator finds Christ and stops manipulating people, it may take years before he is trusted or liked again.

Leadership ultimately functions off the respect people have for the leader. Unfaithfulness and partiality (unfairly playing favorites) undermine the respect of one's followers, and therefore, one's leadership (Pro 20:28; 29:14). A repentant leader will have to spend years earning back the trust and respect he once enjoyed. His leadership will not be returned quickly.

Failure to train and discipline a child properly as it grows up will result in later years of parental depression and grief (Pro 17:21-25). One can pray and work for the adult child's conversion, but there is simply going to be a certain amount of grief and pain.

There are also *good* consequences. Doing the right things over time brings good results over time. Those who raise a wise child can anticipate later years of delight (Pro 23:24). Those who are generous keep being refreshed again and again (Pro 11:25). The diligent do rise to prosper and lead (Pro 10:4; 12:24). Those who plan good keep on finding love and faithfulness from God and others (Pro 14:22).

God operates life such that, when we violate His will, we will likely suffer consequences. Since God is merciful, severe consequences often do not arise immediately upon our rebellion. Since He does not immediately squash us upon our rebellion, we tend to take God's kindness as indication that God is not paying attention to our acts. Therefore, we think we can "get away with it" again (Ecc 8:11). We persist, and the day comes when severe consequences arrive. At that point, we often blame God for being unfair to us, but it is really our own folly that has ruined our lives (see Pro 19:3). When we repeatedly flaunt God's ways, severe discipline will finally arrive.

An old expression I heard as a child said, "The chickens will come home to roost." The idea carried in the expression was that, sooner or later, consequences will come—it is merely a matter of time.

When consequences do arrive, we need to handle them responsibly, lest even worse consequences come (Amos 5:19). And, we need to learn wisdom from them. In the mercy of God, ashes may one day be able to be exchanged for beauty, and mourning for joy (Isa 61:1-3).

- **Loss Of Life**

There is a point at which people have resisted the LORD for the final time. Jesus illustrated this in the story of the selfish rich man (Luke 12:16-21). Herod, regional king in the early church times, finally took his arrogance too far, was cut down by an angel of the Lord, and died of worms (Acts 12:21-23). A believer in Christ who treats the Lord's Supper lightly may also lose his life (1 Cor 11:26-32, see especially *The Living Bible*). Those who are disciplined by the church may have their "flesh destroyed" by the enemy that their soul may be saved (1 Cor 5:5). Some see this as a reference to the destruction of the fleshly tendencies, but even that destruction only occurs at death.

When we are rebuked (severely reprimanded) by the Lord, we need to heed His correction. He rebukes because He loves us. We need to heed and learn from the reproof.

DIFFICULTIES THAT DEEPEN

Not all difficulties in the training program of God come in order to correct or punish us. Many times, they arrive for other reasons, such as the development of mature Christian character. The endurance training done by the Father also results in:

- **Deeper Experience With God**

Sometimes difficulty comes, not to correct or punish, but to take us to new depths of experience with God. Paul describes a desperate situation in 2 Corinthians 1:8-11. He says that the purpose in it was to take him and his team to a new level of trust in God.

Indeed, in our hearts we felt the sentence of death. But this happened that we might not rely on ourselves but on God, who raises the dead. (2 Cor 1:9 NIV)

Job went through a similar circumstance. Unaware of the heavenly dimension of his suffering, he was left with its unexplained mystery until he encountered God directly and knew Him in a deeper way than he would have otherwise (Job 42:5-6).

Though God possesses all knowledge, there was a sense in which even the Lord Jesus learned to follow the Father through the painful things that came His way (Heb 5:8). As intimate as His relationship with the Father had always been, a deepening occurs through the practical living out of the Son's submission amid painful things.

It was this deeper walk with Christ that came from Paul's continued endurance of his "thorn in the flesh." Through the difficulty, he knew experientially the power of God through weakness (2 Cor 12:9-10).

- **Privilege Of Suffering With Christ**

The sufferings of the Lord Jesus are not over. All that was needed for our justification was completed on the cross. But His sufferings in the world go on as His people suffer. As Saul was persecuting the church, he was actually persecuting Christ (Acts 9:5).

After his conversion, Saul, now named Paul, was keenly aware of the Lord's suffering through His people. He recognized that he had been given the privilege of participating in the Lord's sufferings (2 Cor 1:5). Indeed, to Paul's way of thinking, by what happened to him, he was getting the opportunity to make up some of the sufferings Christ was still doing in the world (Col 1:24), especially as he suffered so that others could benefit. So, Paul said he endured everything for the sake of the elect, the people of God, so that they could obtain the salvation God intends (2 Tim 2:10). We also get to participate in Christ's sufferings (1 Pet 1:4), especially as we are persecuted.

- **Ability To Minister To Others**

Paul mentions a second benefit of the difficult time that he had just come through in 2 Cor 1:5-8. Out of their difficulties, he and his team had cried out to God and had been comforted. Now they were able to help the Corinthian church amid its difficulties by sharing with them the comfort God had given.

If we are distressed, it is for your comfort and salvation; if we are comforted, it is for your comfort, which produces in you patient endurance of the same sufferings we suffer. (2 Cor 1:6 NIV)

- **Established Credibility**

Other times, God sends difficulties to toughen and train us. Later, at key moments in our lives and ministries, our endurance through those difficulties will help establish our credibility as a servant of God (see Paul's defense of his ministry by recounting his endurance of troubles in 2 Cor 11:23-12:12).

In the early 1980's I heard a renowned pastor who had suffered under the Communist regime in Russia say, "The KGB (Russian secret police) are God's agents to establish the authority of His pastors." He understood

Satan's intent to destroy through the KGB. But, he had personally experienced God's use of endured suffering to establish the credibility, respect, and leadership of legitimate pastors in his country.

- **Purer Hearts**

Trials also come into our lives to test our faith (1 Pet 1:6-7). It is this kind of challenge to our faith that we must bear up under in order to see mature Christian character take deep root in us (Jas 1:2-4; Rom 5:3-4).

- **Developed Capacities**

God uses difficulties and challenges to develop our abilities, and prepare us for the work He wants us to do.

As the ancient people of Israel left Egypt, God did not take them by the short-cut to the Promised Land. He knew that they were not organized as a nation or skilled in battle and might cave in as they faced military foes. So, He took them on an extended desert camping and training trip (Ex 13:17-18). The inconveniences they faced were part of their preparation for their future. As Israel entered the Promised Land, the LORD said He would not drive all the nations there out quickly, for Israel could not handle the empty land. He would drive them out little by little—which meant an extended time of war for Israel. During the extended war, Israel would grow strong enough to handle the land.

When David, the greatest king of Israel, was a shepherd boy, he defended his sheep, killing first a bear then a lion. David's next challenge was a giant, Goliath. Then, he became a military leader. Next, he became a fugitive, building a guerilla army for six years or so, living on the run. Then, at age 23, he became king over part of Israel. At 30, he became king over all Israel. His difficulties challenged and developed his leadership skills, and also challenged and developed his faith. God used the challenges to prepare him step-by-step for the work God had for him.

He chose David His servant and took him from the sheep pens; from tending the sheep He brought him to be the shepherd of His people Jacob, of Israel His inheritance. And David shepherded them with integrity of heart; with skillful hands he led them. (Ps 78:70-72 NIV)

- **Honor To God**

Sometimes our difficulties arrive to bring honor to God. For example, Peter was told of the kind of death (execution) by which he would honor God (John 21:18-19).

Until that honor to God arrives, we may be clueless as to the reason for our extended troubles. Thus, a man was born blind and stayed that way more than forty years, living as a beggar. His blindness was not due to his sin or his parents, but had been sent by God in order that it may be healed by Jesus and bring glory to God. Until the healing occurred, the man had no clues as to the reason for his difficulties (John 9:2-3).

So, Job also suffered unaware of the heavenly struggle by Satan to impugn the worthiness of God (Job 1&2). When the struggle was over, Job was blessed twice over by God (Job 42:10). And, Job had learned far more deeply *of* God (Job 42:5-6).

When we are amid difficulties and do not know why, we do well to remember Job's words: "Shall we accept good from God and not trouble?" (Job 2:10).

HUMILITY AGAIN

Remember the Biblical statements: "The corrections of *muwcar* are the way to life" and "*muwcar is* your life?" Since correction plays such a role in the acquisition of wisdom, one can understand more deeply why humility is a prerequisite to wisdom. Humility deals with the heart's native arrogance, paving the way for the heart, not only to listen to *muwcar*, but also to *apply* itself to *muwcar* (Pro 23:12) and to find the treasures that come with the end product of *muwcar*: wisdom (Pro 11:2; 15:33; 18:12; 22:4).

Thus, in the church, even today, humility remains extremely important. It is the stuff in which we package our service to the Lord (Acts 20:19), our approach to our fellow Christ-followers (Phil 2:3-4), our approach to our leaders and to our followers (1 Pet 5:5), and indeed, our approach to everyone (Titus 3:2). Humility is to be the spirit that permeates our deeds in this world (Jas 3:13), indicating our wisdom and the change of life that the Lord Jesus brings (Col 3:12).

Those who make it to the staging grounds of humility may embark on the great expedition into wisdom. Those who never make it to humility will never endure *muwcar*. They simply miss the boat.

SUMMARY

There are many happy parts to God's training, such as delightful insights from His Word, fellowship with His people, and comfort and encouragement from the Holy Spirit. We need to realize, however, that God is also using the flow of daily life to correct and grow us. And, contrary to much popular opinion, God *does* use difficulty to do it. So, when the tough times come, we should not lose heart.

And we know that all things work together for good to those who love God, to those who are the called according to His purpose. (Rom 8:28-29 NKJ)

Think About It

Can you identify any "tough times" that are part of God's training program for you right now? What may He be trying to teach you through them?

DOES LEARNING WISDOM HAVE ANYTHING
TO DO WITH CHURCH LIFE?
IF SO, HOW DO THE TWO FIT TOGETHER?
THAT'S COMING UP!

Chapter 14

LEARNING WISDOM IN CHURCH

Instruction, Correction And Church Life

Those who have become Christ-followers have set out on the course of wisdom. As they decided to submit to Jesus Christ as their Lord, they entered the "fear of the LORD," for Jesus Christ, the Lord of the New Testament (NT) is the Alpha and Omega, the LORD of the Old Testament (OT) (compare Isa 41:4; 44:6; 48:12; Rev 1:17-18; 2:8; 21:6; 22:13). The wise are those who seek to put the teachings of Jesus into practice (Matt 7:24). The foolish are those who are aware of Jesus' teachings but do not put them into practice (Matt 7:26).

In the OT, when people decided to humble themselves and began to live in the fear of the LORD, the realm of Wisdom opened up to them (Pro 11:2; 9:10). In the NT, those who yield their lives to Christ, that is, submit to Him, receive the Holy Spirit who has the resources to grant them wisdom. The wisdom granted by the Holy Spirit is not an end in itself, but is given so that the people of God may really know God and do what is pleasing to Him. So, Paul prays that God will grant to the Ephesians wisdom and revelation through the Holy Spirit in order that they may know God better (Eph 1:17). Similarly, Paul prays for the Colossian Christians that God would grant them all spiritual wisdom and understanding so that they might know God's will. Knowing God's will and being strengthened by God's strength, they could live a life worthy of the Lord, please Him in every way, and produce the things God really wanted (fruit): good deeds and a growing knowledge, not just *about,* but *of*, God (Col 1:9-12).

As the pursuit of the Wisdom of God produced a godly and self-controlled person characterized by the profile of the Wise in the OT, so the pursuit of Jesus Christ in the NT produces a godly, self-controlled person (Titus 2:11-14) characterized by the same kind of earmarks, the "fruit of the Spirit" (Gal 5:22-23).

As the wise of the OT rooted themselves deeply in God's Word, so believers in Christ are to "let the word of God dwell in them richly," to have a deep, rich, and copious grasp of the Scriptures (Col 3:16).

The wisdom seekers of the OT gathered, often at the town gates, for discussions and learning from one another (Pro 18:15; 1:5; 24:7) in line with God's Word. Fools missed the point of such discussions, thinking they occurred in order to allow the fools to air their opinions rather than acquire *tabuwn* (Pro 18:2). It was common for the wise to graciously, not rudely or harshly, correct one another (Pro 12:18; 13:14; 15:31). For that reason, mockers stayed away from the wise (Pro 15:12). Among the wise, however, even the mildest correction was heeded (Pro 15:12; 9:8-9; 13:1; 15:5; see Ps 141:5). And, it was deeply appreciated, for the wise understood that correction allowed one to succeed (Pro 12:1; 13:18; 15:5, 32; 29:15). Thus, the one who had corrected them did so out of concern for the one they corrected (Pro 25:12). In essence, the one who corrected them had "spoken the truth in love."

As among the fellowship of the wisdom seekers in the OT, so the wisdom seekers of the NT, the Christ-followers, the members of the church, have an individual relationship to the Lord, but a "corporate assignment." They are not to neglect gathering together regularly for mutual encouragement in doing good (Heb 10:24-25). They are to teach one another and "admonish" one another (Col 3:16). Teaching brings new ideas and insight into the ways of God. The full spiritual development of God's people, however, requires more than ideas and insights. It also requires that they admonish one another. Through wise teaching and admonishing, people become mature in Christ; they reach maturity in Him (Col 1:28).

The NT Greek word translated "admonish" is "*noutheteo*" (noo-thet-eh'-o), meaning literally "to put in mind" and implying to caution or gently reprove (*Strong's Greek & Hebrew Dictionary*). If someone is forgetting something or inadvertently crossing a boundary, one "puts in their mind" the thing they are forgetting or neglecting.

"*Noutheteo*" is much like the Hebrew "*towkechah*," the OT correction. It contains the implication of encouragement, motivation and correction. The thought in Colossians 3:16 is that believers should fill their hearts and minds copiously with the Word of God, and then, instruct and *encouragingly* and *motivationally correct* one another "with all wisdom," that is, in line with God's way of doing things.

The "teaching and admonishing" imply that, as with the wise in the OT, the members of the church are not just teaching one another, but also *learning* from each other. They are not *just* correcting one another, they are also *giving heed and appreciating the correction* given. It is by this mutual willingness to give and receive scriptural correction that each one is kept from being deceived and entrapped by sin (Heb 3:12-13). So, the whole group, the church, is able to strengthen itself and grow as it "speaks the truth in love" (Eph 4:15). Those who become offended at such instruction and correction are foolish and will suffer the fate of the mocker (Pro 9:12; 1 Tim 1:18-20).

Among the wise in the OT, some had greater wisdom, and were highly regarded and sought by others for the wisdom they could impart (Pro 1:5; 1 Kings 4:31). So, also, in the "fellowship of wisdom seekers" in the NT, the church, God grants to some people deeper understanding and greater wisdom, allowing them to probe deeper into the things of God.

Some are given a spiritual gift, a spiritual ability, in the arenas of knowledge and wisdom (1 Cor 12:8). They are to use their gift for the common good, benefiting other believers (Rom 12:7; 1 Pet 4:10-11).

Some have greater wisdom due to increasing spiritual maturity (1 Cor 2:6). That maturity comes as believers practice the Word of God, putting the teachings of the Lord into practice in different situations over time, training themselves by practice to distinguish good from evil (Heb 5:14). It could be, that having made the breakthrough into the realm of wisdom, some believers fail to seize the situational opportunities to practice the Word of God. If so, they fail to mature and can even backtrack, requiring someone to teach them all over again, starting with the simplest things (Heb 5:11-6:3).

Whether coming from a spiritual gift or from increasing maturity, genuine wisdom indicates its presence in the life of a person by his good deeds done in the humility that comes from wisdom, and in his choosing courses of action in line with the character and mind of God (Jas 3:13-17). God grants leadership and responsibility for *major* instruction and correction to certain persons in the church, the NT "fellowship of wisdom-seekers." Angered at the ungodly, self-centered spiritual and governmental leaders of the Old Testament (Isa 56:10-12; Jer 10:21; 50:6; Eze 34:2-10), God promised to come Himself to shepherd His people and to raise up shepherds who would genuinely care for them (Jer 3:15; 23:1-4; Eze 34:11-16; 22-24). Jesus identified Himself as the "good shepherd," in essence, identifying Himself as God come to take care of His sheep in fulfillment of the promise (John 10:11-14). He is "David" (the son of David) set up by God as chief shepherd (Eze 34:23) to whom all other shepherds are accountable (1 Pet 5:2-4), and the "prince" among God's people (Ex 34:24), the head of the church who rules over all (Eph 1:20-23).

As the wise followed the political and spiritual leaders of the people of God in the OT (Pro 24:21-22), so the "fellowship of wisdom seekers," the church follows the shepherds God has appointed now: political leaders (Rom 13:1-7; 1 Pet 2:1-17) and spiritual leaders (Heb 13:17). Indeed, in the church, believers are to make the task of leadership a joy for those who lead them.

Before these spiritual shepherds are appointed to office they are to have already demonstrated their godliness, skill in leading and faithfulness to the Word of God (1 Tim 1:1-7; Titus 1:5-9). They are to continue to set the example in Christian living (1 Tim 4:12; 1 Pet 5:3), in high integrity, and in respectability in their teaching (Titus 2:7-8). Like the wise in the OT, they are to speak and act with a gracious gentleness (1 Thes 2:7; 2 Tim 2:24-26), but they are to *aggressively* teach, encourage and rebuke people within the church with all authority (Titus 2:15).

The shepherds of the church have been assigned their work by the Lord (Acts 20:28). They are literally keeping watch over the souls of the flock members and will have to give account to the Lord for their work (Heb 13:17; 1 Pet 5:4). Their concern is for the welfare of the individual members of the church and for the health of the group as a whole. Their leadership is to be modeled after the pattern of Christ, leading by example, by serving, and out of concern for faithfulness to the Lord (1 Tim 4:12; Titus 2:7-8; 1 Pet 5:2-4)—but definitely leading.

The other members of the "NT fellowship of wisdom seekers," the church, are to learn from their shepherds' lives and teaching, and heed their correction (Heb 13:7; Titus 1:13-14, 2:1-8). They are to hold them in high regard and treat them with great respect (1 Thes 5:12-13), pay them quite well if they work hard (actually, *double* income 1 Tim 5:17-18 TLB), and voluntarily submit to them and obey them (Heb 13:17; 1 Cor 16:15-16). The Greek words used in Hebrews 13:17 for "obey" and "submit" indicate that believers are to "be easily persuaded, not a stubborn hardhead" (obey) and "yield if there is a conflict of opinions" (submit). Indeed, those who are "divisive" may split the church. "Divisive" translates the Greek word *hairetikos* (hahee-ret-ee-kos')—meaning someone who has chosen a stubborn divisive stand on minor issues. It is the root of the English word "heretic." After a couple of warnings, such divisive people are to be excluded from the church (Titus 3:9-11).

When "fierce wolves" (false teachers) attempt to invade and destroy the flock of God (the church), or divisive leaders arise from within it, these shepherds are to deal aggressively with the predators and the divisive (Acts 20:28-30).

Some who have decided to follow Christ, and thus, have entered into the fear of the Lord, may "set up camp" near the *beginning* of wisdom and make little progress in growing in the wisdom and knowledge of God. Some of these are "unruly." They have a rebellious streak, and quickly get out of line. Others are "fearful." Their fears and worries dog their steps and hinder their progress. Some are "weak." They have little strength against the old life and ways (1 Thes 5:14).

Within the NT "fellowship of wisdom seekers," the church, the shepherds are to wisely teach and correct those under their charge in order to present to Christ as many spiritually mature people as possible (Col 1:28-29). In addition, *each* person in the "fellowship of wisdom-seekers" is to take a role in teaching, correcting, encouraging and helping one another. They also are to do these things in a wise manner, not in a rude, crude or thoughtless way (Col 3:16). The church is a realm where we "speak the truth in love" (Eph 5:15).

Not just the pastors, but *the other individuals in the church* are to take initiative to *admonish* (*noutheteo*—gently, but firmly warn) the unruly and rebellious, to "put it in their mind" to get back in line with the will of God.

Fellow church members are to take initiative to *encourage* the fearful or fainthearted. The Greek implies a coming alongside to encourage. Believers are to "run alongside" the fainthearted telling them, "In Christ, you can! Keep on! You can do it!"

It is also the responsibility of fellow church members to take initiative to *help* the weak. The Greek word has the sense of hanging onto them, supporting them, and providing the help they need.

Beyond these specific problem people, everyone in the church needs the patience of everyone else! And, like the wise people of old, the people of God are to turn away from evil, never paying back evil for evil, but exhibit the loving kindness and mercy of God Himself (1Thes 5:15; 1 Pet 3:10-12; Luke 6:36).

The unruly need correction, the fearful need encouragement, the weak need help. One should not mix the prescriptions. Helping or encouraging the *unruly* only makes them worse. The unruly need correction.

The *fearful*, however, need encouragement. Correcting the fearful only increases their fear; helping them only convinces them that they are unable to face their fears alone with Christ. They need to be encouraged by others so that they can step out to meet their fears and discover the adequacy of Christ.

The *weak* need help. Correcting or encouraging the weak only increases their desperation. They already know they are wrong. And, their problem is not a lack of heart! They do not need encouragement. They have the heart, but not the strength. They have the courage, but not the resources. They need help.

As among the wisdom seekers of the Old Testament, so among the church in the New Testament, there is a fellowship of encouragement, instruction, patience, kindness and correction. And, there is great respect for the more mature, and for those given leadership and for their role in teaching and correction. But there is also a *"mutuality"* of instruction, correction and helping one another that *just makes sense* if one really wants to experience the full extent of what God can do in his life (Eph 3:19).

WHAT IF MY CHURCH IS NOT LIKE THIS?

No church is perfect. All churches face the challenge of trying to work with less-than-perfect people in leadership to help other less-than-perfect people grow and minister. All churches will have their "pluses" and "minuses."

However, churches can drift from the will of God and bring themselves to a point of discipline from God due to:

- A preoccupation with busy-ness (and usually also a desire to control) that has eroded concern for loving the Lord and doing what is pleasing to Him (Rev 2:4-5),
- Moral and doctrinal decline, with laxity about sexual immorality and flirting with idolatry (false teachings, participation in other religions or greed) (Rev 2:14-16, 20; Col 3:5),
- Loss of focus and intensity due to resting on the victories of the past (Rev 3:1-3),
- Luke-warmness derived from self-satisfaction based on material wealth (Rev 3:14-17).

Churches drift due to problems in their leadership core, either vocational leaders (staff) or lay leaders—or both. Due to a significant lack of wisdom or pressure from powerful people with wrong values, leaders take the church the wrong direction or let it drift. Once the wrong direction has established itself, the church does not change until a significant number of leaders change.

People do not ordinarily change churches from the bottom up. Change moves from the top down. Unless you have major leadership in the church, you will not make the changes. If mockers have come to lead the church, all you will get for your attempted correction of the situation is resentment and abuse (Pro 9:7-8). If you press your case, all that will result is a major fight as leaders, motivated by selfishness, utilize ungodly strategies to protect themselves from what they perceive as attack (Jas 3:14-116).

If your church leadership core is not wise or is doing wrong, do not imitate them (3 John 9-11). Find a church that is healthy and go there.

Think It Over

Many people "attend church" but do not have a real experience of "fellowship" among "wisdom seekers." To what extent are you "plugged into" a fellowship of "wisdom seekers," a church?

For example, from whom do you consistently learn?

Whom have you given freedom to correct you?

In the upside-down kingdom, the givers are the ones who really receive. How do you contribute (time, effort, emotional energy, money) to the health of the fellowship? What have you received in return?

DID YOU KNOW THAT WISDOM CAN DETERIORATE?
WANT TO KNOW HOW?
READ ON!

Chapter 15

WISDOM'S DECLINE

Wisdom is not a fixed matter. It can grow greatly; it can also decline. It is possible that one can gain *great* wisdom and subsequently live in such a manner that the wisdom deteriorates. We looked briefly at the growth and decline of wisdom in an earlier chapter (see p. 31-32). In this chapter, we will look more closely at the decline of wisdom.

The Scriptures indicate that people can do things that cause wisdom to decay.

IMMORALITY AND INTOXICATION

Harlotry, wine, and new wine take away the understanding (leb) (Hos 4:11 NAS)

Occasionally, we come to points in life where we are under severe stress. Responsibilities or problems have multiplied—or perhaps both have. We bear up under the stress for a time, and then we become worn. We begin to seek some relief, some refreshment, and some comfort. At those times, a person needs to turn to Christ; Jesus will give rest to the weary and heavy-laden. (Matt 11:28-30).

One also needs to seek wisdom, for wisdom, like honey to the taste, will be "sweet to the soul," (Pro 24:14) and as refreshing as a bubbling brook (Pro 18:4). Wisdom will be a life-giving fountain (Pro 16:22). Insight, strength, resources, refreshment and encouragement will keep springing up out of wisdom.

Many people, however, begin to turn back to their old ways of life and think that gratifying their passions will provide comfort. They turn to immorality and heavy drinking or drugs.

They do not find comfort, however. Rather, at the very critical time when the weary one needs clear insight the most, immorality and heavy drinking rob them of their judgment (leb). Immorality and drunkenness only wipe out their perspective and ability to make good decisions. The one who was under heavy stress, now adds to the stress by the stupid things he does as his judgment dims. See Pro 6:32; 20:1; 23:27-35; Isa 28:1, 7-8; Luke 21:23.

Jesus warns us against this, telling us to watch that our lives do not become weighed down with anxieties, drunkenness, and dissipation (see Luke 21-23).

Paul also warns against letting our minds begin to toy with gratification of our sinful desires.

Let us behave decently, as in the daytime, not in orgies and drunkenness, not in sexual immorality and debauchery, not in dissension and jealousy. Rather, clothe yourselves with the Lord Jesus Christ, and <u>do not think about</u> how to gratify the desires of the sinful nature. (Rom 13:13-14 NIV)

Paul tells us to keep away from orgies (the Greek implies wild drunken parties that last until late into the night), intoxication, sexual immorality, and debauchery. Debauchery translates a Greek word that could also be translated as "unbridled lust, excess, licentiousness, lasciviousness, wantonness, outrageousness, shamelessness, and/or insolence." It includes acts or approaches intended to create sexual excitement, such as "filthy words, indecent physical movements, unchaste handling of males and females." (from *Thayer's Greek Lexicon*, Electronic Database. Copyright © 2000 by Biblesoft)

Rather than get into "passion mode" we need to yield ourselves to Jesus Christ. "Lord, I am worn out! Please strengthen me. Give me wisdom about what to do and when to do it." We need to seek scriptural principles for dealing with our situations and talk with wise advisers. And, we need to control our minds. We need to actively fill them with Scripture, keep them busy working on solutions to our situation (not just stewing over it), and refuse to let them drift to getting high and fooling around.

Drunkenness and immorality will only dim our judgment, and lead to doing stupid things that make our situation far worse.

DABBLING IN CIKLUWTH-FOLLY

As dead flies give perfume a bad smell, so a little folly outweighs wisdom and honor. (Ecc 10:1 NIV)

Cikluwth (sik-looth') is the folly of blind desire. When *cikluwth* is in operation, a person sees something that really appeals to him or her, but the thing is outside the will of God, as for example, extramarital sex, adultery, drugs, or a car one cannot afford. Fully inflamed with desire for the forbidden thing, the person then "blinds" himself mentally; he refuses to consider his responsibilities that will be abrogated by his actions. He refuses to consider the certain consequences of violating God's boundaries. He makes everything but the object of his desire fade from the picture. Then, he picks the forbidden fruit; he gratifies himself. Horrendous consequences follow.

King David went through an episode of *cikluwth* (1 Chr 21:1-14). Dead set on having what he wanted, he refused contrary counsel (v. 3-4). When he confessed that he had done *foolishly* (v. 8), he used the word for the Cakal-fool, the practitioner of *cikluwth.* Seventy thousand people died as a result. When a leader indulges in *cikluwth,* he may not be the only one affected by his folly.

Dabbling in *cikluwth* seems to be a real temptation for the wise, even the greatly wise. However, *cikluwth* is the nemesis of wisdom. Even a *tiny* amount of *cikluwth* is adequate to destroy great wisdom and great reputation for wisdom.

This has happened in the sexual arena for a number of political, business and religious leaders over the past fifteen years. Fully focused on their lusts, they took what was not theirs, and their acts destroyed their leadership and reputation.

Cikluwth? Don't even *think* of it!

OPPRESSING OTHERS

Surely oppression maketh a wise man mad (halal); and a gift destroyeth the heart. (Ecc 7:7 KJV)

The oppression that is being talked about involves denying *what is due* to someone (rights, justice, property, etc) until a bribe is paid, either by money or a "gift" of some kind, perhaps property or favors. Even if a wise man does not actually get to the point of perverting justice, the sin ruins his wisdom. He becomes the self-exalting fool, the Halal (see p. 106).

The wise are often chosen as advisers to people making high-impact decisions. Frequently such advisers are approached by those with an interest in the outcome and offered "a gift" (money, property, privileges or favors) if they will advise the decision makers to move in a certain direction. The adviser must refuse the gift or face the dimming of his wisdom.

Occasionally, the wise are asked to serve as a judge or arbiter in disputed matters. The Scriptures are very clear that bribery of judges is forbidden and punished by God (Ex 23:8; Deu 16:19). The wise person should grant to everyone what is due to them (see p. 62). When a wise person decides to use his position in order to gain bribes, he has become a self-exalting fool. His wisdom will go into decline, and he will face the consequences suffered by Halals (see Ps 73:18-20).

Use of position to gain favors or money is a temptation, not only for judges and advisers, but also for leaders. Political leaders who take such "gifts" undermine the stability of their government (Pro 29:4; 16:14; 29:14). Spiritual leaders in the church are to be people *already proven* to *not be* greedy for money (1 Tim 3:3), especially "dirty money" (Titus 1:7). Once they have assumed leadership, they are to serve eagerly, and resist the inclination to serve only when it means money for them (1 Pet 5:2).

This principle might also apply to attempting to use sex in marriage as a bargaining chip to get one's way rather than giving to the other partner what is due to them (1 Cor 7:3-5). If so, then if a wise married person begins to withhold sex from his/her mate in order to gain some favor from the mate, his/her wisdom will begin to deteriorate. The withholder will become ensnarled in the problems that follow. Fading wisdom is of little help with real problems.

ARROGANCE

Two characters in the Old Testament (OT) provide individual case studies in the decline of wisdom: the King of Tyre and Solomon, King of Israel.

The King Of Tyre

Tyre was an ancient city on the seacoast of Palestine. It rose to commercial prominence and was later eradicated by God. In Ezekiel, there is an interesting prophecy against the "king of Tyre."

The word of the LORD came to me: "Son of man, take up a lament concerning the king of Tyre and say to him: 'This is what the Sovereign LORD says:

"'You were the model of perfection, full of wisdom and perfect in beauty. You were in Eden, the garden of God; every precious stone adorned you: ruby, topaz and emerald, ...You were anointed as a guardian cherub, for so I ordained you. You were on the holy mount of God; you walked among the fiery stones.

You were blameless in your ways from the day you were created till wickedness was found in you. ...

Through your widespread trade you were filled with violence, and you sinned. So I drove you in disgrace from the mount of God, and I expelled you, O guardian cherub, from among the fiery stones.

Your heart became proud on account of your beauty, and you corrupted your wisdom because of your splendor. So I threw you to the earth; I made a spectacle of you before kings. (Eze 28:11-17 NIV)

Some interpreters see this passage as a kind of satirical mockery applying to the historical king of Tyre alone. Others see it as a description of the fall of Satan. Many see it as directed toward both: parts about Satan, and parts about the historical king of Tyre. Because of the descriptions of the king being present in the Garden of Eden, I tend to the third view.

Regardless one's interpretive preference, the passage shows a progression from "full of wisdom" to "corrupted...wisdom."

The king of Tyre had been extremely blessed. He had been made

- Full of wisdom (Hokmah)
- Perfect (complete) in beauty
- Splendid in adornment (v. 13)
- Participant in a splendid environment (Eden, the Mount of God)
- For an exalted assignment (Guardian Cherub)

However, the splendid person he was and the splendid life granted him did not stir him to gratitude to God. Instead, his beauty and splendor motivated him to arrogance. He became proud of his splendid beauty, and thus, sinned internally.

His wisdom was then corrupted. The Hebrew word translated as "corrupted" means "decay." His actions deteriorated his wisdom. Out of his pride he took greater privilege to himself than he was due (arrogance), and he began to act independently of God. Then, his broad dealings led into violence (external sin) and the resulting punishment from God.

The king of Tyre's progression in deteriorating wisdom appears to be:

Superior Blessing → Arrogance (Internal sin) → "Decayed" Wisdom → External Sin → Punishment

What began in beauty, splendor, wisdom, honor and the service of God ends in serving self, declining wisdom, expulsion from splendor, and lasting disgrace.

Solomon, King of Israel

King Solomon, however, loved many foreign women... from nations about which the LORD had told the Israelites, "You must not intermarry with them, because they will surely turn your hearts after their gods." Nevertheless, Solomon held fast to them in love...

He had seven hundred wives of royal birth and three hundred concubines, and his wives led him astray. As Solomon grew old, his wives turned his heart after other gods,

He followed Ashtoreth the goddess of the Sidonians, and Molech the detestable god of the Ammonites...Solomon built a high place for Chemosh the detestable god of Moab, and for Molech the detestable god of the Ammonites...

The LORD became angry with Solomon because his heart had turned away from the LORD, the God of Israel, who had appeared to him twice... Although He had forbidden Solomon to follow other gods, Solomon did not keep the LORD's command...

Then the LORD raised up against Solomon an adversary, (1 Kings 11:1-15 NIV).

Solomon became king of ancient Israel about 975 BC. Solomon had been granted *privileges like no other human* since Adam. God had appeared to him twice (v. 9) and granted him to be the wisest mere human to ever live (1 Kings 3:12, 4:29-34). He was blessed with international peace and incredible wealth and splendor (1 Kings 10:18-21).

However, as time went along Solomon began to *violate the boundaries* the LORD had set for Israel's kings (1 Kings 10:26-29).

Earlier, God had forbidden Israel's kings to accumulate horses for national defense (Deu 17:16). God was to be the guardian of Israel and their defense. Horses were necessary in national defense under God—up to a certain point. Part of Solomon's interest in horses was commercial. He sold them to other nations (1 Kings 10:29). However, the vast accumulation of horses might lead the king to trust in his horses and armaments, not in God (see Ps 20:6-8; Isa 2:6-9, 31:1). God did not set an *exact* limit to the number of horses. He just said "don't accumulate." A heart concerned to follow God would have quit accumulating horses at some reasonable point. But, Solomon pushed the limits and built up vast armaments.

God had also forbidden the purchase of horses from Egypt (Deu 17:16). Egypt was a major arms manufacturer, breeding excellent war horses and producing fine war chariots for sale to other nations. However, God had decreed that Israel should never go back to Egypt again for *anything* (Deu 17:16). But, a person willing to violate the "horse limitation statute" could easily talk himself into purchasing Egyptian armaments. Solomon was pushing against the boundaries God had set.

God's word forbade the accumulation of gold also (Deu 17:17). A certain amount of treasure would be okay. Beyond a reasonable amount, the increasing wealth could have been shared with the populace or used for public works, blessing all the people of God. But, Solomon kept accumulating gold. He had crossed over the LORD's boundaries and kept going.

God also forbade the accumulation of wives. The accumulation of too many wives would lead a king's heart astray (Deu 17:17). But Solomon took 700 wives and had 300 concubines (legal live-ins, a second-rank wife).

Solomon not only violated God's *statutes for the king*, he also violated *the general prohibition* against *any* Israelite marrying idolatrous wives. God had said that marriage to idolatrous mates would turn the hearts of His people away from Him to idols (Deu 7:3-4). But a king willing to violate God's "wives limitation statute" would be able to find reasons why marrying idolatrous wives—even hundreds of them—couldn't hurt! Solomon had burst beyond God's limitations.

Solomon went beyond two limits, each of which had promised the violator's heart would be turned from God. *Too many* wives would turn his heart away. *Idolatrous* wives would turn his heart away.

Indeed, Solomon was doubly impacted by his wives. When he grew old, perhaps in his fifties, his wives turned his heart from loyalty to God. He built temples for the idols of his wives and let them worship in them.

Ashtoreth was a fertility goddess whose worship involved immorality. Molech and Chemosh both demanded the live sacrifice of children. Solomon began to "follow" these three.

The picture is almost incredible: the wisest and richest man on earth to whom the true God of the universe had *appeared twice*, now, in his senior years, bowing down in front of gods made of silver and gold, wood and stone!

How far Solomon's wisdom had deteriorated!

God confronted Solomon and told him, that since his attitude was that he did not have to heed God's limits or keep His commands, God would tear most of the kingdom away from his family line in the next generation (1 Kings 11:11-13). In Solomon's own time, God raised up adversaries who created grief for Solomon, chipping away at his empire. Hadad, the Edomite (1 Kings 11:14), tried to rebuild a kingdom in Edom. Rezon gathered rebels, set up a government in Damascus, and ruled in Aram. He added to the grief that Hadad caused (1 Kings 11:23-25). Jeroboam, a former official under Solomon began to foment rebellion (1 Kings 11:36ff). These successful rebels formed the "rod of men" with which God chastised Solomon (2 Sam 7:14).

In the same Scripture passage where God set limits on the king's accumulations, God warned against another *insidious* problem for kings. It is easy for a king to begin to get the idea that he is "better" (of higher and more deserving nature) than his brothers. One who feels better than others begins to *"want what he wants when he wants it and feel like he deserves it!"* He begins to feel that the limitations other people must bear do not apply to him.

In this "exalted" person's way of thinking, God's Law is for the regular people to worry about, but the king gets extra privileges. The king does not have to worry about keeping the law in such *detail.* There is latitude for the king! After all, God has raised him up to the heights he occupies. Obviously the blessing of God rests on him! So he does not have to be *so strict* in his observance of God's word as the ordinary folk.

As an antidote to this creeping arrogance, God commanded the kings to make a personal copy of the Law and keep it with them. The king was to and read it daily so that he might be careful to revere the LORD and follow all the words written in the Law (Deu 17:19). The king was not to get the idea that he was better than his brothers and think, therefore, that he had the option to deviate to the right or left from God's word. Instead, he was to keep God's word in detail (Deu 17:20). Then, God would see that he and his descendants would reign a long time.

Solomon apparently fell into thinking his special appearances from God, the vast wisdom bestowed by God, and the fabulous wealth and status given to him by God meant that he was above his brother Israelites. He did not have to adhere so closely to the word of God. He was privileged to go ahead and push past God's boundaries with impunity.

Perhaps Solomon simply quit reading the Scripture daily. Or, maybe his creeping arrogance distorted what he read. We do not know. We do know, however, of the disaster he created for his kingdom.

The sequence in Solomon's deterioration seems to be a cycle of blessing, creeping arrogance, pushing the limits, and declining wisdom, while God continues to bless—until the step into idolatry occurs.

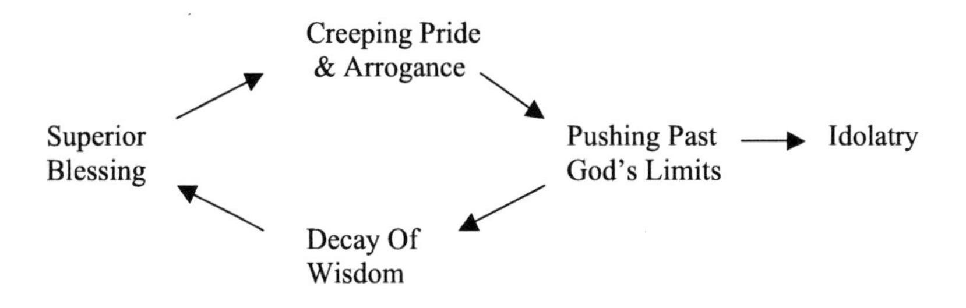

Solomon's Sequence of Decline

Similarities & Lessons

Both the king of Tyre and King Solomon exhibit similar patterns in their decline from glory wisdom to decayed wisdom and shame.

Superior Blessing → Arrogance Pride → Decayed Wisdom → External Sin

When God grants tremendous blessing, it becomes easy for the blessed one to feel "above others" and to feel deserving of greater freedom not to have to keep the word of God so exactly. Blessing leads to pride (inordinate self-esteem) and arrogance (demanding more for oneself than is due). And, pride goes before a humbling fall (Pro 11:12; 16:18; 29:23).

The growth of such pride seems to be especially the province of the rich, the powerful, and those who lead. Ecclesiastes speaks of how much better is a poor but wise youth than an *old and foolish* king who will *no longer listen to advice* or corrective input (Ecc 4:13). Leaders who have had their position for some time need to guard against the creeping arrogance that resists input.

Financial or other blessings granted by God *do not* in anyway affirm a person's freedom to violate any part of God's word, whether it be violations in attitude, following authority (spiritual or otherwise), handling relationships rightly, decision-making, use of possessions, speech, work or any other part of life. Blessing by God only means that you have been given a greater stewardship than others, and therefore, greater accountability than others. Rather than being able to live more loosely, you must live more closely.

In the admonition to "be careful then how you live" (Eph 5:15), the Greek phrase could be worded that we are to live "deviating in no respect from the law or duty." (see *Thayer's Lexicon*). Thus, it is those who live "exactly" who are *wise*, not foolish. There is no blessed position that excuses one from focused obedience.

Humility Again

As God increasingly blesses you, avoid "blessing-induced pride." *Keep on walking in humility*, and pay attention to *doing all of God's Word.*

The decline in wisdom by two persons who were *exceptionally wise* underscores the fact that there is no substitute for humility and the fear of the LORD. No matter how great the fund of knowledge, the skill in analyzing situations, or in drawing conclusions, wisdom will not substitute for walking with God. As Eve discovered, there is no wisdom that can make one independent of God. True wisdom is rooted in God alone. He shares His knowledge and wisdom with us (Ps 94:10). But, whatever degree of wisdom we attain, its vitality will continue to depend on our relationship with God. Our wisdom will never substitute for knowing and loving God. To be wise is a wonderful goal; to be faithful is even greater.

OPPOSING GOD

Sometimes people decide to oppose what is important to the God of the Bible. The opponents may be atheists, refusing to admit God exists, members of another religion, counting on a different god, or those among the people of God who have decided to go against what is right. God deals with some quickly and others slowly, according to His own purposes. But, God deals with opponents quite effectively.

Pharaoh's Advisers

Such it was with ancient Egypt, which followed other gods. The Egyptian Pharaoh had a cabinet of princely advisers, his "wise men," who lived in the cities of Zoan and Memphis. Out of the common grace of God, they had wisdom in dealing with national and international affairs. They were the mainstays of Egypt. All in Egypt were counting on their expert advice to keep the nation safe.

When Egypt decided to oppose God, God sent a perverse spirit, or spirit of distortion, into her top-level decision makers.

11 Surely the princes of Zoan are fools; Pharaoh's wise counselors give foolish counsel. How do you say to Pharaoh, "I am the son of the wise, The son of ancient kings?"

12 Where are they? Where are your wise men? Let them tell you now, And let them know what the LORD of hosts has purposed against Egypt.

13 The princes of Zoan have become fools; The princes of Noph are deceived; They have also deluded Egypt, Those who are the mainstay of its tribes.

14 The LORD has mingled a perverse spirit in her midst; And they have caused Egypt to err in all her work, As a drunken man staggers in his vomit.

15 Neither will there be any work for Egypt, Which the head or tail, Palm branch or bulrush, may do. (Isa 19:11-15 NKJ)

Under the influence of the spirit of distortion, Pharaoh's advisers were led astray. The very mainstay of Egypt became the source of its staggering attempts to deal with the situations that would arise. The top advisers to Pharaoh became the ones who would take Egypt down.

The passage indicates the advisers, became "fools" (v. 13). The Hebrew word indicates the kind of fool who handles his responsibilities loosely. Like a tennis player trying to hit a ball with a loose grip on his racquet, these men took a loose grip on their responsibility to keep the nation strong.

Verse 11 gives the particular way in which the advisers loosened their grip. They are "fools"—the Hebrew word used here indicates they have become 'Eviyl-like. They have become like 'Eviyl, the stubborn, adversarial fool determined to achieve his own agenda no matter what. Under the distorting influence that God has sent among them, each princely adviser became set on his own personal agenda and determined to accomplish it no matter what else happened. As a result, each would give only the advice that would advance his personal agenda, not the advice that would really help the nation. The counsel/advice, therefore, was "foolish." "Foolish" translates a Hebrew word that indicates something like "as stupid as a brute beast of the field," or "as perceptive as a cow." The intense selfish motivation of the advisers led to advice that steered the nation toward disaster.

Under the influence of the spirit of distortion, no one in Egypt could stop the coming disaster, whether they were upper class or a peon. No work could be done to avoid what was coming (v. 15).

The Murderers Of Shechem

Earlier in Israel's history, the citizens of the town of Shechem participated in the mass murder of their former leader's seventy sons, and established a new king over the region (see Judges 9). One son escaped and cursed the men and their new king. In order to avenge the mass murder (v. 24), God sent an evil spirit between the new king and his followers (v. 23). As a result, the followers plotted treachery and rebelled. In the ensuing conflict, both the Shechmites and their new king were killed for their wrongdoing (v. 56-57).

King Ahab

In later times, Ahab, a king of the northern kingdom of Israel rebelled against God for an extended time. During a period of international conflict, God sent a deceiving spirit in among the king's prophets, prophets who did not walk with God. They forecast victory for the king in a coming battle. One prophet of God forecast disaster. The king didn't want to believe the prophet of God, and went with the forecast of the false prophets. He died as a result of battle (1 Kings 22:4-35). The spirit of deception among the highest circle of the king's advisers dealt effectively with God's opponent.

Ahithophel's Counsel

King David's son, Absalom, effectively plotted a rebellion that threatened to kill David and take over the kingdom (2 Sam 15-16). One of

David's key advisers, Ahithophel, sided with the rebellion. His advice had been unbelievably effective over the years for King David. In fact, he was so perceptive that men took his advice almost as the word of God (2 Sam 16:23).

When David heard that Ahithophel had joined the rebellion, he prayed that God would make his advice "into foolishness" (2 Sam 15:31). "Turn into foolishness" translates a Hebrew verb that means to turn the advice into folly like that of the Cakal-fool, the most stupid of all the fools. David basically asked God to "Cakal-ize" Ahithophel's advice to Absalom.

David's other top adviser, Husahi, remained a loyal friend, but pretended to side with the new rebellion. When a critical moment came, Absalom asked the advice of both Ahithophel and Hushai. Ahithophel advised an immediate strike against David. Husahi advised delay. Absalom and the other leaders of Israel rejected Ahithophel's strategically superior counsel and chose Hushai's defective advice (2 Sam 17:1-14). Ahithophel knew that the outcome of Hushai's advice would be the failure of the rebellion. So, he went home, set his estate in order, and hanged himself (2 Sam 17:23).

According to the Scripture, Absalom's preference for Husahi's counsel was from the LORD, in order to bring disaster upon Absalom (2 Sam 17:14).

Thus, even the wisest of advisers cannot effectively oppose the LORD. God sees to it that the wisest advisers end up captive to those they opposed. And, even the shrewdest in judgment are turned into self-exalting fools by Him (Job 12:17).

The LORD is a God who:

...foils the signs of false prophets and makes fools of diviners predictions, who overthrows the learning (da'ath) of the wise and turns it into nonsense... (Isa 44:25 NIV)

When people decide to oppose what is important to God, He will foil the forecasts of their futurists (prophets). He will cause their analysts (diviners) to make arrogant, inflated projections (make them arrogant, self-exalting fools). He "Cakal-izes" the formerly wise perception of the key decision makers, turning their broad, educated perspective (*da'ath*) in an incredibly stupid direction. Key errors in judgment follow, and the opponents of God fall.

No one can come up with a strategy (wisdom) that is effective against God.

There is no wisdom, no insight, no plan that can succeed against the LORD. The horse is made ready for the day of battle, but victory rests with the LORD. (Pro 21:30-31 NIV)

Think About It

When you are under heavy stress, where do tend to go for comfort?
How would one "go to wisdom" to get refreshment during such times?
How can a person avoid unseen, creeping arrogance?

JUST A FEW MORE THOUGHTS...

EPILOGUE

None of us has the option of refusing to make decisions. Daily we must make them, and then we reap the consequences, good or bad.

There is a way to better life by using sharper strokes and living *smarter*, not *harder*. Wisdom gives us an edge to handle both problems and opportunities quite well.

Even if the wisdom one possesses has come only by the common grace of God, that wisdom is a tremendous blessing. It is a shelter and a source of benefit to oneself and others. It can even save one's life (Ecc 7:12).

How much better to have the wisdom that comes through God's indwelling Holy Spirit, who is available to coach us. But the one who would find such wisdom must humble himself and decide to live in the fear of the LORD, under the Lordship of Jesus Christ. All others may pray, cry, or try to buy wisdom, but apart from humility and the fear of the Lord, wisdom will not come.

The one who breaks through into wisdom, will find a vast domain of exciting information, perspectives and abilities. As these are applied to life, life takes on a blessed flavor.

Life will still have its problems. They will come amid the flow of life. Some of them are consequences we have created by bad decisions. Many are surprises; many are completely beyond our control.

Nothing, however, that enters our lives is out of the control of God. Indeed, He will use the events of life to train us in wisdom, if we will just trust Him and "hang in there." Out of the endurance will come a strong character and a joyful outlook on life.

Especially in the church, we have an opportunity to learn wisdom, if we will pull out of our privatism—our exclusive preoccupation with our own concerns—and actually accept God's assignment to be a blessing to a group of people called a "church." By walking with them, we grow, and they grow. "Speaking the truth in love" is a great protection against "creeping pride and arrogance" (see Heb 3:12-13).

For human beings, wisdom is never a "fixed" quantity. It can grow or decline. Decline sets in as we begin to quietly, in our hearts, refuse to deal with God's word in detail. When we decide that we will walk "generally" in line with Christ, rather than "exactly" in line with Christ, we stray into folly, not wisdom. We walk as foolish, not as wise.

Remember, full, genuine wisdom will not be found apart from Jesus Christ, in whom are hidden all the treasures of wisdom and knowledge (Col 2:3). True wisdom keeps asking the question, "How does the Lord Jesus prefer this done?"

I hope you have enjoyed this journey into Wisdom. In later books, I hope to deal with how wisdom operates in the arenas of life that we surveyed in chapter eight.

May God bless your journey and equip you with "sharper strokes." And may you know the love of Christ that surpasses knowledge (Eph 3:19).

Appendix 1

SOCIETY'S VIEW OF "WISE"

Contemporary society has not been silent about what it considers to be the appropriate view of ultimate reality, *and* what constitutes the wise course in life, that is, what it takes to *get what you really want in life*.

Earlier, the societal view of wisdom was communicated through the public schools. Since the 1950's, the schools have increasingly taken a back seat, and the media have become the major instructor in what is "wise," that is, the media now defines for us "what you ought to want and how to get it." We are currently at a hinge point in history where the concept of what is "wise" is changing from a "Modern" view to a "Post-Modern" view. The Modern view still has credence among the older population, especially on university faculties. The Post-Modern view has captured most of the young, and increasingly dominates the media.

We will investigate these because they pressure us to make decisions after their fashion. Both have quite different views of what is wise, different not only from each other, but also from the Bible.

The Popular View Of Wisdom: The Modern Era

The American practice of "leaving god out of the equation," (or, at least, including very little of god in the equation) is in accord with the spirit of the "Modern Era." In the Modern Era, the "wise course of action" was thought to be the one that was atheistic, educated, and most up-to-date in its use of information and technology.

Throughout the first 1500 years after the birth of Christ, western society (Europe) was increasingly shaped by the Christian idea of God. While society was far from perfect, Christian thought impacted the cultural approach to daily life, laws, governments, and the general moral structure and values of society. Among the intellectuals, interest was focused more on spiritual and political matters. Art tended to me more about spiritual subjects, and in a flat, Byzantine style.

In the late 1300's, a strong interest in nature and in human beings developed in Europe. As time went on, artists began to paint realistic, three-dimensional pictures of people, countryside, and daily life. Some of the learned invented telescopes and microscopes with which to investigate nature in more detail. Budding scientists found mathematical relationships in some of the phenomena of nature, and began to propound the laws of physics and chemistry. Philosophers turned their attention to the possibilities of man and what he could achieve by his strength and reason alone.

This "humanism" ultimately grew in two different directions.

One was a God-believing interest in the created world of people and things. Some of the great early scientists and mathematicians were men of deep faith, such as Isaac Newton and Blaise Pascal. These saw their discoveries in science and mathematics as "rethinking the thoughts of God." They were discovering how God had thought up the universe. And, they saw Him as still in control, even of "natural processes."

The other stream of humanism became more centered on man as the key mover in the universe, and finally arrived at the conclusion that, if there were a god, that god made little or no impact on the current world (Deism). Indeed, others argued, there was no god at all (Naturalism). One way or another, it seemed to be up to mankind to study the universe, puzzle over the observations, and come up with the principles behind how the universe operated. With the discovery of such "natural laws," people would surely be able to guide science, technology, art, governments and morality. This second stream of humanism came to dominate the schools and universities. According to *Merriam-Webster's Collegiate Dictionary*, the term "modern" apparently came into use about 1585. It comes from the Latin "modo," meaning "just now" and carries the idea of the latest in methods, techniques or ideas. A "modern person" was someone really trying to keep up-to-date with the latest thought and inventions!

"Modernism" developed as a movement that strove for a complete, radical break with the "superstitious" past, and its reliance on Biblical and traditional wisdom. It strove to create new forms for society, and a life based entirely on "modern" science and "modern" philosophy alone. No God would be needed in the coming "modern world." Modernists thought that, by the use of philosophical reason and the information provided by scientific investigation, mankind would gradually create a nearly perfect world, not only technologically, but also ethically, politically, socially, psychologically, and esthetically.

In the Modern way of thinking, there was no supernatural realm. There was no spiritual reality beyond the physical universe. For this reason, Modernism believed that miracles were not possible. There simply were no gods or spirits to do them. Further, Modernism refused to believe that there were *supernatural* causes to anything in the world. For example, Modernists refused to believe that voodoo could kill anyone. If anyone died in a voodoo-related incident, the death was entirely the result of psychological causes. Since neither demons nor spirits existed, they could not kill or affect a human victim. Death had to occur only because of the victim's psychological belief in the effectiveness of voodoo.

This same attitude affected Modernism's approach to Christianity and counseling. Human problems, such as struggles in marriage, had no "spiritual" component, Modernism reasoned. Human problems were simply the consequence of inadequate information and lack of skill in dealing with life. Psychology alone would come up with the insights needed for relational and emotional health. Such things as prayer, spiritual conversion or church-going were not essential to human well-being and success. Psychology would come up with a completely non-religious (and superior) explanation for the way human individuals worked. Religion was worthless in trying to solve personal problems. Science was everything.

In the early days of modernism, the prophets of a coming utopia seemed to be correct. "Modern" science quickly made incredible strides in technology, with the invention of the steam engine, the development of huge factories and of medicine. Physics, chemistry and engineering were providing wonderful new "time-saving" inventions that made life "better" (easier). Technology seemed to be keeping its part of the utopian promise. Since society was made up of people, building a new form of society without religion required solid, "scientifically accurate" information on how people function, both individually, and in groups. It looked like the newer behavioral science of psychology would provide all the necessary insight into how human individuals ticked, and sociology would provide the needed insights and principles on how people worked in groups, communities and nations.

However, a problem began to develop with the modern agenda. Besides technology and insights on how to deal with people, societies also need *values and ethics* in order to develop adequate social ideals and workable laws. Values and ethics are in the realm of philosophy. Modern philosophers strained to find a rational basis for values, morals and ethics—with no religion involved—but were having difficulty. Without a god, the different schemes for establishing values and morals kept falling short. It began to dawn on some that leaving God out of the discussion resulted in having no way to determine which values or morals were inherently superior to others.

Modernism's optimism and confidence about the future kept up its popular momentum. It kept moving mankind forward into new and improved products and ideas, absolutely sure that blessed progress in the philosophical realm was inevitable. The "superstitious" grip that Christianity had once had on morals began to loosen as Freudian psychology encouraged people to cease repressing many of their psychological urges. Individual liberation from repressive religious morals and needless guilt was on its way. Many, many people were certain something close to utopia lay just ahead!

With the help of TV and the movies, during the 1960's, America cut loose from its religious moorings. Powerful multinational corporations grew and produced new and improved gadgets for all—while the Christian restraint on greed was slackening. A younger generation kicked off the moral restraints of Christianity and set out, sexually unrestrained, to revise morality, marriage and family. Drugs were thought likely to be the door-opener to a happier emotional life. In San Francisco, many young people moved to the Haight-Asbury district, intending to create a morals-free, euphoric (drug induced) new world of "love."

A popular song advised: *"If you're goin' to San Francisco, be sure to wear some flowers in your hair...you're goin' to meet some gentle people there."*

According to recent Modernism (1940's-1990's pop-culture), a *wise person* was the one who acquired a good education, so that he or she understood science and people. Then, the wise one would set out to create a unique life based on the latest (and of course, therefore, the best!) ideas and the findings of scientific research—without worrying about the wisdom of the past (as expressed in the concerns of their parents), religious restraints or a sense of accountability to any God.

Modernism's Failure To Deliver

By the 1980's, the practical results of the modern revolution were rolling in. By the 1990's the failure of the revolution was unmistakable. Haight-Asbury had become a nightmarish place of drug addicts and crime as early as the mid-Seventies. Experiments with unrestrained sexual experience and with new forms of marriage (open marriage, trial marriage, group marriage, polygamy, and homosexual lifestyles) had led to a plague of sexually transmitted diseases, the rise of a new death-plague, AIDS, and the devastation of millions of children. These children had to endure the unstable, damaging family environments created by their "experimenting" parents, and cope with the resulting emotional problems. Crime rose dramatically, and welfare costs skyrocketed, especially as the government increasingly had to care for kids whose parents would not.

At the same time, there was a growing awareness that the wonderful technology that industry produced had come at a high price—the pollution of the environment on a massive scale. Technology had been helpful, but, rather than a savior, it might turn out to be our destroyer!

And, philosophy could not come up with adequate values, ethics or morals based strictly on science and reason. Without a god to say what was right or wrong, or what is of high value or low, morals and values simply become the result of individual preference or societal popularity. For example, rape might be illegal, or even unpopular, but there was no way to say it was *ultimately* wrong. Indeed, Hitler's genocide of the Jews was his own personal preference *and* was backed by the government of his society. Was genocide then ultimately *not* wrong? How could laws for a nation be built on "preferences" or "social popularity?" How could a free and just society be created when "liberty" and "justice" turned out to be only individual preferences, not real values for which it is worth fighting and dying?

Serious disillusionment set in, and along with it, a reaction to the optimistic, hopeful, and logical modernism. Modernism was not going to deliver utopia after all. Even worse, it had created a horrendous mess. Things now appeared worse than before Modernism had taken the field. The philosophical starting point for Modernism was basically an atheistic view of ultimate reality. Since Modernism had failed, would people pick a different starting point and go back to a view of ultimate reality containing some kind of god?

Contemporary Wisdom: The Post-Modern Era

The current fashion is no longer Modernism, but "Post-Modernism" (PM), a doubtful, ironic way of looking at life that wants to be free from having any "right" answers.

Post-modernism has kept the same starting point as Modernism. It still hangs onto the idea that there is no larger "reality" beyond the existence of a bare physical universe where the laws of physics and chemistry operate. There is no *real* god. It readily admits that all values, ethics and morals are merely personal opinions without any basis in actual reality. Because it insists on starting at the same point as Modernism, some thinkers say that Post-Modernism (PM) is the last gasp of Modernism, the last, futile attempt of the Modernist view of ultimate reality to survive (See James Sire, *The Universe Next Door, 3rd Edition*). While PM is a very varied movement, its philosophers still hold onto Modernism's anti-supernaturalism, though they are not as nasty about it.

Though PM starts at the same place as Modernism, PM goes beyond modernism in asserting that, beyond the bare physical reality of the universe, everyone makes up his own personal "reality." One person might prefer to create his own "ultimate reality" in Hindu fashion. Another might adopt a Muslim ultimate reality. Another might prefer the world of fairies, elves and gnomes. One might prefer to construct his world in a homosexual fashion. Another might prefer traditional family and values. Another may create a reality unlike any previous ones. Everyone makes up his own "reality."

Many people who hold such an idea will agree that there is a *physical reality* around us that has consequences *regardless* what we think. So, crossing a street at the wrong time could get you killed by an oncoming bus—whether or not you saw the bus!

But, they continue, there is no ultimately real *god* of any kind. And, there are no *ultimate* "values." What we call values are merely opinions people hold. Beyond survival in a bare, physical universe, all else that people talk about is merely their own views and opinions.

For example, any opinion one holds about "justice" will do, for there is no real, ultimate justice. Any view that one holds on sexuality or about how people ought to be treated in relationships will do—for all views are only mere opinions. Since all such views have nothing to do with *true reality*, one opinion is as good as another. All such personal views are equally valid—and equally invalid!

In this line of thought, if I have truly grasped the real situation we are in, I *will not only accept* the right of other people to make up their own realities, I *will celebrate* the realities they choose to create. To refuse to celebrate the realities and styles that others choose (that is, their non-real views of reality and the way they live based on them) is "bigotry." Even more, to attempt to get others to adopt my "reality" (persuade them that my views are the correct ones) is "oppression." "Bigotry" (refusal to celebrate other's views as equally as valid as my own) and "oppression" (trying to persuade others my views are better than theirs) are about the only two sins recognized by the "post-modern" movement.

What matters is that, given the ultimate meaninglessness of everything, we make up the realities we want, we choose whatever values and morals we want, and we live our lives with *style.* A pronounced or striking style (Goth, multiple body piercing, etc.) is to be preferred.

Also, one wants to live with a questioning attitude, suspecting the illegitimacy of most rhetoric thrust at them and rejecting all attempts at "meta-narrative" (a larger, all-embracing explanation for all things—like the Gospel of Christ).

Lastly, within a PM framework, it helps to have a sense of irony at life and the big joke we have played on ourselves, such as wanting meaning and having none, or thinking we were producing progress when we were poisoning ourselves, etc.

Today, the post-modern notion is center stage in the TV and the movies. And, as our culture "drinks from the media spring," Post-Modernism is absorbed into the lives of more and more people and shapes the outcomes of their lives.

The *wise person* in the post-modern era is someone who believes ultimate reality is only the physical universe, and that all values, morals and such are matters of only personal preference, with no root in ultimate reality. The wise person makes up a reality that suits him or her well, celebrates the realities others choose, lives with style and a sense of the ironic, and abhors bigotry and meta-narrative.

I recently skimmed through a book of advice written for teenagers. One section was built around the idea that "there is no reality; everyone makes up his or her own reality." Based on that idea, the author encouraged teens to alter their views on the events of their lives in a way that would give them a more positive mentality. As teens thought back on experiences that they had previously seen as negative, they should realize their "reality" could be changed so that they could view the experience more positively. One way or another, they should remove the strong negative value they had given such experiences, and re-think them from a more positive angle in order to have a more positive outlook on life.

The author's advice was troubling to me. I agreed with his desire to get teens to consider the possibility that their view of past hurtful experiences may have been inadequate, that they have been mistaken about the intents of people whom they had thought were unkind. And, it is helpful to see past trauma as an opportunity to learn and grow. And, clearly individuals create their own *perspective* on reality. But, to say that each person "creates" his own separate reality introduces several new problems rather than solving the old ones.

Problems With Creating Your Own Reality

The notion that there is no ultimate reality beyond the bare physical universe has several *serious* problems.

First, it suggests that my future quality of life will be determined by my ability to rearrange my mental outlook rather than by the choices I make. And, so, it *removes from life nearly all concern with consequences.*

Second, bare, base-line, non-negotiable "reality" turns out to be more complex than merely the existence of the physics-and-chemistry universe. Not only does "physical" reality (such as, a speeding bus) demand to be observed and obeyed, there are also other "facts of life" that keep intruding into the make-believe "realities" we construct for ourselves.

I once watched a TV talk-show host interviewing a guest, a young man who had just made the statement that evil did not exist in his universe—he simply refused to accept it. The host posed a question, "Suppose Jeffrey Dahmer (the homosexual cannibal serial-killer) came to your door and knocked. You open the door. Now, Dahmer and the evil he has done do not exist in *your* universe. But *you* exist in *his*. What happens next?" The guest could not reply.

Certainly, the laws of chemistry and physics do operate around us. But human beings also tend to operate in certain ways more complex than just chemistry and physics. Thus, there are not only "physical" realities, there are some basic "human realities" with which one must deal.

For example, each human being is selfishly motivated. Indeed, we can have altruistic motivations, but each human has a strong self-concern. A form of government that does not recognize this fact has trouble enduring. Communism depended on its citizens doing top quality work simply for the good of everyone without concern for personal gain. After incredible struggles for nearly three-quarters of a century, the Communist dominated USSR fell apart. It simply could not build an industry and an economy by means of an unmotivated work force. Lenin and his successors could not build a government on human unrealities.

For another example, all human beings have a capacity for both nobility and cruelty. That understanding has led to the system of checks and balances in our form of government in the USA. Without adequate checks and balances, native human selfishness, added to the capacity for cruelty, and enhanced by unchecked power makes the old saying come true: "Power corrupts and absolute power corrupts absolutely." Many nations in the world suffer under the heel of ruthless dictators because of this basic human reality.

These *human realities* not only impact governments, they also shape the joy or sorrow of our daily lives. For example, due to the extended influence of TV and movies, our culture now encourages two people to marry "for love." "For love" usually means out of the strong feelings of attraction the couple feel for one another. Parental input is shoved aside—and perhaps the warnings of friends—as the two "in love" are wed. Sooner or later, it dawns on the couple that they are going to have to *work together* in order to make the marriage succeed. They would have done well to ask some questions before the wedding, such as, *is my potential mate good at teamwork*, at the give-and-take required to make a team effort succeed—or, *is he/she highly selfish and belligerent or manipulative* in order to get his/her way? Marriages live or die based on the attitudes and patterns people have developed in handling relationships—regardless of how attractive that person may seem in courtship.

Certainly, it is easier to recognize the danger from an oncoming bus (physical reality), but the devastation of a failed marriage (human reality) is just as real as any injury from a bus accident. One can create a "reality" of "highly-attractive-wonderful-person-to-marry," but the potential mate, cloaked in that "reality," will ultimately reveal who he or she *really* is.

Reality Has Teeth

Physical reality has teeth! If we do not see the speeding bus coming, and step into its path, it still kills us. The impact of the bus does not go away because I did not see the bus. Reality bites deeply into our lives!

But, *human realities* also have teeth! If I am a highly selfish person (or marry one), my marriage is going to be a kind of "hell on earth" regardless what I thought when we were wed. The reality of two people having to work together will not change to suit my fantasy. Either the selfishness changes, or we both pay the consequences. There are certain things about life that "are the way they are," regardless of what we think.

And, besides the nature of human beings, *other realities* have teeth! The consequences of involvement in sex or drugs turn out to be far less pliable and negotiable than the media teach. "High risk lifestyles" remain "high risk" even though the media promotes homosexuality and heterosexual promiscuity. And, "high risk" means *highly likely to cause you misery and early death* from disease—regardless of the fantasy reality that one constructs. Drugs (alcohol or others) keep on turning out to be the doorway into slavery and degradation for millions—not a door to a higher, more enjoyable life.

Spiritual Reality Has Teeth

Not only are there physical and human factors that shape life for better or worse, Reality also has a *spiritual* dimension, and spiritual reality *also* has teeth.

Contemporary society is inclined to put religious ideas at the head of the list of "non-realities" thought to be *completely unrelated* to the flow of everyday life. That is, you may believe whatever you want to about a god or gods, because ultimately, there is no God who has any influence on the flow of physical reality. All views of god are equally valid and invalid. As long as your god-ideas allow you to cross the street without being hit by a bus, they meet minimum standards, whether you believe in one god, many gods, or no god.

However, the god-ideas that grip a society shape both the life of the society and the quality of life of its citizens. Mayan and Aztec god-concepts demanded human blood and resulted in repeated war to provide adequate numbers of human sacrifices. The citizens who lived under the blood-thirsty gods suffered unrelenting war.

Hinduism, with its focus on the upward journey of the non-personal soul through thousands of rebirths, has produced a culture in which the individual human personal identity is insignificant. And, upward *social* mobility is difficult, if not impossible, because of a rigid caste system through which the soul will ultimately progress as it continues to be reborn at higher and higher levels. Buddhism has had similar results.

Islam has wedded the power of the state and religious ideology. The Islamic state is an ideological state. The state has the duty to punish those who think outside Islamic bounds. Democracy and freedom of thought or freedom of religion do not grow well in Islamic soil. The function of the Islamic state is to establish control, not freedom. The vast majority of Muslims in the world live in a "thought-control" state. Do dissident intellectuals flee the Western world for sanctuary in Saudi Arabia? No!

Atheism, the "un-religion" constructed on the idea of evolution (life evolves to higher and higher levels), has produced governments in which the "more advanced" (the party elite) have a duty to rule over the "less advanced" (the general people), as in Soviet Russia and Communist China. And, somehow, the "more advanced" controllers have lived quite well while the "less advanced" masses have lived deprived lives.

The democracies of the West grew up in the soil of Christianity with its holy God who is unchanging and impartial, and who has a high value on the worth of each individual person because each is made in God's image. The "inalienable right" given to human beings by their Creator flows out of a Christian foundation. The restraint upon government oppression comes from its high value of the individual and the strong concept of justice. The balanced view of human beings both as valuable, and yet capable of nobility and cruelty, has come from a Christian assessment of mankind, and has informed the way the founders structured the American government. The freedom enjoyed by citizens of western governments has religious, not just philosophical, roots.

The god-ideas adopted by human beings turn out to impact *dramatically* the quality of life of the millions of people who have to live under their dominion. Thus, at a basic level, ideas in the spiritual arena *do* matter, for they shape the nature of the state and society, and thereby impact the quality of life of the citizens.

There is yet *another problem* with the thought that one can create whatever god he chooses and his life will work out just fine. The God of the Bible claims the name "Yahweh," meaning "I am what I am," or "I will be who I will" (Ex 3:14). Either translation of the term drives home the same point: "Neither human beings, nor anyone or anything else, will shape who I am. I am completely independent of anything or anyone. Nothing can, or ever will, shape me. I alone determine myself."

God refuses to fit into our opinions of what or who He ought to be.

We may fool ourselves into thinking that we can construct "god" as we see fit, but the Real God will refuse to conform to our ideas. Indeed, he will challenge them. If we persist in our wrong ideas, we will do so to our own pain. The Real God is *not* removed from the flow of physical reality or human reality. Instead, He *controls* the flow. Sooner or later, in this life or the next, we will have to deal with Him based on who He thinks He is and the Reality that He has created, not the one we have made up for ourselves.

According to the Bible, the spiritual realm is not a botanical garden, beautiful and safe for all who stroll there. Rather, spiritual reality includes the presence of demonic beings, predators who easily (but subtly) interact with humans to feed wrong perceptions of life, impact individual, family and national health, and bring bondage and destruction. Those who venture into the spiritual realm need to take care that they do not become prey for these predators (Col 2:7-8, 1 Tim 4:1-5, 2 Tim 2:25-26). Actually, all adventurers desperately need the protective guidance (thy rod and thy staff...Ps 23:4) of the true God of the universe.

In other words, there is a "Reality" (I use capital "R") beyond the mere physical universe that exists *independently* of our opinions. That Reality involves more than just the laws of chemistry and physics. And, that Reality has *teeth*!

So—How Does This Relate To Wisdom?

What does this discussion have to do with Wisdom?

Here it is: We all tend to do our strategies for living (our approach to "wisdom") based on our concept of ultimate reality, our "god-concept." If "reality" is up for grabs (everyone makes up his own reality), then *wisdom is a worthless pursuit.*

If all "realities," beyond the merely physical universe, are *only* personal opinions, then, barring accidents such as being hit by a bus, one can create a happy life simply by imagining a "reality" around us that makes us feel happy. For example:

· We need not be concerned about *which values* we choose to live by, for no "values" (whether predatory or altruistic) are really real. They are just a matter of personal preference. We just need to choose values that we personally like. For one person that may mean a high value on his gratification resulting in greed and sexual predation on others. For another, it may mean a high value on the welfare of others and a life of philanthropy. Both turn out to be equal. No one is better than the other.

· We also do not have to worry about the *components of our "lifestyle,"* such as our views of sexuality or sexual experience, drugs, work, possessions, goals, motives or relationships. Other than survival value, the practices we adopt regarding such issues are ultimately meaningless. *There is no ultimate right or wrong.* No one lifestyle has any greater value or morality than any other—since all values and morals have nothing to do with true reality and are just personal preference. We just need to make up our own views—preferably ones that make us "feel better" right now. Hitler felt better with six million Jews incinerated and had the power to pull it off! Jeffrey Dahmer, the homosexual cannibal, had a different preference regarding morals! We might not like Hitler's or Dahmer's acts, but no one can say they are wrong—*if* morals are merely a personal preference.

· We do not need to worry about developing wisdom, that is, developing the ability to evaluate situations and choose the better or best route to take in life. If there is no ultimate reality beyond the physical universe, then a person would want to gain enough discernment to be able to cross the street without being hit by a bus. However, beyond the issue of staying alive, there really are no better or worse routes in life. "Better" and "worse" are value judgments, and values have nothing to do with true reality. Values are only expressions of personal preference.

In effect, the post-modern attitude and viewpoint leads to the conclusion that, beyond physical consequences, *there are no real consequences in life.*

But If There Is A Larger Reality...

But, what if there *is* a true reality that is greater than the mere, bare physical universe? Then, *having a happy life turns out to be more complicated than merely imagining things that make us feel happy.*

Just as violating physical reality has negative consequences (such as failing to see an oncoming bus), violating other aspects of reality (e.g., human realities or spiritual realities) will also turn out to have bad consequences. Indeed, if there is a greater reality that exists independently of our perception of it—or, of our opinion of it—then, if we want to avoid much pain in life, we would do well to:

- Discern what that reality is, and
- Build our lives (values, morals and lifestyle) in line with that reality.

Even a cursory reading of the evening's newspaper reveals people who have made *value or moral choices* that bring them *destructive consequences*, such as loss, prison or even death. Indeed, as time passes we, ourselves, experience the bite of Reality's teeth. We make choices, and they bring us consequences: trouble or well-being.

With the passage of time, we begin to realize—often too late—that physical survival is not the only issue we need to consider seriously. The realities of life turn out to be larger and more complex than mere physical survival. Decisions we make in the *human* realm have consequences, just like decisions made in the physical realm—and often consequences that are just as painful. Decisions we make in the *values* realm drive our lives in certain directions, with beneficial or painful results. Decisions we make in the *spiritual* realm deeply impact the person we are becoming—and the direction our life takes.

Decisions keep on producing consequences, whether or not we anticipated them. So, the question rises: "Is there a way to make decisions that bring *good* consequences in such arenas as career, marriage, childrearing, emotional health—and *long-term* good consequences, not just short-term good followed by disaster?"

This is the question addressed by true Wisdom. Because there *is* a *real* reality that is greater than the bare physical universe, we *need to discern what that reality is*. Because our decisions and actions *do have consequences,* for better or worse, we need *some way* to make good decisions.

Enter Wisdom.

Appendix 2

ACTUALIZED HUMILITY

If you *really* intend to develop wisdom about life, you are choosing to set out on a journey. The first stage of that journey is humility. If you want to be a wise leader or a counselor to others, or you simply want to make wise choices and reap the benefits of wisdom for yourself, you must become well-practiced in humbling yourself.

It is crucial that you have committed your life to Christ and have the Holy Spirit dwelling in you. He will give power for the growth of humility (Gal 5:21-22).

However, humility will involve repeated choices on your part. In the book of Ecclesiastes, the writer says that we spend all the days of our life with self-exaltation in our hearts (Ecc 9:3). Many translations render the Hebrew word "madness," but it is the participial form of the Hebrew word that means "praising," and designates the self-praising fool. In Ecclesiastes 9:3, the term refers to "self-exalting." The same verse says we have an enduring willingness to hurt others (evil) in our hearts all the days of our lives. Humility can be empowered by the Holy Spirit, but it will continue to involve choices against our native self-exalting tendencies.

Humility must impact your personal view of yourself (psychologically). You need *an accurate estimate of yourself* before God (Rom 12:3). Our tendency is to think of ourselves more highly than we ought, seeing greater things for ourselves than God intends at this time. It is quite important you get to know your strengths and weaknesses accurately, especially the "measure of faith" God has given to you, which impacts the role you will play in His Kingdom.

While we are encouraged to keep an open view of what God could do through us (Phil 4:13), we are also encouraged to *be a good steward of the things* for which God has already made us responsible right now. Humility may pray for great things to happen through our lives, but it does not get an inflated idea of its importance in God plans (Ps 131:1-2). One of the reasons that people become so "down" on themselves is because they are so "up" on themselves. That is, they are *sure* they are capable of so *much*; then they become disappointed in themselves when they are unable to perform to their own high expectations.

Humility must impact you spiritually/religiously. Human beings have an inclination to act like we "have it all together" spiritually. It was this charade that caused many of the religious leaders in first century Israel to reject being baptized by John and so miss God's purpose for them (Luke 7:29-30). Many of us move beyond *pretense* of spiritual perfection to *confidence* of our own spiritual superiority to others (see Luke 18:9). We begin to feel that all things are just fine with us, and with our views of God and life.

However, God *knows the sorry condition* of each human heart (Jer 17:9-10; Luke 16:15). We are all rebels, sinners against God (Rom 3:23), and have deserved only spiritual death because of it (Rom 6:23). Nothing of our religious or other heritage was adequate to save us—only God's grace saved us by sending Christ to die for our rebellion. He is willing to credit Christ's righteousness to us when we trust Him. We only fool ourselves when we brag about our spirituality before God, and we receive *nothing* from Him for our proud religious efforts (see Luke 18:9-14). Also, when we pretend to be like the main character in the Mary Poppins movie, "practically perfect in every way," we lie to others and discourage those who, being so aware of their own struggles, behold our hypocritical shell.
Set your heart to follow Christ. If you have never done it before, admit to God that you have sinned against Him and are a rebel from the heart. Thank Christ for dying for your sins, all of them, past, present and future (1 Pet 3:18)! Ask Him to come into your life and make you into the kind of person He wants you to be. Thank God for forgiving your sins—all of them—because of Christ's death (Col 1:17-22), accepting you as His child (John 1:12), and granting to you eternal life (John 1:11-12). Set your heart to follow Christ, even if the going gets tough (Luke 8:13).

Get used to *admitting any sins to God immediately* upon your awareness of them—it keeps your relationship with Him clear (1 John 1:9). Get used to taking the initiative to explore souring relationships with others to see if you have caused offense. And, get used to asking others for forgiveness when you become aware you have sinned against them (Matt 5:23-24). Get used to acknowledging before others that you, too, have problems. Do it with discretion, but don't play the "I'm perfect" game.

Humility must impact you conceptually and educationally. Get used to *needing to know more* than you already know about God, the Christian life, handling your responsibilities, relating to people, etc. Stop pretending that you already know it all—or *almost* know it all. Don't get the idea that you *know enough*! Humble yourself. Ask questions in areas in which you need to learn. Read books, listen to taped messages and CD's in the areas in which you need to grow.

Humility must impact you socially and relationally. Notice those times during the day or situations in which you put yourself first, or become focused on your own agenda and don't even think about others. Develop a habit of occasionally looking around and *thinking about the interests of those around you.*

Stop "cutting in line." There are a thousand justifications for it, nearly all of which are invalid. It is okay to be first in line (if you got there first), but not to pre-empt the place of others in line It is okay to compete and win—but not at the expense of doing wrongly to others in order to come out ahead. And, it is okay to give focused attention to pursuing your goals—as long as you accomplish your goals in a way that also helps with the interests of others (Phil 2:3-4).

Get used to helping others (also called "serving"). You are not so great that others in the church must take menial tasks and do them while you wait and pray for the great assignment God has in store for you—and do nothing until He reveals it. Get busy being a servant. Humbling yourself to help out in church and in the home will be good for you. Actually, within the fellowship of believers, we are required to love others *sacrificially*—we may even sacrifice some of our agenda for the good of the others (John 13:34-35). If you *ever* want God to bless you in leading God's people, you must become a servant (Matt 20:24-28).

Associate with a range of people. Many times we are ladder climbers. We want to relate upwardly on the social scale. Or, at least, we *don't* want to have to relate to those who are *down* a few rungs from us. God, the highest status person in the whole universe, chose to associate with us—and, not only are we *not* high-ranking angels, but also most of the people that God chose to know him don't even have status among humans (1 Cor 1:28-29). Associate with "lower status" people than yourself (Rom

12:16)—and do it as "one of the guys" not as "the great high status person trying to do a little slumming in order to please God." As, your day goes on and you encounter people of lower status than you, treat them with respect.

Stop bragging. Most of us know how to do it in a socially respectable way. Just quit! Humility doesn't get into comparison and boasting. It boasts only in the Lord and of His great work in our lives (Jer 9:23-24). Those who are intent on comparing themselves with others and boasting to improve their status are not wise (2 Cor 10:12-14).

Humility must impact your decision-making. Get used to taking input on your decisions (getting advice) before you plunge in (Pro 15:22). Get used to checking to see if the Bible says something that would guide a decision you are about to make. When it comes to decision-making, *ignorance is not bliss.*

Get used to needing *correction* by others in "blind areas" of your life (Heb 3:12-14)—and *receive it graciously* when it comes, thanking the person for his concern for you. If you are unsure the criticism is valid, take it to the Lord and ask Him to confirm or disconfirm it to you.

Humility must impact your words. The foolish proudly use their words to beat up others (Pro 14:3). The proud are ready to make fun of (mock) others and to mock serious or holy matters (Pro 21:24). Again and again, when a harsh or "clever" reply is on the tip of your tongue, you are going to need to *choose* only *the words that will be helpful* to your hearers in the situation, words that will build them up, not tear them down (Eph 4:29). If a "smart comment" is "on the tip of your tongue," let it stay there.

Again, stop boasting. Few of us are crass enough to baldly brag in the presence of others—though, indeed, some are so crass. Most of us, however, have developed a socialized skill in letting others know about the excellent things we have done in the past or our excellent heritage, or our excellent possessions in order to get their admiration or jealousy—and to demonstrate our superiority. Stop mentioning the proofs of your intelligence, your wealth or your strength and power. According to the Scriptures, if you just *have to* boast, simply boast about how God has given you the undeserved privilege of knowing Him (Jer 9:23-24). Notice the abilities of others and express your appreciation to them.

Humility must impact your approach to work. Get used to having to work hard for good things to happen. Some people feel they deserve to have a better life without having to exert effort, as though God owed them something. Get used to having, not only to pray, but to *use your head and hands diligently* (Pro 13:4).

Get used to leading in a way that shows *respect for those who work under you.*

Get used to *doing what the boss says* as long as it is not out of line with the Scriptures. Quit balking and just obey (Rom 13:1-4). Get used to respecting people in authority because they have the *position.* The emperors of Rome were not nice, respectable people. Usually, they were debauched and ruthless. Christians still had to show them respect (Rom 13:1-5).

Humility must impact your finances and possessions. You actually are in the position of "steward" of all that God has given to you. Get used to all *your money and possessions belonging to God* (1 Chr 29:14). He is just letting you use them. The question is not "how much of my stuff do I give to God?" but "how much of God's stuff should I keep for myself at this point in life?"

Quit spending God's money on unimportant stuff just so you can proudly impress people (Pro 12:9). *Use God's money* not only to provide for your own family's needs and desires (1 Tim:5:8), but also to advance the Kingdom of God (Phil 4:16-17), and to help others (1 John 3:16-18).

In bringing up all these facets of humility, I am not intending to overwhelm you, just to challenge you to get serious about seeking wisdom. In the Scriptures, humility is not simply a theoretical concept, it is a practical way of living as the minutes of the day tick away and you face hundreds of different situations.

At the bottom of it, humility is a spirit of deference and submission to the Lord, a spirit that intends to honor Him and operate based on His judgments and opinions. That spirit of deference precedes wisdom.

Humility is the departure platform for the train of wisdom. You won't make it onto the train until you get onto the platform. Once on the platform, access to the train is possible.

Appendix 3

WISDOM IN THE BIBLE

In the ancient Middle East, leaders of various societies recognized the need to gather insights into how the world and life really operated in order to be able to make more beneficial decisions. (Gen 41:8; Est 1:13). They gathered around themselves "wise men," people who had exceptional insight into the matters of life and government. Some of the "wise" also delved into the occult. Kings used their prudent counsel on governing and decision-making.

Some of the "wise" were keen observers of life. Based on their observations and discernment, they drew conclusions about how life operated, and packaged their "wisdom" in sayings, similes, metaphors and word puzzles.

By 2500 BC, collections of wise sayings existed in Egypt and in Mesopotamia. The collections were especially used for training the young of the ruling classes for public leadership.

The idea of wisdom was known and appreciated in the time that ancient Israel came into existence as a nation around 1400 BC. But, Israel's first concerns were to develop a nation bonded to God by covenant, a nation that would keep God's Law. So, much of the early history of Israel is focused, not on wisdom, but on learning and living out God's Law. Especially important was the establishment of the system for relating to God and worshipping Him, a system involving Priests and animal sacrifice for sin. The keeping of God's Law would result in the blessing of God upon the nation and demonstrate to the surrounding nations that the people of Israel were a wise nation (Deu 4:6).

From the founding of Israel onward, a person could seek God's guidance. It was understood that God might guide through (see Jer 18:18; Eze 7:26):

o A priest through the law or an oracle (the Urim and Thummim) (Ex 28:30)

- o A prophet through a Word of the LORD (2 Sam 7:4ff)
- o Counsel from the wise (2 Sam 16:23)

It was during the peaceful reign of Solomon (about 975-935 BC), son of David and the wisest of all men, that the interest in wisdom grew in Israel. The "wise" were able to make excellent decisions and benefit from life. So, there was a drive to collect, understand, and use wisdom. Wise men (and women) were in high demand as advisers and teachers. Solomon, himself, put together over 3000 wise sayings (1 Kings 4:30-34).

During the decline of Israel after Solomon, the interest in Wisdom continued. Thus, King Hezekiah's people (about 720 BC) put into the Book of Proverbs many of Solomon's sayings not previously included (Pro 25:1).

But the interest in wisdom increasingly took a *secular twist*. Many people had become convinced that prudent observation of life would lead them to principles on how to succeed in this world. But, they pursued those principles and insights without real concern for obedience to God's Law.

Indeed, the Scribes, supposed to be teachers of God's Law, were radically re-interpreting the Scripture so that much of its content and moral challenge were lost. These "wise ones" were much like the social scientists of today, trying to observe life and discern the principles that would let one live successfully apart from God. They were "wise in their own eyes," and trusted in their own understanding, not God or His Word. See Pro 26:12, Isa 5:21; Pro 3:5-8. Theirs was a false wisdom.

God then raised up prophets who spoke judgment on this kind of "wisdom." (Jer 8:8-10).

Even after the fall of Israel, the Scribes tended to reinterpret the Word of God so as to disembowel it. Their influence continued into the New Testament era. By the time of Jesus, the Pharisees had developed a legalistic approach to God's Law that focused on detailed observance of outer rituals, but ignored the inner condition of one's heart. And, they developed traditions that allowed them to bypass the real intent of the word of God. See Matt 23:23-28; Mark 7:5-13.

It was in the context of such people "wise in their own eyes" that Jesus praised the Father for revealing the truth to the humble people rather than to the "wise and learned" (Matt 11:25-28).

Yet, Jesus spoke repeatedly of the *truly* wise, those who obeyed God's Word, especially the teachings of the Christ. See Matt 23:24-27; 45-51; 25:1-13.

When the Gospel moved out of Palestine into the Greco-Roman world through the Apostle Paul, it had to deal with another form of false wisdom,

Greek speculative ideas about the ultimate nature of reality and how to deal with it based on Greek philosophy. The Greek approach to wisdom started with man's viewpoint, not God's revelation, and depended entirely on man's ability to observe and to reason. Their approach was, at heart, the same as the approach of "modern scientists" (especially the "social scientists") today, who are confident that their use of observation and reason would allow them to deal ultimately successfully with all of life.

Paul condemns the false wisdom of the Greek world in 1 Cor 1-3; see especially 1:18-25. Paul insists that *true wisdom* conforms to the reality of Jesus Christ, for He was the source of *all* Wisdom (Col 2:2-3).

Despite the battle against Greek speculative "wisdom," genuine wisdom had a high value among Christ-followers. They were concerned to *live wisely* according to God's Word, according to the reality of Jesus Christ (Eph 5:15-17; Col 4:5). They understood that the real, true wisdom that led to salvation grew out of the Holy Scriptures as one put his faith in Christ (2 Tim 3:14-15). They also knew that God would give wisdom to His needy children who firmly believed in Him (Jas 1:5-8).

In the NT, the one who was truly "wise" did not merely possess knowledge, for knowledge only inflates one's ego (1 Cor 8:1-2). Rather than being focused on "knowledge," the truly wise person focused on living a life of humility (which precedes and grows out of wisdom) and good deeds—like Jesus Himself (Jas 3:13; see Phil 2:3-11).

In the Biblical view, any strategy for success that was rooted in envy and selfish ambition obviously did not come from God. It came from this world and had its ultimate roots in the demonic. Any wisdom or strategy that actually came from God would have God's characteristic humility and good deeds as an integral part of its fabric (James 3:13-18).

Appendix 4

WISDOM LITERATURE OVERVIEW

Wisdom literature in the Bible tends to:

- Focus on **universal premises**, dealing with realities that impact the life of mankind *regardless of culture*
- Appeal to **observation of**
  - o Nature (Jas 1:11; 3:3-6,11-12; 5:7, etc.)
  - o Human life (2:2-3,15-16; 4:13, etc.)
- Use **concise, antithetical (contrasting) sayings**, contrasts that stick in the memory
- A **cheerful outlook.** See Ecc 3:12-13, 22; 2:24-26; 5:18; 8:15; 9:7-8; Acts 14:7; 1 Tim 6:17; Mt 11:19

The "concise antithetical sayings" are often in the form of a "proverb," which is a short, pithy saying commonly used, and often characterized by shortness, sense and pointed humor. One older writer said that a proverb contains "the wisdom of many and the wit of one."

Certain sections of the Old Testament have been called by scholars "Wisdom Literature," for they deal directly or indirectly with the topic of wisdom. The Wisdom Literature includes the book of Job, several Psalms, Proverbs, and Ecclesiastes. Many scholars also include the book of James in the New Testament.

The following is a brief summary of the content and point of view of the books.

Job. In Job's time, it was widely thought that the righteous person was *always* blessed and the wicked would *always* be troubled. If one were blessed, he was obviously righteous. If he were troubled, he obviously had been wicked. In the popular mind, the troubled and suffering people were to be left alone. They were only getting what they deserved. The book of Job challenges these ideas.

The lesson of the book of Job is that sometimes, for reasons no one but God understands, the godly also suffer. The suffering person needs help, not avoidance or reproof. The book is written in poetic form. After the introduction of Job's suffering, it consists of dialogues between Job, who maintains he has not "sinned," and Job's friends who try to use different arguments to prove that Job must have sinned since he is suffering. The book ends with God encountering Job and his friends, rebuking the friends and restoring Job's prosperity double.

Psalms is a collection of poems/songs about God and walking with God. The ***Wisdom Psalms***

- 19, 104, 147, and 148 show the wisdom and majesty of God revealed in nature.
- 1, 19 and 119 deal with the efficacy of the Word of God.
- 33 shows the sovereignty of God among the nations and the affairs of men.
- 36, 37, 49, 53, and 73 help God's people know how to deal with faith struggles as they face the wicked.
- 32 high-lights the need for confession and forgiveness in walking with God.
- 50, 58, 82, 94, and 125 focus on the trustworthiness of the sovereign, righteous God and His judgment upon the wicked.
- 107 and 111 show God's righteousness and majesty in His deliverance and provision for His people.
- 112 and 128 recount God's blessing upon the man who fears God.

Proverbs is a collection of wise sayings that help people grow in their ability to deal successfully with life from God's viewpoint. While Proverbs is concerned to give guidance on prudent living, its high value on moral living turns out to be more important than practical prudence.

Ecclesiastes is a poetic book that records a search for an adequate philosophy of life. Written by the wealthiest king in Israel (it seems to be Solomon), it surveys what really counts in life and concludes that, at the heart of it all, one needs to fear God and keep His commandments (Ecc 12:13-14).

James was written by the brother of Jesus. It contains many of the characteristics of Wisdom literature and has been called "The New Testament Proverbs." James is concerned to delineate the characteristics of a person who truly walks with God.

Appendix 5

INTERPRETING WISDOM PASSAGES

Most of the Biblical information about wisdom is contained in books written in poetic form: Job, Psalms, Proverbs, and Ecclesiastes. A bit more information is contained in the book of James, a letter in the New Testament. To grasp the Bible's use of some of the wisdom terms, it will be helpful to consider the Bible's use of words and understand the way Hebrew poetry in the Bible was structured.

FLEXIBILITY OF THE BIBLICAL TERMS

The language we use in daily life differs significantly from "scientific language."

Scientific language uses terms with severely restricted meanings. Science strives to create a very exact language so that scientists do not easily get confused in trying to communicate with one another. Thus, physics tries to define carefully words like mass, energy, and momentum, and then use them in such a way that each word always means the same thing.

However, our normal daily use of language doesn't keep such rigid rules. We can use a single word in a variety of ways. For example, the English word "up" has numerous meanings: "Climb up the ladder." "Batter up!" "I feel really up today!" "I wonder what's up." "Up 'til then I was unsure." A few years ago, a world leader was trying to learn English. He became exasperated and quit when he found that the small word "up" could be used in so many very different ways!

The English word "wise" can also be stretched to cover a range of meanings: "She is a very wise person." "I don't like his wisecracks." "What are you—some kind of wise guy?" "Wise guy," itself has more than one meaning. It can refer to a smart aleck or to a man pledged to the mafia. Of course, a given word has a *limited range* of meanings. For example, though "wise" can have several different meanings, we don't use "wise" to mean "whale." But, the words we use in daily life are often flexible; they have a *range* of meanings.

So, how do we determine *which* meaning a person has in mind when he uses a certain word in daily conversation? Say he uses the word "wise." How do we determine which meaning of "wise" he intends?

When another person *speaks* to us, we determine the meaning of their words by understanding, not only the possible meanings of the word, but also the *context* in which the word is used. We look at the situation we are in as well as the tone of voice and other non-verbal cues from the speaker. If a person *writes* to us, we look at the way a word is used in a sentence in order to grasp the word's intended meaning. "You are a really cool person," and "it was quite cool yesterday" imply two different uses of the word "cool."

Thus, it is with the Biblical material. Individual Biblical words are not used with scientific precision. They are used as humans normally use words, often with a range of possible meanings. The wisdom terms used in the Old or New Testaments have some flexibility in their meanings.

Even more, the words are used *poetically*. Poetry tends to push words or concepts beyond their normal range of meaning in order to give striking perspective to the reader or listener. The statement "wisdom is a shelter" in Ecc 7:12 does not mean that there is a physical building called "wisdom." We read the phrase and understand that the term "shelter" is being used in a *metaphorical* sense, a comparative sense, *comparing* wisdom with a physical place of refuge. As one pieces together an understanding of the wisdom terms and how they relate to one another, he needs to remember the flexible, poetic sense with which they are used.

It also helps to understand the way Old Testament poetry was structured.

HEBREW POETIC STRUCTURE

The Old Testament Wisdom Literature is poetic in form. Since the Wisdom material of the Old Testament is primarily in the Hebrew poetic form of "parallelism" (rhyming ideas), the type of parallelism helps one to determine meanings and the relationship of different Hebrew wisdom terms to one another.

Popular English poetry often contains rhymed sounds at the end of lines (moon/June). Hebrew poetry in the Old Testament consisted of *rhymed ideas* not rhymed sounds. The second line of a Hebrew poem would, in some way, elaborate on the ideas of the first line. This "parallelism" helps one to determine meanings and the relationship between different Hebrew wisdom terms to one another.

Except for chapters 1-9, 30 and 31, the material in Proverbs is made up of balanced couplets (pairs of lines) of rhyming ideas. The two lines usually relate in one of the following manners:

- **Synonymous** parallelism: the 2nd line repeats or reinforces the first.

Pro 11:7 When a wicked man dies, his expectation will perish, and the hope of the unjust perishes. (NKJ)

- **Antithetic** parallelism: the 2nd line is a contrast or reversal to the first.

Pro 15:1 A gentle answer turns away wrath, but a harsh word stirs up anger. (NIV)

- **Synthetic** parallelism: the 2nd or 3rd line adds to that of the first.

The blessing of the LORD makes one rich, and He adds no sorrow with it.
(Pro 10:22 NKJ)

Stern discipline awaits him who leaves the path; he who hates correction will die.
(Pro 15:10 NIV)

Do not let your heart envy sinners, but always be zealous for the fear of the LORD.
There is surely a future hope for you, and your hope will not be cut off.
(Pro 23:17-18 NIV)

Some time back, I wrote an *English* poem about *Hebrew* poetry. It summarized for me what was going on as I deciphered the intents of the writers.

Hebrew Poetry

Line coupled with line,
Not words, but thoughts rhyme,
Stating a thought
Then amplifying
By comparing, contrasting or applying.

THE DIVINE NAME

In the Wisdom Literature one frequently encounters the term "the LORD" with the second word in all caps. The Hebrew term behind this translation is "Yahweh," God's "personal name," the name God used when He revealed Himself to Moses. Yahweh identifies God, not as a god-in-general, but as the God associated with the Exodus and the making of the Covenant on Mt. Sinai, and the one who gave the Law. Out of respect for God, the actual name "Yahweh" was not pronounced by the Hebrews when they read the text aloud. Rather, they would say the word 'Adonai, meaning "lord" or "master."

When the Hebrew text *actually uses* the term Adonai, addressing God as Master, the translation is written *without* all caps: Lord. When it uses "Yahweh," addressing God by his revealed name, the translation is written in all caps: LORD.

HEBREW CONCRETENESS

Hebrew has a very concrete quality about its terms. Greek contains many abstract ideas, but in Hebrew rather concrete terms are used to represent abstractions. For example, "torah" (a teaching, a precept) can represent the Law of God, a particular teaching, or the religion of another nation. The concreteness of the Hebrew keeps the poetry linked to real life rather than indulging in flights of philosophic fancy. The poetry deals with the stuff life is made of, rather than theoretical speculations about life.

TYPES OF PROVERBS

Different kinds of sayings are found in the Proverbs. Some are

• **Rules of life** (Heb: mashal [maw-shawl']). These are tersely cogent sayings that may involve a simile or a comparison.

Like snow in summer or rain in harvest, honor is not fitting for a fool. (Pro 26:1 NIV)

Like an earring of gold or an ornament of fine gold is a wise man's rebuke to a listening ear. (Pro 25:12 NIV)

• **Riddles or puzzles** (chiydah [khee-daw']). These are verbal puzzles and conundrums intended to provoke effort to derive the point.

Pro 26:4-5
4 Do not answer a fool according to his folly, or you will be like him yourself.
5 Answer a fool according to his folly, or he will be wise in his own eyes. (NIV)

• **Adages** (meliytsah [mel-ee-tsaw']) **with a satirical** or terse, taunting edge. These concisely state a principle.

As a door turns on its hinges, so a sluggard turns on his bed.
(Pro 26:14 NIV)

The sluggard buries his hand in the dish; he is too lazy to bring it back to his mouth.
(Pro 26:15 NIV)

"There are three things that are stately in their stride, four that move with stately bearing:
a lion, mighty among beasts, who retreats before nothing;
a strutting rooster, a he-goat, and a king with his army around him.
(Pro 30:29-31NIV)

A very few number of times the Hebrew of a verse is capable of several different interpretations. Some of these situations may be due to accidents in the copying of the text in the past. Other situations do not appear to be due to accidents, but arise from different ways the Hebrew can be translated. In such cases, different versions of the Bible will have rather different interpretations of the verse. An example is Proverbs 26:10.

The great God that formed all things both rewardeth the fool, and rewardeth transgressors. (KJV)

The great God who formed everything gives the fool his hire and the transgressor his wages. (NKJ)

Like an archer who wounds at random is he who hires a fool or any passer-by. (NIV, see NAU)

The master may get better work from an untrained apprentice than from a skilled rebel! (TLB)

INCLUSIVE INTERPRETATION

When various translations are possible, I think it is wise to remember that we are dealing with "crafted" sayings. The Proverbs were crafted to compact a tremendous amount of insight into a short saying. Designed by wise men, they do not necessarily yield all their meanings immediately. Many times, a great deal of thought is required to extract the meanings. Jesus taught in much the same manner and challenged His listeners to process what He was saying: "He who has ears to hear, let him hear!" (Mark 4:9, 23; Luke 8:8, 14:35)

When the Hebrew text can be interpreted in different ways, I think it good to look at all the interpretations and come up with the linkages behind the different meanings. The wise verbal artist who created the verse may have intended *several* messages in his brief statement.

One way or another, God has left the text in this form. So, I tend to *look for the range of meanings and try to stay alert to all as* I seek to apply the verse to life.

SYNONYMS: THE FACETS OF WISDOM

In the Old Testament, several different Hebrew terms convey different aspects of wisdom. Occasionally, some of the terms are used synonymously, as is the case with wisdom and knowledge in Ecclesiastes 7:12.

Ecc 7:12 Wisdom is a shelter as money is a shelter, but the advantage of knowledge is this: that wisdom preserves the life of its possessor. (NIV)

"Wisdom" and "knowledge" appear interchangeable in the verse. Here, they are synonyms. It is the nature of synonyms that, while each synonym has a *common core of meaning*, each also conveys meanings that are *somewhat distinct.* For example, the English word "wise" (an adjective) has several synonyms—wise, sage, sapient, judicious, prudent, sensible and sane. *Webster's Tenth Collegiate Dictionary* gives their common core of meaning as "having or showing sound judgment." While all these synonyms share the same core of meaning, they also convey separate shades of the core meaning. For example, *sapient* suggests great sagacity and discernment, *judicious* stresses an ability to reach wise conclusions or just decisions, and *prudent* refers to the restraint generated by sound practical wisdom and discretion.

In a similar manner, the Hebrew wisdom terms *that are used synonymously also have distinctions among them. For example, while Ecclesiastes 7:12 treats knowledge and wisdom as synonymous, the parallelism of Proverbs 2:6 seems more to treat wisdom as a larger category, and knowledge and understanding as components of wisdom, not just synonyms of wisdom.*

For the LORD gives wisdom, and from His mouth come knowledge and understanding. (Pro 2:6 NIV)

The Greek language also has flexibility in the way its terms are used, though it tends to be more exact than Hebrew. One has to study the Old Testament and New Testament passages where the wisdom terms are used in order to discover how the terms are similar to one another and how they also differ.

—END—